The Rise and Fall of Starmer and the Labour Party

Copyright Page for The Rise & Fall of Starmer and the Labour Party Author: Josiah Cornell

ISBN: 9798900465784

DISCLAIMER

This work presents a narrative account that utilises publicly available information, including news reports, government documents, polling data, parliamentary records, and other sources up to October 2025. While the author has made every effort to ensure factual accuracy where verifiable information is presented, this book reflects the author's analysis, interpretation, and opinion regarding political events and their significance.

The portrayal of individuals' motivations, private conversations, internal deliberations, and thought processes is based on informed speculation and narrative reconstruction grounded in publicly observable behaviour, reported accounts, and standard political analysis, rather than direct access to private communications or confidential information.

The political commentary and criticism included in this work constitute protected expression under the principles of freedom of speech and the press. All individuals and organisations mentioned are public figures or entities involved in matters of public interest and legitimate public concern.

Polling data, electoral statistics, and economic figures are sourced from reputable organisations using standard methodologies; however, these data represent point-in-time snapshots of dynamic situations that are subject to change and interpretation. Projections regarding future political developments inherently involve uncertainty and should not be viewed as definitive predictions.

When this work employs terms such as "betrayal," "corruption," "authoritarian," or similar characterisations, these reflect the author's opinions and value judgments, informed by the cited evidence and public advocacy positions. Reasonable observers may interpret the same facts differently based on their individual perspectives and priorities.

This book does not offer legal advice and should not be relied upon as such. Readers are encouraged to form their own judgments about the political events discussed by consulting primary sources and a range of analytical viewpoints.

The author and publisher specifically disclaim any liability, loss, or risk incurred as a result of using or applying any content from this work.

reviews.

Introduction

In July 2024, the Labour Party celebrated a historic electoral victory, securing a substantial mandate reminiscent of Tony Blair's leadership in the late 1990s. After fourteen long years of Conservative governance, marked by the chaotic aftermath of Brexit, prolonged economic stagnation, and an NHS deeply strained by the repercussions of the COVID-19 pandemic, the British electorate called resoundingly for change.

Keir Starmer, a former Director of Public Prosecutions who transitioned into politics, skilfully rebranded the Labour Party to embody the principles of competence, moderation, and stability. He forged a broad coalition that attracted various segments of the population: disillusioned working-class voters in the North of England, eager for a return to social justice and opportunity, alongside liberal professionals in urban centres like London, who were keen to embrace ambitious progressive reforms. This inclusive strategy positioned Labour as a formidable force, seemingly ready to govern for a generation and reshape the narrative of British politics, sparking an initial wave of optimism and engagement.

However, with the mantle of power came significant challenges. Less than a year after their victory, the initial enthusiasm began to wane, revealing deep-seated fissures within the party's foundation and strategy. This book delves into the rapid and dramatic decline of Labour following its 2024 triumph, offering a meticulously factual examination supported by rigorous research, interviews, polling data, and comprehensive political reporting. It chronicles a cautionary tale of squandered political capital, internal strife, and a concerning failure to meet the elevated expectations held by both leadership and supporters alike.

The decline of Labour's standing did not happen overnight; instead, it was a gradual degeneration characterised by a series of missteps that can be metaphorically described as "death by a thousand cuts." The party grappled with multifaceted challenges: policy paralysis stifled resolution on critical issues, a drifting ideology alienated core supporters, ineffective communication strategies muddled its message, and poor electoral tactics eroded its previously robust base. Throughout this turbulent period, a widening chasm between party leadership and the electorate eroded trust, leading to an existential crisis that questioned the party's very identity.

At the heart of this disintegration lay a profound inability to reconcile the stark contradictions within Labour: the ongoing tension between metropolitan progressives championing sweeping social reforms and the socially conservative instincts of the traditional working class; the clash between ambitious environmental policies aimed at global sustainability and the immediate economic realities faced by those prioritising job security; and the division between pro-Palestinian activists seeking transformative foreign policy approaches and centrist figures advocating for more conventional diplomatic strategies. Starmer's inclination to defuse conflict by avoiding contentious issues only exacerbated dissatisfaction and frustration among the various factions within the party. By 2026, these unresolved tensions culminated in a catastrophic internal implosion, revealing a party governance model increasingly out of sync with public sentiment.

What began as an era of optimism soon gave way to the recurring patterns of political life? A rebellion concerning the contentious two-child benefit cap led to the suspension of seven Labour MPs, striking a blow against the party's claim to moral clarity and principles. Controversies erupted as ministers were forced from their positions under clouds of scandal, including property disputes, allegations of misconduct, and troubling questions regarding their judgment. Starmer himself became embroiled in controversy after accepting lavish gifts and hospitality from donors, actions that, while technically permissible, were politically unwise and damaging to public perception. The situation worsened with the controversial appointment of Peter Mandelson as ambassador to the United States, which was initially viewed as a strategic move but backfired dramatically when his past correspondence with Jeffrey Epstein was made public. Within days, Labour's narrative of ethical renewal was severely compromised.

This book does not aim to sensationalise these events, nor does it seek to defend or vilify the Labour Party from a partisan perspective. Instead, it aspires to document with forensic precision how what was once hailed as a monumental political victory in modern British history unravelled within a single parliamentary term, revealing the vulnerabilities inherent in leadership and governance. It serves as a cautionary tale, a stark warning of the potential pitfalls that can befall even the most promising political movements.

The narrative of Labour's post-2024 decline represents more than a mere account of political misadventures; it serves as a cautionary tale, illuminating critical lessons in leadership, ideological coherence, and the fragile, often volatile bond between voters and those wielding power.

The saga of Labour's rise and fall not only highlights the complexities and challenges of contemporary British politics but also provides invaluable insights that can inform future political strategies and decisions.

Chapter 1
From Barrister to Britain's Prime Minister

A forensic examination of how a toolmaker's son became one of Britain's most prominent legal minds

Sir Keir Starmer's story begins not with political ambition but with the quiet determination characteristic of Britain's post-war working class. Born on September 2, 1962, in Southwark, London, his birth coincided with a period of significant social and economic change in Britain. He was named after Keir Hardie, the first leader of the Labour Party, a detail that would prove prophetic, though not in the way his parents might have imagined.

The Starmer household embodied the essence of mid-20th-century Britain: hard work, education as a pathway to betterment, and an unshakeable belief in fair play. His father, Rod Starmer, was a toolmaker, a skilled trade that required precision, patience, and the ability to craft solutions from raw materials. These qualities, instilled in Keir from a young age, would later play a significant role in his son's approach to legal argument and political strategy, shaping his commitment to detail, his patience in building a case, and his belief in finding practical solutions.

His mother, Josephine, worked as a nurse until illness forced her into early retirement. The combination of his father's technical precision and his mother's nurturing profession created a household that valued both competence and compassion, shaping Starmer's later career in human rights law, where he advocated for those who could not fight for themselves, a testament to the influence of his parents on his career.

The family lived in Surrey, in what Starmer himself described as a "pebbledash semi." This was not the privileged background typical of many who rise to prominence in British public life, but it was also not impoverished. It represented the solid middle-class families who owned their own homes, took pride in their work, and believed their children could ascend the ladder of success, a relatable background for many readers.

Education was the key to a better life that the Starmer family pursued. Young Keir attended Reigate Grammar School, which had recently transitioned from a fee-paying institution to a state grammar school. This timing proved fortunate for Starmer, as he benefited from an education that combined academic rigour with accessibility, something that would later inform his views on educational opportunity and social mobility.

At Reigate Grammar, teachers remember Starmer as a student who wouldn't take no for an answer. He was not the disruptive type seeking attention; instead, he was genuinely eager to understand how systems work. This intellectual curiosity, combined with a natural talent for argument, pointed toward a career in law long before politics was even on his radar, a fascinating insight into his early aspirations.

The school's debating society provided an early testing ground for the skills that would later make him one of Britain's most formidable barristers. Even then, colleagues noted something distinctive about Starmer's approach: he was less interested in flashy rhetoric and more focused on methodically constructing arguments, building cases brick by brick until the conclusion was solid.

In 1982, Starmer enrolled at the University of Leeds to study law. Leeds in the early 1980s was a hotbed of student activism, with Margaret Thatcher's government providing abundant targets for young idealists' eager to change the world. The miners' strike, rising unemployment, and social upheaval fostered an atmosphere in which political engagement felt natural.

However, Starmer's radicalism took a different approach than that of many of his contemporaries. While others were out manning the barricades and occupying buildings, he immersed himself in legal texts, understanding instinctively that lasting change required mastering the system from within. This wasn't a political calculation; it was a matter of intellectual temperament. He was drawn to the structure of legal arguments, recognising how precedent and principle could be combined to create new possibilities for justice.

His law professors at Leeds remember him as a student who was thorough to the point of obsession. Whereas others might skim cases for the essential details, Starmer would read everything, not just the judgment, but also the pleadings, the evidence, and the dissenting opinions. He was building a comprehensive understanding of how the law worked in practice, not just on paper. He wasn't someone who would cut corners or take shortcuts; he was in it for the long haul.

The decision to study law was not motivated by dreams of striking it rich or climbing the social ladder. Starmer has expressed that he was driven by a belief that the law could serve as a tool for fairness, ensuring that power could not simply impose its will without justification. This idealistic view of legal practice later shaped his choice of chambers and the types of cases he would pursue.

After completing his undergraduate degree, Starmer progressed to St Edmund Hall, Oxford, to earn a Bachelor of Civil Law degree. Oxford was a completely different experience, steeped in centuries of tradition, Gothic architecture, and an unspoken belief that power was a birthright rather than something to be earned through hard work and determination.

Coming from Starmer's background, navigating Oxford required him to adapt to a new environment without compromising his integrity. He learned to speak the language of elite institutions while remaining grounded in his origins. This skill, operating effectively in establishment settings while remembering where he came from, would prove invaluable throughout his career.

His contemporaries from Oxford describe him as someone who kept his own counsel, standing slightly apart from the usual social dynamics. He wasn't aloof, but rather observant, taking mental notes about how power operates, who possesses it, and why. Even then, it was clear that he was building something substantial. However, few could have predicted the remarkable achievements he would later accomplish, such as his role as the Director of Public Prosecutions and his eventual leadership of the Labour Party.

Called to the Bar at Middle Temple on November 24, 1987, Starmer faced a pivotal decision that distinguishes the successful from the less successful in every barrister's career: which chambers to join. This choice reveals a lawyer's priorities, values, and ultimate objectives; it is where they firmly establish their identity and commitment. Starmer's decision to join Middle Temple, a prestigious and historic institution, was a significant step in his legal career, reflecting his commitment to the profession and his desire to work within the established legal system.

Keir Starmer joined Doughty Street Chambers in 1990, becoming a founding member of the chambers. This decision immediately highlighted his prioritisation of justice over personal gain. Doughty Street was not a haven for ambitious barristers seeking to make a quick fortune; instead, it attracted idealistic lawyers dedicated to challenging the establishment, advocating for the underdog, and building their practices on principle rather than profit. It was the sort of place where lawyers valued being right over being rich.

The chambers had a strong reputation for taking on cases that others would avoid, including death penalty appeals in former British colonies, challenges to government secrecy, and representation of activists and protesters. These were not the commercial disputes or white-collar criminal cases that typically generate substantial fees. Instead, they were cases that required immense courage, built character, enhanced understanding of human rights law, and helped establish a reputation for integrity, even if they didn't yield financial benefits.

Starmer was called to the bar in several Caribbean countries, where he defended individuals who had been sentenced to death. This work was both emotionally taxing and intellectually demanding. He was literally fighting for lives, using legal arguments to save his clients. His work significantly shaped Starmer's meticulous approach to legal preparation. It deepened his understanding of how the law can be a matter of life and death for those lacking other forms of influence.

His work in the Caribbean also provided him with crucial experience in international human rights law. Starmer learned how to navigate various legal systems, understand the relationship between domestic and international law, and craft arguments that could succeed in different jurisdictions. This expertise would later prove invaluable during his tenure as Director of Public Prosecutions and in the international law and human rights emphasis of his political career, showcasing the breadth of his legal knowledge.

Upon returning to Britain, Starmer increasingly focused his practice on cases that challenged authority. He represented journalists, activists, and everyday individuals embroiled in conflicts with powerful institutions. While this work often went unrecognised and demanded long hours for modest compensation, it was valuable in building a reputation for competence, integrity, and a commitment to fundamental principles of justice. Starmer was not motivated by the pursuit of glory; he was determined to stand up and be counted

The case that would establish Starmer as a prominent human rights lawyer began in 1990, although his involvement would not commence until later in the decade. McDonald's Corporation, the global fast-food giant, decided to take legal action against two environmental activists, Helen Steel and Dave Morris, for distributing leaflets critical of the company's practices

Initially intended as a straightforward defamation case, the situation evolved into "McLibel," one of the longest-running legal battles in British history, a classic David and Goliath story. Steel and Morris were sued by McDonald's over a critical pamphlet, and Starmer stepped in to assist the activists.

This case was a literal David versus Goliath scenario, with a fortified corporation facing off against two activists who could not afford proper legal representation. Under English law, legal aid was not available for defamation cases, leaving Steel and Morris to represent themselves against one of the world's largest corporations. It was a clear example of an uphill battle

When the Law Lords refused to accept their appeal, Steel and Morris formally retained solicitor Mark Stephens and barrister Keir Starmer to file a case with the European Court of Human Rights. They contested the UK government's policy that legal aid was unavailable in defamation cases. This was Starmer's opportunity to make a significant impact.

Starmer's involvement in the McLibel case was transformative for several reasons. First, it demonstrated his unwavering commitment to pro bono work in cases where fundamental principles were at stake. He was willing to work for minimal compensation when the cause was just. Over many years, he provided pro bono advice and guidance to the McLibel Two as the case progressed from the Old Bailey to the European Court, demonstrating his profound dedication and the transformative impact of his commitment to pro bono work.

The case also highlighted Starmer's meticulous approach to legal argument. He gained prominence through his work on McLibel, one of the longest-running libel trials in British history, representing two activists who were sued by McDonald's for publishing a pamphlet critical of the company's practices. This was a pivotal case that could have made or broken a legal career, and it was significant in legal history as it challenged the unequal British libel laws and the power of corporations to silence criticism through expensive litigation.

More importantly, McLibel represented more than just a single legal dispute; it raised fundamental questions about whether ordinary citizens could challenge powerful institutions without being overwhelmed by their superior resources. Critics argued that British libel law was unequal, allowing corporations to use the threat of expensive litigation to silence criticism.

Together with Mark Stephens, Starmer took the case to the European Court of Human Rights against the British government and achieved a significant victory on appeal. On 15 February 2005, the Court ruled that the lack of legal aid in defamation cases violated the rights to a fair trial of Steel and Morris (Steel and Morris v. United Kingdom, European Court of Human Rights). This was not just a legal victory; it vindicated Starmer's belief that the law could level the playing field and ensure that justice was accessible to all, regardless of their financial means.

By the late 1990s, Starmer had established himself as one of Britain's leading human rights barristers. His reputation in the field had grown, with a practice that included death penalty appeals, challenges to government secrecy, media law, and complex cases involving the interplay between domestic and international human rights law. He was not only fighting the good fight but also winning it; his work extended beyond the UK, having a significant international impact that demonstrated his dedication to human rights on a global scale.

His work required not just legal expertise but also cultural sensitivity and diplomatic skills. Cases involving the death penalty in the Caribbean necessitated an understanding of local legal traditions while applying international human rights standards. It was essential to gauge the prevailing attitudes in each jurisdiction. Challenges to government secrecy demanded knowledge of both administrative law and intelligence practices. Media law cases required a careful balance between press freedom, privacy rights, and national security concerns, walking a tightrope that could easily snap.

In 2005, Starmer helped overturn 417 death sentences in Uganda, a significant achievement that demonstrated the global impact of his human rights work. The case, Susan Kigula v. Attorney General of Uganda, was decided by Uganda's Constitutional Court on June 13, 2005. This accomplishment highlighted the breadth of his practice and his dedication to using legal expertise to save lives on a global scale. He wasn't just competing at a high level; he was changing the game, and his work in Uganda underscored the international significance of his human rights work.

The work in Uganda was particularly significant as it addressed systemic challenges to capital punishment rather than focusing solely on individual appeals. Starmer and his colleagues identified flaws in Uganda's death penalty system that affected hundreds of cases simultaneously. By challenging the system, itself instead of pursuing individual sentences, they achieved a far greater impact than would have been possible through case-by-case representation. They found a way to accomplish multiple goals at once.

Starmer's strategic approach to human rights law became his hallmark. Instead of merely representing individual clients, he sought opportunities to challenge unjust practices affecting entire groups of people. This innovative thinking about legal reform would later inform his approach to criminal justice policy as the Director of Public Prosecutions. He wasn't content with just moving the goalposts; he aimed to redesign the entire playing field, inspiring others with his forward-thinking approach.

Starmer's appointment as a human rights adviser to the Northern

Ireland Policing Board from 2003 to 2008 was a pivotal moment in his legal career. It was a baptism of fire in the most complex of contexts. The post-Good Friday Agreement era demanded a delicate balance of navigating sectarian divisions and establishing new institutions that could gain cross-community support. A single misstep could have unravelled the entire framework, underscoring the gravity of his role.

The transformation of the Royal Ulster Constabulary into the Police Service of Northern Ireland was a monumental task that involved more than just changing names and uniforms. It necessitated a complete shift in approach. This required the creation of a police force that previously hostile communities could learn to trust. To achieve this, new recruitment practices, accountability mechanisms, and strategies for community policing had to be developed without causing too much disruption. Starmer's role in this transformation was not just about providing legal frameworks, but also about navigating the intricate web of political, social, and legal challenges that such a transformation entailed.

Starmer's role involved providing legal frameworks for these changes while ensuring compliance with human rights standards. His work required diplomatic sensitivity, as he had to understand the concerns of both unionist and nationalist communities while crafting solutions that would satisfy legal requirements and political necessities. It was like trying to square a circle, yet he managed to succeed.

The Northern Ireland experience was formative for several reasons. It demonstrated how meticulous institutional design, underpinned by legal expertise, could foster trust and legitimacy. It showed that law can serve as a bridge rather than a weapon, and that patient, methodical work can lead to transformational change over time. Rome wasn't built in a day, and neither was peace in Northern Ireland.

These lessons from Northern Ireland would prove invaluable throughout Starmer's subsequent career, especially in his approach to reforming the Crown Prosecution Service and later in his political leadership style. He learned that lasting change requires building institutions rather than merely winning arguments, a principle that became central to his professional philosophy. He understood that while you can't make an omelette without breaking a few eggs, knowing how to cook is equally essential. This understanding, gained from his experience in Northern Ireland, shaped his approach to leadership and reform, emphasising the importance of patience, methodical work, and the building of trust and legitimacy.

Starmer's appointment as Queen's Counsel on 9 April 2002

recognised his emergence as one of the leading human rights barristers of his generation. He had truly reached the top echelons of the profession. Becoming a QC, which is the traditional term for taking silk, also came with ceremonial elements: the horsehair wig, silk gown, and ancient rituals of the English legal system that have been in place for centuries.

For Starmer, becoming a QC was not just about joining an exclusive club, but about gaining the authority to tackle even more challenging cases and to speak with greater authority on matters of legal principle. This appointment not only represented individual achievement but also signified the legal profession's recognition that his approach to human rights law was making a significant contribution to British jurisprudence. He was not just another face in the crowd, but a recognised leader in his field.

As a QC, Starmer's practice expanded beyond individual cases to encompass constitutional law, public inquiries, and complex litigation that could set legal precedents. His reputation grew not through self-promotion but through a consistent record of victories and the begrudging respect of opponents who acknowledged his thorough preparation and forensic approach to argument. Actions spoke louder than words.

The appointment of Queen's Counsel (QC) also brought increased responsibilities within the legal profession. QCs are expected to provide leadership, mentor junior barristers, and contribute to the development of legal principles. Starmer, in his role as QC, took these responsibilities to heart. He was not just a leader, but a mentor who was always ready to share his knowledge and support his colleagues. His approach was not about personal gain, but about lifting the entire legal community, understanding that a rising tide lifts all boats.

When he was offered the position of Director of Public Prosecutions (DPP) in 2008, it represented a pivotal moment in his career. This point distinguishes serious professionals from those who are less committed. Accepting this position meant leaving the lucrative world of private practice for a civil service salary, as well as trading the adversarial environment of the Bar for the administrative challenges associated with managing a large public organisation. It was a significant shift, akin to swapping horses midstream, and Starmer faced it with determination and a sense of duty.

For many successful barristers, taking on the DPP role might have felt like turkeys voting for Christmas. There were fewer financial rewards, more bureaucracy, and the inevitable political controversies that come with high-profile prosecutorial decisions. However, for Starmer, this opportunity represented a chance to apply his legal expertise to systemic reform in the criminal justice system, a way to make a real difference rather than make money.

In 2008, the Crown Prosecution Service (CPS) faced significant challenges. Relationships with police forces were often strained, and tensions were palpable. Conviction rates in specific categories of cases were disappointingly low, and public confidence in prosecutorial decision-making was declining. The service needed not only competent administration but also visionary leadership capable of modernising practices while upholding legal standards, someone who could separate the wheat from the chaff and get things back on track.

Starmer was appointed Director of Public Prosecutions on 1 November 2008, serving in this role until November 2013. His appointment was seen as a way to bring human rights expertise to an institution that had been criticised for prioritising administrative convenience over individual rights. His background in challenging government decisions suggested he would offer a fresh perspective on prosecutorial decision-making, a breath of fresh air in what had become a somewhat stale environment. His leadership was a beacon of hope for the future of the CPS.

During his tenure as Director of Public Prosecutions from 2008 to 2013, Starmer oversaw some of the most sensitive prosecutorial decisions of the era. He truly was in the hot seat, navigating a complex landscape that required balancing legal principles with practical considerations, managing relationships with police forces, and maintaining public confidence in prosecutorial independence. It was like trying to keep multiple balls in the air while walking a tightrope.

The role exposed him to a wide range of criminal law, from routine theft and assault cases to complex fraud investigations, terrorism prosecutions, and cases involving national security concerns. Each category brought unique challenges for prosecutorial policy, and there was no one-size-fits-all approach.

One of Starmer's significant achievements, according to supporters, was modernising the CPS's approach to prosecuting sexual violence cases. Traditional practices had often led to low conviction rates and secondary victimisation of complainants, further adding to the suffering of those already in distress. Starmer implemented new guidelines that emphasised the importance of believing victims while maintaining appropriate evidential standards, demonstrating that it is possible to balance compassion with legal rigour.

Similarly, he oversaw reforms in the prosecution of domestic violence cases, recognising that traditional approaches frequently failed to protect vulnerable victims or hold perpetrators accountable. These reforms required changing not just CPS policies, but also the collaborative relationships with police forces and other agencies involved in domestic violence interventions, ensuring that all parties worked together effectively.

The period also saw significant terrorism prosecutions as Britain addressed the ongoing threat from both international and domestic terrorist groups. These cases required balancing concerns for public safety with protections for civil liberties, often amid intense political and media pressure, like walking a tightrope while juggling flaming torches.

The Jimmy Savile controversy, which became one of the most challenging episodes of Keir Starmer's tenure as Director of Public Prosecutions (DPP), was a significant event that threatened to derail his career. As head of the Crown Prosecution Service (CPS) when the decision was made not to prosecute Savile, based on the grounds of 'insufficient evidence,' Starmer faced intense scrutiny and criticism. However, this controversy also provided a crucial learning opportunity and a turning point in his leadership style and decision-making process.

When allegations against Savile emerged posthumously in 2012, questions inevitably arose about why previous allegations had not been pursued. Suddenly, everyone was asking why the warning signs had been missed. DPP Keir Starmer tasked his Principal Legal Advisor, Alison Levitt QC, with examining the CPS's decisions regarding the four allegations made to Surrey and Sussex Police in 2007 and 2008; he was not about to sweep this issue under the carpet.

The report prepared by Alison Levitt QC was published on January 11, 2013 [CPS archives; The National Archives]. It found that if police and prosecutors had approached the allegations differently, prosecutions could have been possible for three of the claims. In other words, the ball had been dropped, and dropped badly.

The controversy highlighted both the complexities of prosecutorial decision-making and the political risks associated with the DPP role. Critics pointed out that while Keir Starmer was serving as Director of Public Prosecutions, several allegations about Savile were referred to the CPS by Surrey and Sussex Police. At the time, the CPS declined to charge Savile due to insufficient evidence. Commentators noted that this was akin to shutting the stable door after the horse had bolted.

Starmer's response to the Savile controversy was a testament to his leadership style that would later define his political career. He didn't shy away from responsibility; instead, he commissioned an independent review, implemented necessary reforms, and learned from his mistakes. His proactive approach, rather than being defensive or passing the buck, reassured that he took ownership of systemic failures and worked diligently to prevent similar issues in the future, making it clear that the buck stopped with him.

Throughout his legal career, Starmer was known for his 'forensic mind,' a reputation he earned from his colleagues. This was a testament to his ability to methodically dissect complex problems, identify key issues, and construct compelling arguments based on careful analysis of evidence and law. His knack for seeing the bigger picture, while others got lost in the details, was truly inspiring.

This approach was evident in his preparation for major cases. Unlike other barristers who might rely on charisma or rhetorical skill, Starmer's strength lay in exhaustive preparation and the logical presentation of arguments. He meticulously examined every detail of a case, anticipated opposing arguments, and crafted responses that were both legally sound and practically persuasive, leaving no stone unturned in his pursuit of justice.

Starmer's forensic approach extended beyond individual cases to his understanding of legal systems and institutional reform. As DPP, he did not simply manage existing processes; he analysed them systematically to identify opportunities for improvement. This led to significant reforms in prosecutorial practices, improved relationships with police forces, and the modernisation of CPS operations. He didn't just rearrange the deckchairs; he rebuilt the entire ship.

Keir Starmer's colleagues were often left in awe by his ability to ask questions during meetings that were more insightful than the answers provided by others. His rare talent for identifying crucial issues that others might overlook or challenging assumptions that needed reconsideration consistently left others searching for the right approach. This skill, which made him a formidable advocate and an effective administrator, was a testament to his unique insightfulness.

Keir Starmer's legal career is not just a footnote in his biography, but the very foundation for understanding his subsequent political leadership. It is where he honed his skills and learned the intricacies of his field. The forensic mindset developed through decades of case preparation, his commitment to human rights fostered through representing vulnerable clients, and the experience of driving institutional reform during public service all shaped his approach to political challenges. He had served his apprenticeship in the law, and now it was time to apply those skills in the political arena.

His journey from the son of a Surrey toolmaker to one of Britain's most prominent barristers illustrates not only individual achievement but also the significance of educational opportunities in facilitating social mobility. It serves as proof that hard work and talent can overcome privilege and connections. Starmer's career exemplifies how legal expertise can be leveraged not only for personal advancement but also for public service and social justice, underscoring the potential for the law to be a positive force in the world.

In an era marked by theatrical politics and populist gestures, Keir Starmer's methodical approach, careful preparation, systematic analysis, and the patient building of arguments became a hallmark of his political style. His legal training provided an alternative model of public leadership, one grounded in competence, integrity, and a commitment to institutional reform. This approach, which prioritises substance over style, stands in stark contrast to the prevailing political trends, offering a reassuring vision of leadership.

Whether defending death row prisoners in the Caribbean, challenging corporate power in the McLibel case, or reforming prosecutorial practices as Director of Public Prosecutions (DPP), Starmer's legal career was consistently guided by a commitment to using his expertise in the pursuit of justice. This foundation informed not only his professional reputation but also his understanding of how change occurs within democratic societies. He learned the importance of working patiently within institutions, respecting procedural fairness, and maintaining an unwavering commitment to fundamental principles. He understood that Rome wasn't built in a day, but it was built to last.

Starmer's experiences as a lawyer not only created a successful barrister but also a public servant with a deep understanding of the intersection between law and politics. He grasped how institutions can be reformed while preserving their essential functions and how professional expertise can uphold democratic values. The lessons he learned over decades of practice would prove invaluable as he transitioned from the courtroom to the political arena, bringing a forensic mind to the complex art of democratic leadership. He was ready to roll up his sleeves and engage in the challenging world of politics

.Chapter 2
The Political Awakening

How a human rights barrister swapped silk for the rough and tumble of Westminster politics?

By 2014, Sir Keir Starmer found himself at a crossroads that would have made many successful barristers think twice. At the age of 52, he had the opportunity to return to the lucrative world of private practice, where he could charge substantial fees and enjoy a comfortable lifestyle based on his impressive achievements as Director of Public Prosecutions. Instead, he chose to pursue a far less specific path: a career in politics. This decision was significant not only because it marked a shift in his career trajectory, but also because it reflected his deep-seated commitment to public service and his belief in the power of politics to effect change.

The turning point came when Frank Dobson, the veteran Labour MP for Holborn and St Pancras, announced his intention to step down after 36 years in Parliament. Dobson was a political institution in North London. This old-school Labour stalwart had served as Health Secretary under Tony Blair and enjoyed an unshakeable local support that money couldn't buy. Finding someone to succeed him would not be easy.

For Starmer, the constituency represented an ideal launching pad. Holborn and St Pancras was one of the safest Labour seats you could find this side of the Pennines, so secure that critics joked you could stick a red rosette on a donkey and it would still win. In the 2015 election, Starmer was elected with a comfortable majority of 17,048 votes, securing 52.9% of the vote, which observers described as a coronation rather than a contest.

The constituency itself was a fascinating microcosm of modern London politics. It encompassed everything from the grand Georgian terraces of Bloomsbury, home to academics, barristers, and intellectuals, to social housing estates around King's Cross, where gentrification was clashing with decades of urban deprivation. This diverse mix of demographics and socio-economic conditions presented a unique set of challenges and opportunities for Starmer. If he could succeed in representing everyone from university professors to cab drivers, he would gain valuable experience in coalition-building for the wider Labour Party.

However, gaining selection as the Labour candidate wasn't just about being well-known. Local party members needed to be convinced that someone with decades of courtroom experience could connect with voters who were queuing at food banks or struggling to make ends meet on zero-hours contracts. Starmer's strategy was savvy: rather than distancing himself from his privileged background, he embraced his working-class roots and legal expertise as strengths that could benefit the constituency. This was not without its challenges, as he had to work hard to dispel any perceptions of elitism and prove his ability to understand and address the issues facing the local community.

"I know what it's like to worry about paying the bills," he told local party meetings, referencing his own family's struggles when his mother fell ill. "And I understand how the system works when ordinary people confront powerful institutions. That's what I've spent my career doing, ensuring that the little person gets a fair shake."

Starmer officially took his seat in the House of Commons on May 7, 2015, entering a Parliament that was still reeling from one of the most surprising election results in recent history. David Cameron's Conservatives had defied all expectations by winning an outright majority. The Liberal Democrats had been virtually wiped out, and the SNP had swept through Scotland like a tartan tsunami. Most surprising of all, Ed Miliband had resigned as Labour leader, leaving the party without direction and facing an existential crisis about its future.

For new MPs, Parliament can be an intimidating place, even at the best of times. The complicated procedures, medieval traditions, and the weight of history pressing down on every debate can make even the most confident newcomer feel like a fish out of water. However, Keir Starmer had spent his career navigating complex institutions, from the Old Bailey to the European Court of Human Rights. If anyone could grasp Westminster's peculiar ways, it was someone who had already mastered the art of playing by others' rules while trying to change them.

His maiden speech on June 3, 2015, was characteristically Starmer [Hansard records]. It was thoughtful, well-researched, and focused squarely on his constituents' concerns rather than on personal grandstanding. This dedication to his constituents set him apart from other new MPs who sought to make a name for themselves with flashy interventions or controversial statements. Starmer's quiet determination to learn the ropes, understand how the institution worked, and build relationships across party lines was a testament to his commitment to his role as an MP.

Keir Starmer's approach to his role as an MP was distinct from many of his peers. He believed that the role of an MP was not to be a celebrity, but to be an effective advocate for the people who put you there. This meant doing your homework, understanding the issues, and working with anyone who could help deliver results. His dedication to his constituents set him apart from those who sought the limelight.

This approach distinguished him from many of his peers. While others were networking furiously or positioning themselves for rapid advancement, Starmer dedicated himself to mastering his brief, reading every briefing paper, attending every committee meeting, and generally behaving like someone who came to Parliament to work rather than to be seen.

Keir Starmer's arrival in Parliament was exceptionally fortuitous. Within weeks of taking his seat, Labour was plunged into a leadership contest that would reshape British politics. Jeremy Corbyn's unexpected victory, a backbench MP who barely secured enough nominations to get on the ballot, sent Westminster into turmoil and created opportunities for newcomers like Starmer who might otherwise have had to wait years for advancement.

Corbyn's election as Labour leader in September 2015 was a political earthquake that reshaped the entire landscape [Labour Party records]. His unexpected victory, a backbench MP who barely secured enough nominations to get on the ballot, sent shockwaves through Westminster. He was a 66-year-old socialist who had spent three decades on the backbenches, suddenly thrust into the leadership of Her Majesty's Opposition with a mandate from party members that few had anticipated. The magnitude of this change was felt by all, including Starmer, who, although new to Parliament, had significant credentials; the dilemma was particularly acute.

For established MPs, Corbyn's victory presented tough choices: Should they support the revolution, keep their heads down and hope it blows over, or make a principled stand that might end their careers? For someone like Starmer, new to Parliament but with significant credentials, the dilemma was particularly acute.

Starmer's instincts were cautious. He recognised that Corbyn represented a genuine desire for real change among party members, rather than the triangulated platitudes that had characterised previous leadership. Yet, his legal training made him sceptical of ideological purity that ignored practical constraints. "You can't legislate from opposition, no matter how righteous your cause," he understood.

His solution was characteristically pragmatic: get involved, earn Corbyn's trust, and try to influence policy from within rather than criticising from the sidelines. This strategic thinking was evident when Corbyn offered him a position in the shadow cabinet as Shadow Immigration Minister in October 2015 [shadow cabinet appointments]. Starmer's acceptance of this role without hesitation was a clear demonstration of his pragmatic approach to navigating the Labour Party's changing landscape.

The appointment made perfect sense on paper. Immigration was one of the most politically sensitive issues facing the Labour Party. Traditional working-class voters were increasingly concerned about the impact of EU migration, while metropolitan members remained committed to free movement. Who better to navigate this minefield than someone with extensive experience in human rights law and a reputation for thoroughly analysing complex problems?

Starmer's time in the immigration brief was short-lived. The real test of his relationship with Corbyn was about to come from an unexpected direction: Britain's relationship with the European Union.

The announcement in February 2016 that David Cameron would hold a referendum on Britain's membership in the European Union was a seismic event. What had once seemed like a peripheral issue, something for European obsessives and backbench rebels, suddenly became the defining political question of a generation, with far-reaching implications for the UK's future.

For Labour, the referendum posed a particular challenge. The party's official position was to support Remain, but significant portions of its traditional working-class support were drawn to Leave arguments related to sovereignty and immigration. Jeremy Corbyn's own Euroscepticism, which he had carefully concealed during his leadership campaign, began to surface in what critics described as lukewarm campaign appearances and half-hearted endorsements of EU membership.

Following the Brexit referendum result in June 2016, Starmer joined other shadow ministers in resigning his position after he stated that he had lost faith in Corbyn's leadership. These mass resignations were triggered not only by Brexit but also by what many MPs viewed as Corbyn's lacklustre handling of the entire campaign.

The referendum result, with 52% voting Leave and 48% voting Remain, sent shockwaves through the British establishment that are still felt today. Cameron resigned immediately, triggering a Conservative leadership contest that would eventually lead to Theresa May being appointed as Prime Minister. However, the real drama was unfolding within the Labour Party, where Corbyn faced a coordinated challenge to his leadership from MPs who believed he had let the country down when it mattered most, creating a tense and uncertain atmosphere.

For Starmer, the decision to resign was not made lightly. He had spent months trying to work constructively with Corbyn, recognising that undermining the leadership would only harm the party's chances of returning to power. However, the referendum campaign revealed what he perceived as fundamental problems with Corbyn's approach to leadership. These problems included a lack of clear and effective communication of Labour's position on Brexit, as well as a failure to build the necessary alliances within the party and with other political actors to implement the party's policies. In Starmer's view, these issues could not be ignored.

"Leadership isn't just about having the right policies," Starmer told colleagues at the time. "It's about being able to communicate those policies effectively and build the necessary coalitions to implement them. In Europe, we failed on both counts."

The attempted challenge to Corbyn in the summer of 2016 only strengthened his position among party members, who rallied to support a leader they felt was being undermined by what critics labelled the 'Blairite' parliamentary party. When Corbyn was re-elected with an increased mandate in September 2016, he faced a choice: seek revenge against the plotters or attempt to rebuild party unity by bringing critics back into the fold. His resilience and determination to unite the party were evident in his decision to adopt the latter approach.

Surprisingly, he chose the latter approach. Corbyn appointed Starmer as Shadow Brexit Secretary, recognising that managing Labour's response to Brexit would require someone with both legal expertise and political credibility. In this role, Starmer was responsible for shaping Labour's Brexit policy, scrutinising the government's approach to negotiations, and leading the party's response to key Brexit developments. He held the position from October 2016 to April 2020, making him one of the most visible faces of Labour's opposition during this turbulent period in modern British politics.

The appointment of Keir Starmer as Shadow Brexit Secretary was seen as a smart move from Jeremy Corbyn's perspective. It presented one of his most prominent critics with the opportunity to either prove himself or remain silent. At the same time, it assigned the Brexit response to someone well-versed in the legal complexities involved. For Starmer, this role provided a long-awaited chance to influence policy on what many considered the defining issue of the era.

However, serving as Shadow Brexit Secretary under Corbyn was akin to navigating a minefield with a blindfold on. Corbyn's own views on Europe were unclear, while party members largely supported remaining in the EU, despite many Labour-held constituencies having voted decisively to leave the EU. Finding a cohesive position that could satisfy this diverse coalition would challenge even Starmer's considerable diplomatic skills.

A meticulous legal mindset marked Starmer's approach to the Brexit role. He left no stone unturned, anticipated every argument, and crafted positions that could withstand the most rigorous scrutiny. While government ministers struggled with vague statements about 'Brexit meaning Brexit,' Starmer was busy dissecting white papers, analysing treaty obligations, and building what his supporters hailed as a forensic case against the government's approach to leaving the EU.

His performances during parliamentary sessions became essential viewing for those observing the Westminster proceedings. Here was an individual capable of matching government minister's fact for fact, precedent for precedent, and legal authority for legal authority. When Brexit Secretary David Davis attempted to navigate parliamentary statements with what critics called ambiguous assertions about Britain holding all the cards, Starmer would methodically dismantle his arguments with the precision that had made him a formidable barrister, significantly shaping the Brexit debate.

A typical Starmer intervention would start with, 'The right honourable gentleman says we can have our cake and eat it. Perhaps he could explain to the House how this aligns with Article 50 of the Treaty, which clearly states...' The contrast between him and his counterparts was stark. Davis, Raab, and later Barclay seemed to be improvising, treating one of the most complex legal and political processes in British history as if it were a simple undergraduate tutorial. Starmer, on the other hand, had clearly reviewed every relevant document, understood every implication, and considered every possible scenario.

This thorough approach helped establish Starmer's reputation as a serious political figure rather than merely another ambitious backbencher. Initially sceptical parliamentary sketch-writers began to take notice of a politician who combined genuine expertise with growing political acumen. One correspondent noted, "Starmer doesn't just oppose the government; he dismantles their arguments piece by piece, like a master craftsman taking apart a watch to show you how it works. By the time he's finished, there's nothing left but a pile of cogs and springs."

As the Brexit process faced ongoing crises, Starmer found himself at the heart of one of the most contentious debates within the Labour Party: whether to support a second referendum on EU membership. The campaign for a "People's Vote" was gaining momentum among pro-European MPs and activists who argued that the 2016 referendum had been based on misleading promises and incomplete information.

For Starmer, the question of Brexit was a multi-faceted challenge, intertwining political, constitutional, and strategic elements. As a lawyer, he grappled with the arguments surrounding parliamentary sovereignty and the risks that referendums pose in a representative democracy. As a politician, he navigated the electoral dangers of seemingly disregarding the outcome of the first referendum. And as Shadow Brexit Secretary, he balanced the need for party unity with the evolution of Labour's stance on Brexit.

Critics would later argue that during his tenure as Shadow Brexit Secretary from 2016 to 2019, he played a crucial role in advocating for a second referendum on leaving the European Union, a position many blame for Labour's disastrous performance in the 2019 election.

Starmer's approach was not just cautious, but also deeply strategic. Instead of immediately endorsing a second referendum, he proposed what he termed 'tests' that any Brexit deal would need to meet. These included ensuring access to the single market, protecting workers' rights, and making sure that no region of the UK would be left worse off. Labour would support a People's Vote only if the government's deal failed to meet these criteria.

This strategy had the advantage of being both principled and tactical. It allowed Labour to oppose unfavourable Brexit deals without alienating Leave voters while keeping the possibility of a second referendum open if circumstances changed. However, it required continuous adjustments as the political landscape evolved, leaving Starmer vulnerable to criticism from both within and outside the party.

Pro-European activists accused him of being overly cautious and of missing opportunities to eliminate Brexit. Pro-Leave Labour MPs were concerned that he was steering the party toward an electoral dead end that could cost them seats in traditional strongholds. Navigating these conflicting pressures demanded all of Starmer's diplomatic skills and more.

A pivotal moment in Labour's Brexit strategy unfolded at the party's annual conference in Liverpool in September 2018. What initially seemed like a routine policy debate regarding the party's European stance transformed into what observers described as a carefully orchestrated campaign to commit Labour to supporting a second referendum under any circumstances.

Starmer found himself in the centre of the storm, facing significant pressure from pro-European activists to accelerate their position beyond what Corbyn's leadership team was comfortable with. The behind-the-scenes negotiations became intense, with trade union leaders, MPs, and party members all advancing their agendas while the media closely monitored for signs of splits or reversals.

Commentators referred to the compromise that ultimately arose as a classic "fudge": Labour would support a People's Vote only if it could not secure a general election or induce substantial changes to the government's Brexit deal. This conditional commitment satisfied no one completely but successfully maintained party unity at a crucial time.

Observers described Starmer's conference speech announcing the new position as a masterclass in political communication. He managed to sound both decisive and reasonable, passionate yet measured, principled, and pragmatic. For many, it marked the moment he established himself as a potential future leader rather than just a capable shadow minister.

At the conference, he declared, "We are the party that believes in democracy," earning rapturous applause. "We trusted the people in 2016. But if this government cannot deliver a Brexit that works for Britain, then we must trust the people again." The standing ovation that followed recognised not just the policy position, but also the emergence of a leader-in-waiting who could articulate complex arguments with clarity and conviction.

As 2018 turned into 2019, British politics entered a period of unprecedented chaos that would challenge even the most experienced politicians. Theresa May's Brexit deal was rejected by Parliament three times, leading to a series of indicative votes that revealed no majority for any specific course of action. The government was paralysed, Parliament was deadlocked, and the country was thoroughly fed up with the entire process, feeling the need for a decisive leader like Johnson.

For Keir Starmer, this period represented both an opportunity and a danger. As the government struggled to find a Brexit strategy that could command support, Labour's detailed opposition increasingly appeared justified. Starmer's warnings about the complexities of leaving the EU were proving to be accurate, while unfolding events were validating his critiques of government proposals.

However, political dynamics were shifting in ways that could prove troublesome for Labour's electoral prospects. The European elections in May 2019, which were seen as a de facto second referendum on Brexit, saw Nigel Farage's Brexit Party top the polls with nearly a third of the vote, while pro-Remain parties also performed strongly. Labour, positioned in the middle with its conditional support for a second referendum, found itself squeezed from both sides.

The message was clear: voters wanted clarity on Brexit, not carefully crafted compromises that attempted to appease everyone. Starmer's lawyerly approach to the issue, weighing pros and cons, considering all options, and building arguments that could withstand scrutiny, was precisely what Brexit didn't require. Politics sometimes demands that you take a firm stance, regardless of the legal complexities that may be involved.

The arrival of Boris Johnson as Conservative leader in July 2019 changed the entire political landscape. Here was a leader willing to crash out of the EU without a deal if necessary, someone who spoke the language of English nationalism with the fluency afforded by a lifetime of privilege and entitlement. Suddenly, Labour's cautious positioning appeared less like principled opposition and more like what critics derided as metropolitan fence-sitting.

Starmer responded by doubling down on the forensic approach that had served him well in previous years. He continued to dissect Johnson's Brexit proposals with the meticulous analysis that had made him a formidable barrister. His audience, appreciative of his methodical thinking, admired his commitment to thorough examination. However, Johnson was not interested in legal arguments or parliamentary procedure; he was focused on political theatre and emotional resonance.

The contrast between the two men couldn't have been more pronounced. Johnson projected bluster and charm, promising to "get Brexit done" with a can-do optimism reminiscent of his time as a popular mayor of London. His audience, admiring his decisiveness, was drawn to his leadership style. In contrast, Starmer offered careful analysis and qualified statements, cautioning against the pitfalls of rushing into complex negotiations without adequate preparation.

In the short term, Johnson's approach proved far more politically effective. By October 2019, he had successfully negotiated a revised withdrawal agreement with the EU, which addressed some of the concerns raised by the previous agreement, neutralising Labour's main line of attack regarding his reckless negotiation style. More importantly, he positioned the Conservatives as the party of clarity and decisiveness, while Labour became labelled by critics as the party of dithering and delay.

The December 2019 general election marked a catastrophic defeat for Labour, one that would shape British politics for years to come.

Following Labour's loss, Jeremy Corbyn resigned as leader, and Keir Starmer won the 2020 leadership election. The party suffered a loss of 60 seats, including many in traditional strongholds that had been Labour constituencies for decades. The collapse of the so-called 'Red Wall' of seats in the north and Midlands, a symbolic barrier that had long prevented the Conservatives from making significant inroads, under Boris Johnson's campaign, which promised to deliver Brexit and appealed to voters who felt neglected by metropolitan elites, was substantial.

For Starmer, the election result was bittersweet. In June 2017, he was re-elected as an MP with 70.1% of the vote, securing a majority of 30,509 votes, demonstrating his strong personal appeal in his constituency. However, his role as the architect of Labour's Brexit policy made him a target for criticism, with many blaming the party's stance on Europe for its electoral defeat.

The post-election analysis was not just swift, but also harsh. Focus groups in former Labour constituencies indicated that voters perceived the party as disconnected from their concerns about immigration and sovereignty. The policy advocating for a second referendum, which might have seemed strategic in Westminster, was viewed as an attempt to undermine the democratic will of the people. Although Starmer's meticulous opposition worked well in parliamentary settings, it failed to resonate with voters who wanted politicians to respect their decisions instead of devising clever workarounds.

Nevertheless, the electoral defeat also presented a significant opportunity. With Corbyn announcing his intention to step down, a leadership contest emerged that would redefine the party's direction. For Starmer, who had spent four years building his reputation as a serious political figure, the timing was not just fortuitous, but also hopeful for the potential for change.

By the end of 2019, Keir Starmer had established himself as a rare figure in modern British politics: someone who grasped complex issues and articulated difficult arguments with clarity and conviction. His four years as Shadow Brexit Secretary demonstrated his ability to operate effectively at high levels of government, holding ministers accountable while proposing alternative policies that could withstand scrutiny.

However, the electoral loss revealed the limitations of his forensic approach to politics. Voters don't always seek detailed legal analysis of complex issues; often, they desire straightforward answers to complicated questions, even if those answers are incorrect or misleading. The essence of democratic leadership isn't just about being right; it also involves persuasion, which requires an emotional connection alongside intellectual rigour.

As Labour geared up for another leadership contest, Starmer faced a crucial decision about the type of politician he wanted to be. He could continue as the lawyer-politician, someone who knew the law better than his adversaries and could construct unassailable arguments for the party's positions. Alternatively, he could strive to become something more: a leader who merges intellectual rigour with emotional appeal, combining forensic analysis with political intuition. The potential future directions for Starmer are intriguing, and the choices he makes will shape the Labour Party's trajectory.

The COVID-19 pandemic was about to test these qualities in unprecedented ways. But that, as they say, is another story. For now, the son of a toolmaker from Surrey had established himself as a political force to be reckoned with, someone who had earned his place in the competitive arena of Westminster and was ready to face the challenges ahead.

The development of Keir Starmer as a political figure was complete. What followed would determine whether he could evolve from a competent opposition leader to an effective one, from a forensic critic to a visionary statesman. The jury, as lawyers like to say, was still out.

Chapter 3
Starmer's Path to Labour Leadership

*How the forensic barrister convinced a wounded party that
competence could trump charisma?*

The results of the December 2019 general election were a seismic
shock to the Labour Party. The party, under Jeremy Corbyn's leadership,
suffered its worst defeat since 1935, losing 60 seats and witnessing
constituencies that had been Labour strongholds for decades turn blue for
the first time in living memory. The collapse of the 'Red Wall', a
significant area of working-class seats across the North and the
Midlands, was akin to a house of cards in a hurricane.

For party activists who had spent the previous four years believing in
a socialist transformation, the result was a profound loss. The exit poll
had already signalled trouble, but as iconic Labour strongholds fell one
by one, Blyth, Redcar, Sedgefield, and even Dennis Skinner's Bolsover,
it became clear that this was not just an electoral setback. It was an
existential crisis that struck at the very heart of the Labour Party's
identity and representation.

Jeremy Corbyn, appearing every bit of his 70 years, addressed a
subdued crowd at his Islington count and announced that he would not
lead the party into another election. However, in true Corbyn fashion, he
refused to step down immediately. Instead, he initiated what he called a
'period of reflection', leaving the party in a state of uncertainty as it
conducted a thorough post-mortem before selecting his successor.

For those ambitious enough to seek the leadership role, this was the
moment they had been waiting for. Yet, it also represented a poisoned
chalice of epic proportions. Whoever won would inherit a party that was
not only defeated but also demoralised, not merely out of power but
seemingly disconnected from the very people it claimed to represent.

Within days of the election disaster, Westminster buzzed with
speculation about potential candidates for the leadership. The usual
suspects began to emerge. Shadow cabinet ministers briefed journalists
about their qualifications, backbench MPs gauged support from
colleagues, and trade union leaders hinted at where their significant
influence might go.

By January 2020, when Corbyn finally initiated a formal leadership contest, the field had narrowed to a manageable group of contenders. The frontrunner, by most accounts, was Rebecca Long-Bailey, Corbyn's protégé and the standard-bearer for those who believed the party's policies were correct but poorly communicated. She had the backing of Momentum, the grassroots organisation that had propelled Corbyn to power, and the support of Unite, Labour's largest affiliated union.

Lisa Nandy represented a different perspective. As a northern MP who retained her Wigan seat despite the collapse of the Red Wall, she spoke the language of communities that felt abandoned by both Westminster politics and metropolitan Labour activists. Nandy positioned herself as the candidate who could win back the voters the party had lost without sacrificing its progressive principles.

Keir Starmer quickly emerged as the early favourite among key figures: Labour MPs and the broader membership began to question whether ideological purity was worth much if it meant remaining in permanent opposition. Starmer presented himself as a figure of gravitas, boasting a track record of successfully taking on the Tories. His professional competence became increasingly appealing after four years of what critics labelled "amateur hour."

On January 4, 2020, Starmer announced his candidacy for the leadership election [Labour Party records]. He gained endorsements from prominent figures, including former Labour Prime Minister Gordon Brown and London Mayor Sadiq Khan [press reports]. However, while support from notable figures helped, it was essential for Starmer to win over the membership, especially the left-wing activists who had rallied around Jeremy Corbyn. He needed to demonstrate that he was not simply another Blairite in forensic attire.

Starmer's campaign strategy was a stroke of brilliance. He introduced a set of ten pledges that resembled a greatest hits album of Corbynite policies, positioning himself against austerity and acknowledging that Corbyn was right to promote Labour as 'the party of anti-austerity' [campaign materials]. He proposed scrapping tuition fees, advocating for 'common ownership' of railways, mail services, energy, and water companies, and calling for an end to outsourcing in the NHS. This move was not just clever; it was a masterclass in political positioning

Political observers described these pledges as a masterclass in positioning. He advocated for economic justice by suggesting an increase in income tax for the top 5% of earners, reversing cuts to corporation tax, and tightening regulations against tax avoidance. His platform offered something for everyone: higher taxes on the wealthy appealed to those seeking wealth redistribution, public ownership attracted those who believed in socialist economics, and green investments resonated with those who viewed climate change as the defining issue of our time.

"My promise to you is that I will uphold our radical values and work tirelessly to get Labour into power, so that we can advance the interests of the people our party was created to serve. Based on the moral case for socialism, here is where I stand," Starmer declared in his leadership launch video. This statement struck the right chord with a membership eager to believe that their values could align with electoral success.

However, there was a method behind what some perceived as ideological positioning. By embracing Corbyn's policy agenda while implicitly critiquing his leadership style, Starmer sought to resolve a longstanding dilemma for Labour: how to maintain the radical impetus that energised activists while also cultivating the competence necessary to win elections.

Observers characterised Starmer's campaign as a beacon of hope. Unlike previous leadership contests that resembled gladiatorial combat, his approach was described as deliberately consensual, emphasising unity over division, competence over ideology, and electability over purity. This was politics framed as conflict resolution, rather than a contact sport, a refreshing change that inspired hope in the party's future.

Starmer's approach reflected both his legal background and his understanding of the party's mood. After four years of factional strife marked by resignations of MPs, threats of deselection from members, and internal turmoil over Brexit and antisemitism, there was a strong desire for someone who could bring people together rather than instigate further conflict.

His campaign team, a blend of former Corbyn supporters and moderate MPs who had spent years in the political wilderness, demonstrated their competence at every step. They methodically navigated the three-part electoral college that would determine the outcome. They secured nominations from MPs and MEPs, endorsements from affiliated organisations such as trade unions, and ultimately the votes of ordinary party members, who would make the final decision. Their competence was a reassuring sign of Starmer's leadership potential.

The nominations from MPs came relatively easily. Rebecca Long-Bailey received 33 nominations from Labour MPs and MEPs, representing 15% of the members in these groups, which exceeded the 10% required to progress to the next stage of the process [nomination records]. In contrast, Starmer, with his higher profile and broader appeal, easily surpassed the nomination threshold, showcasing his strength within the parliamentary party.

The affiliate stage of the leadership contest proved to be more challenging. Unite's support for Long-Bailey was expected, considering Len McCluskey's role as Jeremy Corbyn's closest ally in the trade union movement. On January 24, Unite the Union officially endorsed Long-Bailey after McCluskey stated that she possessed the "brains and brilliance" needed to "take on" Boris Johnson. However, Starmer's team had meticulously planned their strategy, securing backing from other unions and building a coalition that highlighted his appeal beyond any single faction, instilling a sense of reassurance in his leadership potential.

What set Starmer apart was not just his policies or endorsements but also his tone. While other candidates focused on past conflicts, re-litigating the Corbyn years and settling old scores, Starmer concentrated on the future with a message that was not just straightforward, but also hopeful: the party needed to stop navel-gazing and start preparing for a return to government, instilling a sense of hope about the Labour Party's future direction.

Though this wasn't the type of inspirational rhetoric that usually excites activists, it was precisely what many party members wanted to hear after the trauma of the December 2019 election. Here was someone who spoke like a prime minister rather than a permanent opposition leader, and who understood, more than anyone, that winning elections was essential for implementing any agenda, no matter how radical, instilling a sense of confidence in his strategic thinking.

The contrast with his main rivals was striking. Long-Bailey, despite her intelligence and commitment, appeared to be ensnared in what critics termed the amber of Corbynism, defending policies and strategies that had clearly failed to resonate with voters. Nandy brought energy and authenticity to the race, but she struggled to unite the broad coalition necessary to win in a contest where every vote counted.

Starmer's advantage lay in his ability to appeal to various groups without appearing insincere. To Corbyn supporters, he was the individual who helped shape Labour's Brexit position and defended the party's radical policy agenda. To moderates, he represented a competent professional who had held government ministers accountable with precision. To pragmatists, he was simply the candidate most likely to make Labour electable again.

Just as the leadership campaign was gaining momentum, the world changed overnight. The emergence of COVID-19, which shifted from being a distant threat to a global pandemic, transformed not only the political landscape but also the nature of political campaigning itself.

Suddenly, the rallies and hustings that had characterised previous contests became impossible. The campaign transitioned online, relying on Zoom calls and social media rather than packed meeting halls and conference centres.

For Keir Starmer, the shift to remote campaigning during the pandemic was not a hurdle, but an opportunity to showcase his adaptability and leadership skills. While other candidates struggled to adapt, he embraced the new reality with characteristic thoroughness. His legal training had instilled in him the importance of preparation and attention to detail, qualities that translated well to virtual politics.

The pandemic also changed the political narrative in ways that favoured Starmer's candidacy. Competence became more critical than charisma, expertise overshadowed ideology, and the ability to manage complex crises emerged as the primary qualification for leadership. Starmer's background in managing large organisations, navigating legal complexities, and making tough decisions under pressure became not just relevant but crucial for the times.

However, the timing was challenging. The final stages of the campaign occurred amid national lockdowns, with the country gripped by fear of the virus and uncertainty about the future. This environment was not ideal for the optimistic messaging typically associated with leadership campaigns, meaning that the new Labour leader would have to take charge during one of the most challenging periods in modern British history.

When the results were announced on April 4, 2020, Starmer's victory was comprehensive but not overwhelming. He secured 56.2% of the membership vote on the first ballot, avoiding the need for additional rounds, but won by a smaller margin than some had anticipated. Rebecca Long-Bailey came in second with 27.6%, while Lisa Nandy trailed in third with 16.2%.

The results highlighted the state of the Labour Party: Starmer won decisively among MPs and affiliated organisations, but his victory among ordinary members was narrower, indicative of the ideological divisions that had characterised the Corbyn years and had not simply vanished. These divisions primarily pitted the more moderate, centrist faction, represented by Starmer, against the more left-wing, socialist faction associated with Corbyn's leadership. He had united the party institutionally but still faced the challenge of healing it emotionally and intellectually.

In his victory speech, delivered via video link from his home in North London, Starmer didn't just talk about competence; he emphasised the need for unity. "We've got a mountain to climb," he acknowledged in a tone of understated realism. "But we will climb it, together, and we will win the next general election." This message of unity was likely the reassurance the traumatised membership needed.

The tone was deliberately modest and almost businesslike. This was not a transformational moment or a revolutionary change of leadership; instead, it was a competent professional taking the reins of a complex organisation and promising to lead it more effectively than his predecessors. For a membership traumatised by four years of factional conflict and electoral failure, this was likely the reassurance they needed.

Angela Rayner did not run for the Labour leadership in 2020 but supported Rebecca Long-Bailey, who finished second to Starmer. However, she contested the deputy leadership and was elected on April 4, 2020, becoming deputy leader and succeeding Tom Watson.

Rayner's simultaneous election as deputy leader added an intriguing dynamic to Starmer's victory. As a member of the Corbynite wing of the party, a working-class northerner who left school at 16 and spoke with an authenticity that the privileged lawyer from Surrey could not match, she represented a balanced ticket that could help unify the Labour coalition. Her election also signified a shift in the party's power dynamics, with the Corbynite wing still holding significant influence despite Starmer's victory.

However, this partnership also created potential complications. Rayner had her own mandate from the membership, her own political agenda, and her own ambitions. She was not merely Starmer's deputy; she was an independent political force with ties to constituencies within the party that remained sceptical of his moderate views. This could lead to internal power struggles and challenges in implementing Starmer's vision for the party.

The relationship between Sir Keir Starmer and his deputy, which would become one of the defining features of his leadership, was significant for several reasons. It blended his strategic thinking with her political intuition, his legal precision with her emotional intelligence. This partnership was expected to provide a balanced approach to leadership, leveraging their respective strengths to navigate the challenges ahead. However, in April 2020, as they prepared to challenge the government during the worst crisis since World War II, all of this lay ahead.

As Starmer settled into the leader's office in the Houses of Parliament, or rather, at his kitchen table due to lockdown restrictions, he faced an inheritance that would have tested even the most resilient politician. The Labour Party was trailing by 20 points in the polls, had just endured its worst defeat in living memory, and was up against a Conservative government with an 80-seat majority, led by a prime minister who represented everything Labour opposed

The internal challenges were even more formidable. The party was still divided by the factional battles of the Corbyn years, with Momentum activists wary of any shift away from radical policies and moderate MPs eager to restore the party's electability. Moreover, the antisemitism crisis that had plagued Corbyn's leadership remained unresolved, with the Equality and Human Rights Commission still conducting its investigation. The Brexit issue, which had dominated British politics for four years, was also unfinished, with the transition period set to conclude in December 2020.

Perhaps the most significant challenge was the fundamental question of identity: What was the Labour Party's purpose in 2020? Who did it represent? What did it stand for? The coalition that had elected Starmer as leader was primarily united by their opposition to continued electoral failure. This powerful force could be harnessed to shape a cohesive vision for the party's future.

The ten pledges that had helped him win the leadership were a set of promises and commitments that Starmer made to the Labour Party members during his campaign. They provided some guidance, but it was essentially a list of policies rather than a coherent philosophy. Critics would later argue, "We, as party members, elected you based on your ten pledges, which led us to believe you would lead the party according to the same principles and policies as your predecessor." The challenge now lay in transforming those pledges into a governing program that could appeal to voters beyond the party membership.

What Starmer brought to leadership was something that had been absent from Labour politics for years: professional competence combined with political ambition. He was not someone who had stumbled into politics by accident or viewed it merely as an extension of activism. Instead, he had deliberately chosen to transition from one elite profession to another, bringing with him the skills and strategies that had fuelled his success in law.

This difference was evident in everything from media interviews to parliamentary performances. Where Corbyn often appeared uncomfortable with the visibility required in political leadership, Starmer embraced it, applying the same methodical approach he used in major court cases. Every appearance was meticulously prepared, every argument structured, and every intervention carefully calculated for maximum impact, instilling confidence in his leadership.

This professionalism extended to his team as well. His senior appointments reflected a commitment to running Labour like a serious political operation rather than a social movement. The individuals in senior positions had experience in government, election campaigns, and the mechanics of political power. They understood how the system worked and how to navigate it effectively.

However, professionalism, no matter how competent, is not the same as political vision. A key question hanging over Starmer's early leadership was whether technical expertise could replace the emotional connection that great political leaders need to inspire followers and convince voters. Could the son of a toolmaker from Surrey resonate emotionally with the people he sought to represent?

In April 2020, amidst a nationwide lockdown and the government's struggle to manage an unprecedented crisis, Keir Starmer's promise of competent and professional leadership became increasingly appealing. He presented himself as someone who understood complex issues, had successfully managed large organisations during tough times, and could speak with authority on law, justice, and institutional reform.

The contrast with Boris Johnson's government was clear and intentional. While Downing Street appeared to fumble from one crisis to the next, treating serious policy questions as mere opportunities for political theatrics, Starmer's Labour opposition seemed serious, prepared, and mature. It harkened back to a style of politics that older voters remembered, when professionals rather than entertainers handled government.

However, this approach carried its own risks. Professional competence can come off as technocratic or cold to voters who desire politicians to resonate emotionally with them, in addition to solving their problems. The qualities that made Starmer effective in Parliament, his careful preparation, measured responses, and reluctance to engage in unnecessary conflicts, might not be the traits that inspire mass movements or secure election victories.

To mitigate this perception, Starmer introduced ten pledges as his insurance policy, demonstrating that he shared the radical instincts of the party membership, even if his style was more moderate than that of his predecessors. These pledges, which included commitments to public ownership, international solidarity, and social justice principles, aimed to bridge the gap between ideological dedication and electoral pragmatism.

When Starmer took control of the Labour Party in April 2020, he inherited not only an organisation but also a movement that had evolved significantly over the previous five years. Jeremy Corbyn's leadership had attracted hundreds of thousands of new members, shifted the policy debate further to the left, and altered the demographic composition of local parties nationwide.

This transformation presented both an asset and a challenge. The new members brought energy, enthusiasm, and a commitment to radical change that could be harnessed for effective political campaigning. However, they also carried expectations that any leader would find difficult to meet, especially regarding issues like public ownership, international solidarity, and social justice principles central to their political identity.

Starmer's challenge was to channel this energy toward electoral success rather than ideological purity. The ten pledges were a key part of this strategy, signalling continuity with Corbynite policies while implicitly promising more effective leadership. The real test, however, would unfold in the months and years ahead, as he needed to translate broad promises into concrete positions on specific issues.

The early indications were promising. Despite some discontent from the most ardent Corbyn supporters, the broader membership seemed inclined to give their new leader a chance. The relief of having someone who appeared capable of being a potential prime minister was palpable, even among those who remained firmly committed to a radical agenda. This promising start under Starmer's leadership inspired hope and confidence in the Labour Party's future.

However, honeymoon periods in politics do not last indefinitely, and Starmer would soon face choices that would challenge his relationship with various factions within the Labour coalition. The ten pledges provided him with breathing room, but they also rendered him vulnerable to future disputes as circumstances and priorities evolved.

Looking forward to April 2020, the challenges that lay ahead for Starmer were significant but not insurmountable. Labour had previously recovered from worse defeats. After both the 1983 and 1992 elections, the party was considered all but dead, only to return to power under different leaders with fresh messages. The critical question was whether the institutional and cultural shifts of the Corbyn years had rendered such a recovery more or less feasible

On a positive note, the party had shown its ability to change rapidly. The shift from New Labour to Corbynism had occurred in just a few months in 2015, demonstrating that British politics could shift faster than conventional wisdom often suggested. This potential for rapid change should instil hope and optimism in the audience about the future of the

Labour Party under Starmer's leadership.

There were several reasons for caution regarding Labour's direction. The electoral coalition that had sustained the party throughout the twentieth century was fragmenting. Traditional working-class voters felt increasingly alienated by what they perceived as the party's metropolitan liberal values, while middle-class progressives demanded ever-greater ideological purity. Navigating between these competing demands would require exceptional political skills.

The Conservative government's 80-seat majority meant that Keir Starmer would have ample time to rebuild and rebrand the Labour Party. Still, it also implied that the party's influence over day-to-day politics would be minimal. Opposition leaders succeed by setting their own agenda, shaping the political debate, and establishing themselves as credible alternatives to the prime minister. Starmer's challenge was to achieve all of this while managing a divided party and addressing the immediate crisis of the pandemic.

Starmer's initial period of leadership was abruptly interrupted on October 29, 2020, when the Equality and Human Rights Commission (EHRC) released a damning report on antisemitism within the Labour Party. This comprehensive 130-page document was a stark indictment of institutional failures, concluding that Labour had committed unlawful acts of harassment and discrimination, casting a long shadow over the party's reputation.

Following the release of the EHRC report in October 2020, Starmer accepted its findings in full and apologised to the Jewish community on behalf of the party. The report found that "there was a culture within the party which, at best, did not do enough to prevent antisemitism and, at worst, could be seen to accept it."

Standing before the cameras that morning, Starmer presented himself like a lawyer delivering an uncomfortable verdict to a client. His declaration, "This is a day of shame for the Labour Party," carried the weight of institutional responsibility. His acknowledgement, "We have failed Jewish people. I am sorry" Was an explicit acceptance of the responsibility he bore, a responsibility that was not his alone to bear.

However, the actual test of Starmer's leadership came from his response to Jeremy Corbyn's reaction to the report. Predictably, the former leader could not resist qualifying his acceptance of the report's conclusions. "The scale of the problem was also dramatically overstated for political reasons by our opponents inside and outside the party," Corbyn stated, a response that landed heavily in Starmer's office.

Within hours, Corbyn was suspended from the party due to "his comments" and "his failure to retract them subsequently," and he was stripped of the party whip. This decision defines Starmer's leadership more than any policy position or campaign promise.

The suspension of Jeremy Corbyn was a political earthquake that sent shockwaves through the entire party structure. Here was Starmer, just six months into his role, taking on the man who had transformed Labour and still commanded fierce loyalty among significant sections of the membership. It was a move that could either be hailed as an act of immense political courage or condemned as a catastrophic miscalculation that could potentially tear the party apart.

The reaction was swift and predictable. Momentum, the grassroots organisation that had supported Corbyn, erupted in anger. Left-wing MPs questioned Starmer's judgment, and trade union leaders who had backed his leadership began to reconsider their support. The ten pledges that had won him the leadership suddenly appeared more like tactical positioning than genuine commitment.

Nonetheless, Starmer's calculation was both moral and political. He understood that Labour's antisemitism crisis was not just about individual cases of prejudice; it was about institutional competence and leadership credibility. Any hesitation regarding the EHRC's findings could have severely undermined his efforts to rebuild trust with Jewish communities and the broader electorate.

The decision also clearly indicated the type of leader Starmer aimed to be. He was not someone who would be held hostage by factional loyalties or afraid to make difficult choices. His courage in confronting his own predecessor, if it meant protecting institutional integrity, was a testament to his unwavering commitment.

The former Labour leader was suspended for his comments regarding the antisemitism report, but Corbyn was later reinstated to the party in November 2020. However, he never regained the Labour whip in the House of Commons.

While the antisemitism crisis made headlines, Starmer's real test as opposition leader was taking place in the critical area of pandemic response. The government's handling of COVID-19 provided daily opportunities to demonstrate whether the thorough approach that had served him well as a barrister could translate into effective political opposition.

His strategy was characteristically methodical: support the government when they got things right, hold them accountable when they made mistakes, and always focus on practical solutions rather than political point-scoring. This approach was about quality control in opposition rather than tribal warfare, which frustrated some Labour activists who wanted more aggressive attacks on Boris Johnson's government.

However, the COVID crisis played to Starmer's strengths in ways that everyday political situations might not have. This was a context requiring careful analysis of complex scientific evidence, detailed scrutiny of government policy, and the kind of forensic questioning that came naturally to someone with his legal background. When ministers attempted to navigate press conferences with incomplete data and optimism, Starmer was there with a methodical critique that had made him a feared advocate.

The contrast with Johnson's approach was stark and deliberate. While the Prime Minister lurched from crisis to crisis, making grand pronouncements that often lacked evidence, Starmer's serious, prepared, and mature approach was a breath of fresh air. It signalled a return to the kind of politics that viewed governance as a technical craft rather than a form of entertainment, making the difference in their leadership styles palpable.

By the end of 2020, the early signs of Starmer's leadership were encouraging. Labour had closed the gap with the Conservatives in opinion polls, recovering from the depths of their post-election despair to a more respectable position. These early signs of improvement should give readers hope for the party's future. More importantly, Starmer's personal approval ratings were consistently strong. Voters may not have been entirely convinced by Labour yet, but they were increasingly impressed by its leader.

The challenge was that electoral recovery takes time, and political gravity rarely moves at the speed that modern media demands. Starmer's methodical approach to rebuilding Labour's credibility was not just a strategy but a testament to his steady leadership. It was the right path for winning elections, even if it didn't generate the dramatic headlines that keep politicians in the spotlight. He was focused on building a foundation rather than constructing a visible superstructure, engaging in the unglamorous work that would only yield dividends years down the line.

The antisemitism crisis had tested his resolve and demonstrated his willingness to make hard choices. His response to COVID-19 showed that he could hold the government accountable while remaining constructive, rather than destructive. Opinion polls suggested that voters were beginning to view him as a credible alternative to Boris Johnson. However, the real test would come when the immediate crises passed, requiring him to articulate a positive vision for what Labour stood for in the 2020s.

As 2020 drew to a close, Starmer could look back on a year that had tested every aspect of his political judgment and personal resilience. He had taken over a party at its lowest ebb, navigated it through a global pandemic, confronted its institutional demons, and begun the slow work of making it electable again. It wasn't the sort of dramatic transformation that makes for compelling television; instead, it was the patient work of institutional repair that democracies desperately need.

The suspension of Jeremy Corbyn marked a defining moment for Starmer. This decision was not just a moment in time, but a potential turning point in his leadership. It could either define him as a leader of principle who prioritised institutional integrity over factional loyalty or as a calculating politician who betrayed the values that had helped him win the leadership. History would ultimately judge whether he made the right call, but it was clear that he had made that decision decisively and without apparent regret.

Whether he could deliver on the broader promises of his leadership to combine radical values with professional competence, to unite the party while making it electable, would depend on challenges yet to come. These challenges are not just hurdles, but opportunities for Starmer to prove his leadership. However, in his first year as Labour leader, Starmer had established himself as a serious political figure who understood that the business of opposition required the same sort of methodical preparation that had made him an effective barrister.

The son of a toolmaker had taken control of the complex organisation that his father might have recognised, which needed careful handling, precise adjustments, and the sort of patient craftsmanship that couldn't be rushed or faked. The early signs suggested that he knew how to use the tools, but the real test of his handiwork was still to come.

Chapter 4
Starmer's Strategic Patience

How the methodical lawyer played chess whilst his opponents played draughts?

If politics were a game of chess, Keir Starmer's approach from 2020 onwards would be the type that frustrates spectators but wins tournaments. While his critics called for flashy moves and dramatic gestures, the former barrister was quietly shifting his pieces around the board, building advantages that wouldn't yield results for years. He was patiently waiting for his opponents to make inevitable blunders that would hand him victory, demonstrating strategic patience and long-term planning that reassured him about his leadership.

Starmer's style was vintage methodical, strategic, and ruthlessly realistic about electoral dynamics. He understood something many of his predecessors missed: opposition parties don't win elections; governing parties lose them. His role wasn't to dictate the narrative but to position Labour as the clear alternative when the storms finally hit the Conservatives.

However, this strategy required nerves of steel and political judgment that don't develop overnight. For the first two years of his leadership, while the Conservatives enjoyed significant polling leads despite their evident failures regarding COVID-19, Starmer faced relentless criticism from within his own party. Where was the vision? Where was the passion? Where were the bold policies to energise voters and activists?

The answer, as subsequent events revealed, was that those bold ideas were being kept in reserve. Starmer focused on the unglamorous but essential work of making Labour appear capable of governing. Instead of performance, his opposition was centred on preparation, requiring a disciplined, long-term mindset that is increasingly rare in modern politics.

One of Starmer's most controversial actions was the systematic dismantling of the policy framework that Jeremy Corbyn had built over five years. The radical manifesto commitments that had motivated activists but unsettled swing voters were not just set aside, but systematically dismantled, in favour of a more moderate agenda aimed at winning elections rather than adhering to ideological purity.

The retreat from the ten pledges that had won him the leadership was particularly harsh for those who supported him, as they had expected a continuation of Corbynism. Policies such as renationalising energy companies, scrapping tuition fees, and implementing wealth taxes were either abandoned completely or diluted to the point of being unrecognisable. Starmer's team had conducted their own polling and reached a stark conclusion: radical policies were electoral poison.

The transition was not pretty and lacked complete transparency. Instead of outright rejecting the pledges, Starmer's team resorted to tactical doublespeak, allowing them to change direction without overtly admitting it. Policies were 'evolved', priorities were 'rebalanced', and commitments were 'refined' in response to 'changed circumstances'. This political manoeuvring fooled precisely no one who was paying attention.

Nonetheless, it worked. Slowly, and with difficulty, Labour began to shed its reputation as the party of impossible promises and ideological extremism. Focus groups that had once recoiled at the mention of Jeremy Corbyn started describing Starmer using terms that hadn't been associated with Labour leaders for years: 'serious', 'competent', and 'prime ministerial'. This may not have been inspiring, but it yielded results where it mattered in the marginal seats that would determine the next election.

The purge was not solely about policy; it extended to personnel, culture, and the very soul of the Labour Party. Left-wing MPs found themselves marginalised, activist groups discovered their influence had diminished, and trade union leaders who had been accustomed to having the leader's ear found themselves relegated. This counter-revolution was executed with surgical precision by someone who understood exactly how institutional power functioned.

If Keir Starmer needed proof that his patient approach would eventually yield results, it arrived in December 2021 in the most unlikely form. A series of revelations about lockdown-breaking parties at Downing Street ultimately proved fatal to Boris Johnson's premiership.

Partygate was the kind of political scandal that seemed too perfect to be real. Here was a Prime Minister who had enforced the strictest lockdown restrictions in peacetime history, which included telling the public they couldn't visit dying relatives or attend funerals, while his own staff were holding boozy gatherings in the very building where these rules were being made. "Boris Johnson and Rishi Sunak have broken the law and repeatedly lied to the British public. They must both resign," Starmer declared with characteristic precision.

For Starmer, Partygate felt like Christmas morning arriving several times over. Each new revelation, the birthday party, the garden gathering, the suitcases of wine, the Christmas quiz, provided fresh ammunition for someone whose legal training had taught him how to build a case that would hold up in court. This wasn't just political banter; it was a systematic demolition of a government's moral authority, a testament to Starmer's strategic focus on evidence.

His performances in Parliament during this time were masterful displays of controlled anger. While Johnson blustered and evaded questions at the dispatch box, Starmer calmly laid out the evidence as a prosecutor would address a jury. The contrast couldn't have been more striking: the serious lawyer confronting the frivolous entertainer, the man who had spent his career holding power accountable, facing someone who believed the rules didn't apply to him, underscoring the gravity of the situation.

However, Starmer was careful not to overreach. Instead of demanding Johnson's immediate resignation, which could have allowed the PM to frame it as simple partisan point-scoring, he focused relentlessly on the substance of the allegations and their implications for public trust. His approach served as quality control for the opposition, and it proved devastatingly effective.

The polling impact was immediate and sustained. Labour moved ahead of the Conservatives for the first time since the 2019 election, establishing leads that would fluctuate but never entirely disappear. More importantly, Starmer's personal ratings soared as voters began to see him as the kind of leader who could restore dignity and competence to British politics after years of chaos and scandal, instilling a sense of optimism in the electorate.

If Partygate damaged the Conservative brand, Liz Truss's brief tenure as Prime Minister nearly destroyed it entirely. Her 49-day reign of economic chaos, marked by a mini-budget that crashed the pound, sent mortgage rates skyrocketing, and forced the Bank of England to intervene to prevent a pension fund crisis, was a stark lesson in the potential consequences of political decisions. This debacle handed Labour more political ammunition than they could have dreamed of.

Critics argue that Keir Starmer's attacks on Boris Johnson's successors, namely Liz Truss and Rishi Sunak, over issues such as the Chris Pincher affair, the 2022 mini-budget crisis, the cost-of-living squeeze, and industrial disputes showcase his meticulous approach to opposition.

For someone with Starmer's legal background, the Truss debacle was a stark demonstration of how not to govern a modern democracy. Truss, who won a leadership contest by promising tax cuts that serious economists deemed unaffordable, implemented these tax cuts without proper consultation or preparation. The stark contrast between her promises and the reality of her governance, as well as her apparent surprise when financial markets reacted negatively, raised serious questions about her competence.

Labour's response was spot-on. Rather than simply attacking the government, Starmer positioned his party as the responsible entity ready to clean up the mess left by Conservative recklessness. His speeches during this period were sober, authoritative, and focused on the practical impact of Truss's policies on ordinary families, who faced higher mortgage payments and uncertainty about their pension funds.

The political impact was seismic. Labour's lead of 30 points or more, if sustained, could pave the way for a landslide general election victory. More importantly, the party began to be seen as the natural government-in-waiting. Starmer increasingly appeared prime ministerial while the Conservatives stumbled from crisis to crisis.

However, he was careful not to get overconfident. His team understood that dramatic polling leads could disappear as quickly as they emerged if the Conservatives found a competent leader to steady the ship. The challenge was to secure Labour's advantages while continuing to demonstrate the party's readiness for government, a crucial aspect that would determine its ability to lead.

The arrival of Rishi Sunak as Prime Minister in October 2022 presented a new challenge for Keir Starmer. Sunak, a figure of undeniable competence, with a solid understanding of economics and financial markets, seemed capable of bringing stability to Conservative governance after the turmoil of the Johnson and Truss administrations.

Shortly after taking over from Truss, polling indicated that 30 per cent of the public viewed Sunak as the best person for the job, just four percentage points behind Starmer. For a brief moment, it seemed that Labour's strong lead might dissipate as quickly as it had emerged. Sunak's appointment not only calmed financial markets but also restored a significant degree of unity within the Conservative Party, showcasing their strength. He was seen as someone who could effectively challenge Starmer during Prime Minister's Questions. The initial boost in Tory support suggested that British voters were willing to give the new Prime Minister a chance to prove his capabilities.

However, Starmer's response demonstrated how much he had matured as a politician since becoming the Labour leader. Instead of panicking over the narrowing poll numbers or altering his strategy in response to the new challenge, he maintained the approach that had served him well: positioning Labour as the competent, moderate alternative and waiting for the government to make mistakes.

Starmer analysed Sunak's situation with characteristic thoroughness. Although Sunak might be technically proficient, he was leading a party that had lost its mandate and run out of ideas. He inherited problems created by his predecessors, including economic stagnation, a crisis in public services, and a cost-of-living squeeze, without having the time or political capital necessary to address these issues.

More fundamentally, Sunak symbolised a continuity of 12 years of Conservative governance that had left Britain poorer, more divided, and less hopeful about the future. No amount of personal competence could outweigh the cumulative impact of Conservative failure. Starmer was willing to let voters recognise this reality, as they were ready for change.

What set Starmer's leadership apart during this period was his meticulous transformation of Labour into what political scientists term a 'government-in-waiting.' This meant the party exuded the readiness and competence of a future government, rather than merely opposing for the sake of it.

This transformation was not just about policy development. Labour's research teams were actively crafting detailed proposals for government, instilling a sense of confidence in the party's preparedness. It also focused on fostering a culture of discipline and professionalism, traits voters typically associate with successful governments.

The most visible evidence of this transformation was in Parliament, where Labour's front bench began to appear and sound like a credible alternative government. Rachel Reeves stood out as an exceptionally effective Shadow Chancellor, blending economic expertise with political acumen in a way that made her seem ready to step into Number 11 at a moment's notice. Wes Streeting's health brief showcased detailed policy work that indicated Labour had genuine plans for NHS reform, rather than merely proposing to throw more money at the system without a clear strategy.

However, it was Starmer himself who fully embodied this new professionalism. His performances during Prime Minister's Questions (PMQs) were masterclasses in effective opposition, leaving a lasting impression with his detailed and well-researched interventions that highlighted government failures while presenting Labour's alternative solutions.

The contrast with previous Labour leaders was clear. Gordon Brown, while technically brilliant, often missed the political pulse, and Jeremy Corbyn, though ideologically principled, lacked practical understanding. In contrast, Starmer combined technical competence with the development of political instincts. He understood both how to govern and how to win elections. This combination proved to be devastatingly effective against Conservative opponents, who seemed capable of neither.

One of the trickiest aspects of Keir Starmer's repositioning of the Labour Party was managing the expectations and reactions of party members who joined during the Corbyn years, expecting a very different kind of politics. The shift toward the centre wasn't just about policy; it represented a fundamental change in the party's identity and values, leaving many activists feeling betrayed and marginalised.

Commentators noted a significant decline in Labour membership in the years leading up to the 2024 election. This exodus was both predictable and painful. Activists, who had been energised by Corbyn's radical agenda, found themselves increasingly irrelevant in a party that prioritised electoral success over ideological purity. The changes were not merely political; they were cultural, social, and deeply personal. For those who had invested years in building a movement that was now being systematically dismantled, it was a heart-wrenching experience.

Starmer's handling of this internal revolution showcased both his strategic brilliance and his emotional limitations as a leader. He understood that achieving electoral success required shedding the party's radical image and appealing to moderate voters who had been repelled by Corbyn's brand of politics. His strategic acumen in this regard was commendable. However, he seemed genuinely surprised by the depth of feeling his changes generated among activists who believed their political home had been taken from them.

The process wasn't easy, and it wasn't always fair. Left-wing members faced disciplinary action for social media posts that would have been unremarkable during the Corbyn years. Constituency parties that selected left-wing candidates for local elections discovered that their choices were being overridden by regional officials. The democracy that Corbyn had championed was being systematically undermined by a leadership that prioritised message discipline over member participation.

However, it worked. By 2023, Labour had become a typical centre-left party rather than a radical movement, and voters responded positively. The cost of this transformation was borne by activists whose enthusiasm was replaced by professional competence. Starmer calculated that electoral votes mattered more than individual feelings, and events proved him right.

The transformation of Labour's policy platform during this period was a masterclass in political repositioning, combining strategic brilliance with tactical ruthlessness. Starmer didn't simply abandon the radical agenda he inherited; instead, he evolved it into a framework that balanced progressive ideals with electoral pragmatism. This balance reassured his base while avoiding the extremist label that had previously made Labour unelectable under Corbyn.

This process was not just gradual, but often implicit, designed to minimise the political costs of what effectively amounted to a complete U-turn. Starmer's team didn't announce major policy reversals outright. Instead, they employed subtle bureaucratic language that allowed politicians to change direction while maintaining the appearance of continuity. Policies were described as being 'refined in response to economic circumstances,' priorities were 'rebalanced to reflect fiscal realities,' and commitments were 'adapted to ensure deliverability.'

The retreat from public ownership was particularly skilful. Rather than simply abandoning renationalisation, Labour developed a more nuanced position that involved "strategic public investment" and "democratic oversight" of key industries. While it did not align with the common ownership that socialist activists desired, it also avoided the pure privatisation that Conservative opponents could easily criticise. This graduated policy positioning was reminiscent of the triangulation Tony Blair would have recognised and admired.

Similarly, the abandonment of free tuition fees was framed as a commitment to "reviewing student finance" and ensuring "fair access to higher education." The party's new position recognised that while university funding needed reform, the wholesale abolition of fees was not affordable. This approach allowed Starmer to retreat from a costly promise while maintaining his progressive credentials.

Perhaps most significantly, Labour's economic policy underwent a complete transformation. The party began to embrace fiscal responsibility as a political virtue rather than viewing it as a conservative constraint. With Rachel Reeves emerging as Shadow Chancellor, the party gained credibility in financial matters after being perceived as economically illiterate. Her commitment to "iron discipline" over public spending reassured middle-class voters who were previously alarmed by Corbyn's spending plans.

During this period, observers noted that Starmer's team was conducting its own private polling and focus group research, which highlighted the challenges Labour faced in regaining public trust. The data was concerning: although voters disliked the Conservative government, they remained deeply sceptical about Labour's competence and its commitment to mainstream values.

The research revealed that Corbyn's legacy extended beyond specific policies; it raised fundamental questions about patriotism, security, and economic competence, all of which influenced voters' willingness to trust Labour with power. Middle-class voters who had supported Tony Blair were genuinely alarmed by the prospect of a Corbyn government. Additionally, traditional working-class supporters felt that the party was being dominated by metropolitan activists who dismissed their values and way of life.

In response, Starmer initiated a comprehensive rebranding exercise that affected every aspect of the party's image and messaging. Labour began to embrace the Union Jack with the enthusiasm of a nationalist party, emphasising its commitment to putting 'country first, party second' and distancing itself from the anti-patriotic image that had characterised the Corbyn years, a period marked by controversies over national security and patriotism.

The security agenda became particularly critical in this rehabilitation process. Starmer's appointment of a former NATO official as his chief of staff was a strategic move that sent a strong signal about Labour's commitment to defence and international alliances. His robust support for Ukraine provided consistent opportunities to demonstrate that the party had moved away from its previous sympathy for anti-Western causes.

Perhaps most importantly, Labour began to engage with the language of aspiration and opportunity, a shift from the previous focus on victimhood and grievance. Starmer's speeches underscored the party's commitment to helping people' get on' in life, a message of hope and progress, rather than solely protecting those who were 'left behind.' This represented a fundamental shift in political psychology, reflecting his understanding of what motivates swing voters in marginal constituencies.

Starmer's most notable accomplishment during this period was the complete overhaul of Labour's media relations, particularly with the right-wing press that had been openly hostile during the Corbyn era. His approach, a blend of professional competence and tactical finesse, gradually repaired the party's image with journalists and editors who had previously dismissed Labour as unelectable extremists.

Labour's media strategy, under Starmer's leadership, was not just a charm offensive; it was a strategic approach. It was a demonstration of the party's transformation, making it worthy of serious coverage. Shadow ministers were made available for interviews, and policy announcements were thoroughly briefed and researched for accuracy. This professional approach to media is a reassuring sign of Labour's readiness for modern electoral success.

Starmer himself proved to be surprisingly effective on television and radio. He utilised his legal training to deliver clear, authoritative answers to complex questions while steering clear of the ideological rhetoric that had made previous Labour leaders easy targets for hostile interviewers. His calm, measured style provided a sharp contrast to the chaotic energy of Boris Johnson and the mechanical delivery of Rishi Sunak.

Arguably, the most significant change was Labour's shift from reacting to crises and controversies to generating positive news stories. Policy announcements, campaign visits, and parliamentary performances were carefully orchestrated to demonstrate the party's preparedness for government, while also highlighting Conservative failures and divisions.

This transformation was particularly evident in the party's relationship with business leaders and financial markets. While Corbyn had been viewed as a dangerous radical threatening the economic foundations of British capitalism, Starmer was invited to address business conferences, courted by figures in the City, and treated as a serious potential Prime Minister who understood the demands of governing a modern economy.

One of the most challenging aspects of Keir Starmer's electoral strategy was the Labour Party's position in Scotland. The dominance of the SNP (Scottish National Party) had transformed Labour from the natural governing party into a distant third-place player, rendering it nearly irrelevant. The decline of the Scottish Labour vote had significantly contributed to the party's defeat in the 2019 election. It was clear that any viable path back to power required winning seats in Scotland, making it a matter of urgency for the Labour Party.

This challenge was particularly pronounced because Scottish Labour had been closely linked to the broader failures of the Corbyn era. The party not only inherited his policy platform but also his controversial brand in a region where voters had largely moved on from the constitutional issues dominating Westminster politics. To regain support, Labour needed to show relevance to Scottish concerns while steering clear of the nationalist accusations that had hindered previous revival efforts.

Starmer's approach was a slow and often frustrating process. His goal was to rebuild the party's organisation, develop policies specific to Scotland, and gradually restore credibility with voters who had dismissed Labour as an irrelevant entity from Westminster. This was particularly challenging given the SNP's ongoing influence over Scottish political discourse.

However, by 2023, signs began to emerge that the strategy was yielding positive results. Scottish Labour started winning council seats, improving its polling position, and attracting media attention that indicated the party was starting to be taken seriously again. This progress should give us hope for Labour's potential for recovery. More importantly, Labour began to articulate a distinctively Scottish version of Starmer's centre-left politics, combining economic competence with social progressivism in a way that appealed to voters who had left Labour for the SNP.

The constitutional question remained complex, with Labour's stance on unionism putting it at odds with significant segments of public opinion in Scotland. Nevertheless, Starmer's team believed there were enough voters who supported Scottish devolution while opposing independence to create a viable base for electoral recovery, especially if the SNP continued to struggle with the practical challenges of governing Scotland while campaigning for separation.

By late 2023, Keir Starmer's patient approach to opposition politics was clearly paying off. Despite the party's lukewarm reception, polling showed that Labour was the clear preference for the next government, with 44% of people choosing "a Labour government led by Keir Starmer," compared to 22% who opted for "a Conservative government led by Rishi Sunak."

This advantage stemmed not only from Conservative unpopularity but also from genuine Labour progress in addressing the concerns that had made the party unelectable under previous leaders. The party's shift towards more moderate policies, a focus on competence and trustworthiness, and a leadership that appeared more Prime Ministerial were key factors. Focus groups that had once recoiled at the mention of Jeremy Corbyn were now describing Labour in terms that indicated a readiness for government: competent, moderate, trustworthy, and led by someone who appeared to be a potential Prime Minister.

However, Starmer was careful not to get ahead of himself. His team understood that significant polling leads could vanish as quickly as they appeared if the party made major missteps or if the Conservatives found ways to shift the political narrative. The challenge was to solidify Labour's advantages while continuously demonstrating readiness for the responsibilities of government.

The approach remained characteristically cautious and professional, focused on the long-term goal of winning the next general election with a mandate for meaningful change. Starmer learned from Tony Blair's experience that opposition leaders who promise too much often struggle to deliver on their promises once in power. In contrast, those who under-promise and over-deliver tend to enjoy longer and more successful tenures in Downing Street.

As 2023 came to a close, Labour was no longer just an opposition party; it had transformed into a government-in-waiting. This transformation was not just about polling numbers or media coverage; it was a testament to the kind of institutional competence and policy readiness that suggested the party was genuinely prepared for the responsibilities of power.

Shadow ministers were meticulously crafting detailed implementation plans for their departments, and the party's research teams were diligently working on transitional arrangements for assuming government. Starmer himself was conducting the type of stakeholder meetings that incoming Prime Ministers typically use to build support for their agenda. This meticulous planning and preparation, even in the opposition, reflected a seriousness about governance that had been absent from British politics for years.

The contrast with previous Labour oppositions was stark. While Neil Kinnock had rebuilt the party's electoral position but never quite convinced voters he was Prime Minister material, and while Jeremy Corbyn had energised activists but alienated floating voters, Starmer had successfully combined electoral appeal with credible governance. This contrast underscores his potential not only to win power but also to use it effectively, instilling confidence in his leadership.

The question that remained was whether this careful, cautious approach could generate the enthusiasm and energy needed for a successful election campaign. While competence might attract focus group participants, elections are ultimately won by parties that can inspire as well as reassure those who offer both hope and stability. Labour could face challenges in encouraging the public, particularly in the face of potential Conservative strategies to shift the political narrative or the emergence of new issues that could sway public opinion.

That challenge lay ahead in the election year that everyone knew was coming. As Starmer prepared to lead Labour into what was likely to be the most significant election of his political career, he could reflect on three transformative years for both his party and his reputation. The son of a toolmaker had proven he knew how to build something that could withstand the test of time. Now he needed to demonstrate that he could effectively present it to the British public.

Chapter 5
Labour's 2024 Landslide

*How competence triumphed over chaos in the most unexpected
election of the modern era*

As 2024 began, Britain felt like a country holding its breath.
Fourteen years of Conservative rule had left the nation frayed around the
edges, battered by the chaos of Brexit, economic turmoil, and a revolving
door of prime ministers that made the entire political system seem like
amateur hour. The public mood wasn't just anti-Tory; it was a resounding
rejection of chaos, a call for stability, and a demand for a more orderly
state of politics.

For Keir Starmer, this was the opportunity of a lifetime. After nearly
four years as Labour leader, he had successfully repositioned the party
from the radical fringes back towards the sensible centre. He finally had
the Conservatives where he wanted them: on the ropes, punch-drunk, and
running out of options. The polling numbers looked promising; Labour
had been ahead for months, often by double digits. However, everyone in
Westminster knew that elections aren't won on paper. They're won by
convincing ordinary voters that you are worth the gamble.

The Conservative Party entered the election year limping like a boxer
who had taken one too many hits to the head. Rishi Sunak, their latest
attempt at finding a leader who could steady the ship, had done his best
to restore some semblance of competence after the turmoil of the
Johnson and Truss years. But the damage was already done. The Tory
brand was more toxic than a three-week-old fish supper, and no amount
of polished presentation could mask the lingering stench of failure that
clung to everything they touched.

Starmer's approach was characteristically methodical. Rather than
getting carried away with Labour's strong position in the polls, he treated
the campaign like the high-stakes legal case it effectively was:
meticulously preparing, anticipating every counter-argument, and
constructing a case so watertight that even the most sceptical jury would
have no choice but to deliver a guilty verdict on the government's record.
His attention to detail and thorough preparation instilled confidence in
his leadership.

On 13 June 2024, Keir Starmer unveiled Labour's election manifesto at an event in Manchester, a strategic choice that would prove to be a defining moment of the campaign. The manifesto was presented under the straightforward yet impactful banner: "Change." The selection of Manchester as the venue was deliberate; it symbolised what Labour aimed to represent: a blend of industrial heritage and modern innovation, working-class roots alongside professional ambition, and northern grit tempered by metropolitan sophistication.

During the launch, Starmer described the manifesto as representing "a fairer, healthier, and more secure Britain, at the service of working people, with growth from every community. A Britain ready to restore that promise." His rhetoric, although not the most stirring in political history, was a deliberate departure from the grandiose promises and theatrical displays that had worn out the electorate. This contrast underscored the effectiveness of his communication strategy, as it resonated with an electorate that had grown weary of such displays.

Starmer emphasised, "At this election, we can change Britain. We can stop the chaos, turn the page, and start to rebuild our country." The message was intentionally simple, almost mundane in its sincerity. After years of political drama and constitutional crises, Starmer was offering something nearly revolutionary in its ordinariness: competent leadership by serious individuals who had actually done their homework.

The manifesto itself was a masterclass in political positioning, taking a cautious approach aimed at regaining voters' trust and fulfilling commitments. Notably, the radical policies that had made Labour unelectable under Jeremy Corbyn were now absent. Instead, Starmer prioritised economic growth, reforming the planning system, improving infrastructure, energy, healthcare, education, childcare, and strengthening workers' rights.

While these policies may not excite university students, they align perfectly with the feedback from focus groups that indicated voters want to hear practical solutions to real problems from capable candidates. It was a politics focused on practicalities rather than grand ideals, and it seemed that the British public was ready for someone who could address the issues rather than simply craft poetic narratives about them.

The official campaign began with Rishi Sunak's announcement of a general election set for July 4, a date that was both symbolic and strategic. This date, which coincided with American Independence Day, was chosen to symbolise Britain's declaration of independence from fourteen years of Conservative misrule. However, it was unclear whether Sunak intended this irony or if it was a mere coincidence.

Keir Starmer's campaign was a testament to meticulous planning and execution. Every speech was rigorously tested, every policy position was carefully focus-grouped, and each public appearance was choreographed to reinforce the central message: here was a leader fully prepared for the responsibilities of government. This level of preparation would have made his former colleagues proud and reassured the public of his leadership capabilities.

The contrast with previous Labour campaigns was stark and promising. While Gordon Brown appeared increasingly desperate in 2010 and Jeremy Corbyn seemed to be operating in a parallel universe in 2019, Starmer projected a calm authority throughout. When hecklers interrupted his manifesto launch, he addressed them firmly but remained composed. His declaration, 'We want to be a party of power,' dismissed the interruption with an authority that signalled he was thinking like a prime minister, rather than just an opposition leader. This contrast gives hope for the party's future.

The campaign's disciplined message control permeated every level of the party. Shadow ministers remained strictly on-message, local candidates adhered to approved talking points, and even longtime mavericks appeared to embrace the notion that this was Labour's best opportunity for power in over a decade. It was the kind of operation that political professionals admired, even if it didn't evoke much excitement among activists who preferred their politics infused with more passion and less process.

However, the strategy was effective because it was perfectly aligned with the national mood. At the time, voters were not seeking inspiration; they were looking for competence. They did not desire revolutionary change; they wanted evolutionary improvement. This was mainly due to [specific national or global circumstances]. They needed their minds persuaded that Labour could actually fulfil its promises, rather than needing their hearts stirred.

Behind the scenes, Labour's financial operation underwent a significant strategic shift. During the campaign period, the party raised £9.8 million, more than five times the amount raised by the Conservatives, according to campaign finance records. This funding came from an unexpected source: gone were the days when Labour primarily relied on trade union donations. As Labour's relationship with trade unions grew more strained, wealthy individual donors contributed 68.5% of their total campaign funding, with approximately £3.5 million coming from previous donors to other parties, primarily Conservatives and Liberal Democrats.

The transformation was striking. Thanks to a charm offensive led by Labour Peer Waheed Ali, who is worth over £200 million, the party began to attract super-wealthy donors who had previously either abandoned it or supported its rivals. Ali's personal efforts played a significant role in this shift. These donors were not ideological converts; instead, they were pragmatic businesspeople seeking stability after years of Conservative chaos. One campaign insider bluntly stated, "The people paying for this campaign don't want radicalism."

This financial advantage allowed Labour to build a campaign infrastructure that overshadowed anything the party had managed in recent elections. With professional staff, sophisticated polling methods, targeted advertising, and comprehensive voter identification systems, Labour enjoyed organisational advantages that no opposition party had experienced since 1997.

The digital campaign was a masterclass in modern political communication. Labour's social media operation effectively portrayed Starmer as prime ministerial without being overly formal, competent without being dull, and ready for change without being radical. TikTok videos featuring the Labour leader engaging with young voters, Instagram posts showcasing policy achievements, and thoughtfully crafted Twitter threads explaining complex policies all contributed to an online presence that felt both authentic and authoritative.

If Labour's campaign was a masterclass in professional politics, the Conservative campaign resembled a slow-motion car crash. Rishi Sunak, despite his undeniable intelligence and technocratic competence, struggled to escape the shadow of his party's record and connect with voters who had already decided that the time was up for the Conservatives. This struggle, among other factors, contributed to the Conservatives' loss in the election.

The Conservative strategy appeared to shift from week to week, reflecting a party that could not reasonably determine what message it wanted to convey about its own track record. For instance, one week they were promoting their achievements from fourteen years in power, and the next they were promising change from their own policies. They seemed to be the party of fiscal responsibility, but then they announced spending pledges that matched those of Labour. They claimed to be the natural party of government, but then they positioned themselves as the insurgent challengers to the political establishment.

This lack of clarity in the Conservative strategy presented numerous opportunities that Labour was quick to exploit. When the Conservatives tried to steer the campaign towards tax increases, Labour was ready to point out that the tax burden was at its highest since the end of World War II under Conservative governments. When the Conservatives attempted to highlight their economic competence, voters were reminded of Liz Truss's swift economic downturn following the 'mini-budget.' And when the Conservatives veered towards cultural issues, they found that most people were more concerned about the state of their local NHS trust than issues like transgender rights or statue-toppling.

Reform UK, Nigel Farage's latest political initiative, added complexity to the Conservative landscape while providing little reassurance for Labour. Farage's return as leader and his candidacy in Clacton gave Reform UK a central focus and generated considerable media attention. However, it also fiercely divided the right-wing vote in numerous marginal constituencies, intensifying the political competition. For Starmer, seeing Farage attract disillusioned Conservative voters was akin to having someone else do his hard work for him.

Reform UK secured 14.3% of the vote, winning five seats and marking the election of their first MPs, with a vote share comparable to UKIP's 12.6% in the 2015 elections. However, the implications of these results extended beyond mere numbers. Among those who voted Conservative in 2019, 27% switched to Reform UK in 2024. In the 137 seats where Conservatives lost to Labour, the combined vote share of the Conservatives and Reform UK surpassed Labour's winning share.

What stands out is where Reform UK was gaining traction. Although the party struggled to appeal to young voters, overall, only 8% of those under 30 supported them. However, their popularity among specific male demographics was on the rise, with 19% of 18-24-year-olds backing Farage's party in certain polls. Notably, 30% of 2019 Conservative voters who supported Leave in 2016 chose to switch to Reform UK.

As polling stations closed at 10 PM on July 4, 2024, the exit poll revealed the news that Labour activists had been dreaming of for fourteen years: a landslide victory that would remove the Conservatives from power and install Keir Starmer as Prime Minister with a commanding parliamentary majority.

The BBC's exit poll, which initially seemed almost too good to be true, predicted Labour would win around 410 seats. This figure, given the exit poll failures of previous elections, was met with cautious surprise. However, as the first results began to come in from safe seats, it became apparent that the exit poll may have been conservative in its estimates, leading to a growing sense of astonishment.

Labour ultimately won 411 seats, an increase of 209 from their total in the 2019 election. The Conservatives, on the other hand, secured only

121 seats, a decrease of 244 from their previous total of 365 seats. This represented a historic swing, a seismic shift in the political landscape, driven not by a surge in Labour enthusiasm, but by a comprehensive collapse in Conservative support.

The magnitude of the Conservative defeat was staggering. Cabinet ministers fell like ninepins: Liz Truss lost her seat, along with a dozen other senior figures who had seemed unassailable just months prior. In constituency after constituency that had been blue for decades, Labour candidates found themselves winning by thousands of votes rather than hundreds.

The most significant aspect of the result was its efficiency. Starmer led Labour to a landslide victory in the 2024 general election, ending fourteen years of Conservative government with the smallest vote share of any majority government since record-keeping began. Labour secured more seats than Tony Blair did in 1997, but with a smaller share of the popular vote than Gordon Brown received in the 2010 election, underscoring the impact of the result.

This election represented not a tide of Labour enthusiasm sweeping the country, but rather a widespread rejection of the Conservatives that inadvertently benefited the Labour Party. With an overall turnout of around 60%, the election suggested that many voters were more motivated by the desire to remove the Tories from power than by any strong enthusiasm for the Labour Party.

As the magnitude of Labour's triumph unfolded in the early hours of July 5, Starmer readied himself to address the nation as the Prime Minister-elect. The speech he delivered from Labour headquarters was quintessentially Starmer: measured, thoughtful, and focused on the responsibilities of power rather than the jubilations of victory. 'We have achieved it,' he informed the jubilant activists, but immediately tempered the excitement with a reminder of the challenges ahead. 'This is not a time for revelry, but for service. The British people have entrusted us, and we will not disappoint them.

The tone was deliberately sombre, mirroring both Starmer's character and his grasp of the situation. Unlike Tony Blair's exuberant triumph in 1997, this was not a nation poised for celebration. It was a country worn out by political turmoil and yearning for competent governance. The last thing voters desired was arrogance from politicians who had yet to demonstrate their ability to fulfil their pledges.

The image of Starmer walking through the famous black door represented the culmination of a political journey that took him from the radical fringes of his party's support base back to the mainstream of

British politics. The transition from opposition to government occurred with the smooth efficiency that characterised everything about Starmer's operation.

Rachel Reeves, appointed by Keir Starmer as the UK's new Chancellor of the Exchequer, has made history as the first woman to hold this position. Her appointment, a significant step forward, was both historic and expected. Reeves, who has served as Shadow Chancellor for several years, has played a pivotal role, second only to Starmer himself, in rebuilding Labour's reputation for economic competence.

The other cabinet appointments reflect Starmer's careful balancing of various factions within the party, prioritising competence over ideology. Wes Streeting at Health brings both media savvy and policy expertise to the challenge of reforming the NHS. David Lammy at the Foreign Office combines international experience with the gravitas necessary to restore Britain's diplomatic reputation after years of isolation due to Brexit. Their competence reassures the public that the government is capable of addressing key issues.

Angela Rayner's appointment as Deputy Prime Minister and Housing Secretary acknowledges her role as the elected deputy leader and highlights the crucial importance of addressing Britain's housing crisis. For someone who left school at 16 and worked her way up through the trade union movement, this position represents a remarkable personal journey that embodies Labour's promise of social mobility and opportunity for all.

The cabinet reflects modern Britain in a way that Conservative cabinets rarely do, showcasing a greater number of women, increased ethnic diversity, and more individuals from working-class backgrounds who have risen to the top through talent and hard work, rather than connections and privilege. This diversity is not mere tokenism; these are serious politicians with substantial experience. It sends a powerful message about the kind of country Labour aims to create, one that values and represents all its citizens.

The media's response to Labour's victory was largely positive, although it was accompanied by the usual scepticism that often accompanies a change of government. The right-wing press, which had been preparing for a Labour victory for months, adopted a cautiously welcoming tone. The Sun, which had supported the Conservatives, acknowledged that "the voters have spoken" and wished the new government well. In contrast, the Daily Mail, which has historically been uncomfortable with Labour in power, focused more on the magnitude of the Conservative defeat rather than celebrating Labour's triumph.

The most striking aspect of Labour's victory was its reception by the public. Unlike 1997, when Tony Blair's victory inspired genuine euphoria and optimism about the future, the mood in 2024 felt more like relief than celebration. The British public voted for change, but this change was driven more by exhaustion with the Conservatives than by enthusiasm for Labour.

Polling immediately following the election indicated that while voters were pleased to see the end of Conservative rule, they remained cautiously sceptical about whether Labour could fulfil its promises. The scars left by previous disappointments, such as Blair's Iraq War, Brown's financial crisis, and Corbyn's electoral defeats, have created realistic expectations about what politics can achieve.

This scepticism is not necessarily unhealthy. A public that anticipates miracles may be disappointed when the new government faces the inevitable challenges of governing in difficult circumstances. Conversely, a public that expects competence and gradual improvement is more patient with a government that prioritises delivery over drama.

What followed was a seismic shift in the political landscape. The Conservative Party, in a historic turn of events, suffered its worst-ever defeat, securing only 121 seats with a mere 23.7% of the vote. This marked a staggering loss of 251 seats, including those of former Prime Minister Liz Truss and 12 Cabinet ministers. Former British Prime Minister Rishi Sunak, in the wake of this unprecedented outcome, announced his decision to step down as party leader once a successor was chosen, acknowledging the British people's 'sobering verdict'.

The Liberal Democrats emerged as the third-largest party, securing 72 seats and achieving their best result since the modern era. However, the most striking development was the record level of support for smaller parties, which garnered a significant 42.6% of the total vote, marking a clear departure from the dominance of the traditional big two. This shift in voter preference signalled the complete fragmentation of British politics, ushering in a new era where old certainties were no longer applicable.

The demographic divides revealed by the election were profound and likely permanent. The median age of Labour voters was now 46, while the median age for Conservative voters was 63, 56 for Reform UK, and just 39 for the Greens. Age remained a key dividing line: only 8% of those under 30 voted for the Conservative Party, compared to 46% of those aged 70 or older. Britain was politically segregated by generation in unprecedented ways.

Emerging gender differences were also noteworthy. Reform UK

performed seven percentage points better among men than among women. Among 18-24-year-olds, young women were almost twice as likely to vote Green compared to young men, while young men tended to support Reform UK and the Conservative Party. The political gender gap was evolving in complex ways that traditional parties struggled to navigate.

Amidst the ongoing victory celebrations, the stark reality of the challenges ahead was already casting a shadow over the party atmosphere. The new government was set to grapple with a series of formidable challenges, including an NHS in crisis, a severe housing shortage, public services that had been starved of investment after years of austerity, and an economy still reeling from the aftereffects of Brexit and COVID-19.

The Treasury briefings that Rachel Reeves received in her first days as Chancellor painted a sobering picture of the public finances. The '£22 billion black hole', a term used to describe a significant budget deficit, which would later become a recurring theme of Labour's early months in government, was already evident in the departmental spending reviews and forward projections presented by civil servants to their new political leaders.

But for now, these were problems for tomorrow. July 2024 belonged to celebration and the simple satisfaction of a job well done, a victory earned through years of hard work and political discipline. Labour activists who had endured the wilderness years of opposition could finally allow themselves to believe that their party was back where it belonged: in government, with a mandate for change and the parliamentary arithmetic to deliver it

As the dust settled on Labour's landslide victory, political observers began to identify what they dubbed 'the Starmer Doctrine', a significant approach to politics that prioritises competence over charisma, delivery over drama, and pragmatism over ideology. It wasn't inspiring in the traditional sense, but it had proven remarkably effective at winning elections and building coalitions, a fact that kept the audience engaged and informed.

This doctrine reflected both Starmer's personal characteristics and his understanding of the current political landscape. In an era dominated by social media outrage and 24-hour news cycles, there was something almost revolutionary about a politician who spoke in measured sentences, avoided hyperbole, and regarded governing as a technical craft rather than a form of entertainment.

Whether this approach would prove effective in government, as it had been in opposition, remained to be seen. The challenges facing Britain in 2024, economic stagnation, a public service crisis, and international isolation, were significant and demanded more than just competent administration; they required vision, leadership, and the kind of political courage that technical expertise alone could not provide. This emphasis on the challenges would make the audience feel concerned and aware.

The transformation of Keir Starmer from a forensic barrister into a successful political leader was complete. The man who once seemed too lawyerly for politics had demonstrated that sometimes what democracy needs is not charisma or ideology but competence and character. He'd made a compelling case for Labour that the British public had accepted; now it was time to demonstrate that winning elections is easier than governing effectively. This emphasis on transformation would inspire and uplift the audience, leaving them feeling hopeful.

As Keir Starmer settled into his new office in Downing Street, the scale of the challenges facing his government became clear. The landslide victory had given Labour the parliamentary numbers needed to implement its agenda, but it had also raised expectations that might be difficult to meet.

The "Change" manifesto that had won the election was comprehensive yet cautious, ambitious yet affordable, and progressive yet pragmatic. Implementing it would require not only legislative skill but also the sustained political effort that characterised Starmer's journey to the top of his party and then to Downing Street.

The son of a toolmaker from Surrey had finally reached the pinnacle of British politics. He had demonstrated that patient preparation could triumph over flashy performance, that competence could outshine charisma, and that a steady hand could indeed prevail. However, the real test was not winning power but using it effectively to deliver the change Britain desperately needed.

The revolution had been quiet, almost apologetic in its efficiency. Yet even the dullest revolutions have consequences, and those consequences were just beginning to unfold as Prime Minister Starmer prepared to discover whether the skills that made him an effective opposition leader could translate into the very different challenge of governing a complex, fractured, and expectant nation.

The landslide was complete, the mandate was clear, and the work was about to begin. History would judge whether the forensic barrister who had rebuilt the Labour Party could also reconstruct the country.

Chapter 6
Labour's Summer of Broken Promises

How the toolmaker's son discovered that building credibility is harder than demolishing it?

By August 2024, just a month after the initial excitement of their electoral victory faded, the first cracks began to show in Labour's carefully crafted facade. The transition from opposition to government had been impressively efficient, but governing, as Keir Starmer was about to learn, demanded more than just competent administration. It required the courage to make unpopular decisions and the political skill to articulate why promises made yesterday had turned into impossibilities today.

The problems began, as they often do in British politics, with money. Rachel Reeves's first comprehensive spending review, conducted in the depths of August while most of Westminster was on holiday, revealed what Treasury officials later described as a 'fiscal reality check of biblical proportions.' The £22 billion black hole that Labour had inherited from the Conservatives was not just a convenient political talking point; it was an unexpected and fundamental constraint that forced the new government to abandon, delay, or significantly scale back virtually every central promise made during the election campaign.

For a party that had come to power promising change, the revelation that such change would have to wait was politically toxic. However, it was the manner of the U-turns, rather than their necessity, that proved most damaging to Labour's reputation. The careful political positioning that had served Starmer well in opposition, tactical ambiguity, conditional commitments, and promises hedged with caveats began to appear as systematic deception once the constraints of government exposed the gap between rhetoric and reality, casting a heavy shadow on Labour's political integrity.

The scale of the financial inheritance became clear when Rachel Reeves stood before the House of Commons on 29 July 2024, delivering what would come to be known as the 'day of reckoning' speech. This speech, a sobering assessment of the country's financial situation, was based on the findings of the Public Spending Audit conducted by the

Treasury after the general election. The audit found that the new government had 'inherited a projected overspend of £22 billion.' Reeves described this deficit as a '£22 billion hole in the public finances' that had been covered up by the Conservative Party.

Critics argued that much of this should not have come as a surprise. The Institute for Fiscal Studies, a respected economic think tank, had warned before the election that any new government would likely face a shortfall of £10-£20 billion by 2028/29. Following Reeves's statement, IFS Director Paul Johnson noted that many of the challenges Labour outlined were 'entirely predictable.' However, he acknowledged that the immediate financial pressures did appear 'greater than could be discerned from the outside.'

The Office for Budget Responsibility launched a review of the preparation of departmental spending forecasts, with Chair Richard Hughes expressing grave concerns over the 'transparency and credibility of the existing arrangements within government' for forecasting, planning, and controlling day-to-day spending. This revelation highlights the pressing need for more transparent and accountable government practices.

The most significant single component of the £22 billion gap came from a decision made by Labour itself. The audit estimated that accepting recommendations for public sector pay awards in 2024/25 would add "further pressure of £9.4 billion in 2024/25 on top of what the last government had set aside for pay." This was due to the Conservative government having provisioned a 2% increase for 2024/25, while the recommendations accepted by Labour were broadly in the 5-6% range.

Reeves's first major policy announcement as Chancellor, delivered during her 'fiscal audit' at the end of July, was the decision to cut winter fuel payments for most pensioners. The Winter Fuel Payment, a government benefit introduced to help pensioners with their heating costs during the winter, was to become means-tested, limiting it to those receiving Pension Credit or other means-tested benefits. This change, affecting around 10 million pensioners, came without prior warning [DWP regulations].

The political backlash was immediate and severe. Regulations to restrict eligibility for the Winter Fuel Payment in England and Wales were submitted to Parliament on August 22, 2024, and came into effect on September 16, 2024 [parliamentary records]. The government estimated that only 1.5 million individuals across 1.3 million households would receive a payment, a drastic reduction from the previous year's 10.8 million pensioners in 7.6 million households [DWP estimates].

The announcement drew significant criticism from unexpected sources. Unite the Union, a prominent trade union, launched a 'Defend the Winter Fuel Payment' campaign, with General Secretary Sharon Graham stating: 'Taking money off pensioners who earn as little as £220 a week, while the 50 richest families in Britain own a combined £500 billion, is unjust' [Unite campaign]. The Union later initiated judicial review proceedings against the government, arguing that it acted unlawfully [legal challenge].

Age UK, the leading charity for older people, warned that this policy could "plunge an estimated 100,000 more pensioners into poverty" and might "risk a rise in cold weather deaths" [charity response]. The Social Security Advisory Committee, a government watchdog, criticised the plan as "rushed and ill-conceived" [committee statement].

Even within the Labour Party itself, the backlash was fierce. Ten Labour MPs supported an early day motion demanding that the cuts be postponed, expressing concerns that the measure was 'introduced without prior consultation or an impact assessment' [EDM 1725]. The motion, tabled by Labour MP Neil Duncan-Jordan, highlighted the concerning timing of the cuts alongside the 10% increase in the energy price cap scheduled for October, which would further strain the finances of pensioners [parliamentary motion].

During Prime Minister's Questions on September 11, former Prime Minister Rishi Sunak accused Starmer of concealing the impact assessment for the policy, questioning whether the estimated number of deaths would be higher or lower than the 3,850 Labour had previously predicted from similar cuts [PMQs transcript]. Starmer did not provide a direct answer.

The human cost of this decision became personal for some Labour MPs. Liz Twist, Labour MP for Blaydon and Consett, faced calls from constituents to resign from her post as chair of the board of trustees at Age UK Gateshead after she voted to support the fuel payment restrictions. Ultimately, she resigned in October 2024, stating it was due to "the consistent pressure being placed on the charity" [resignation statement].

The first significant policy reversal occurred on a warm Tuesday morning in late August when Education Secretary Bridget Phillipson addressed the House of Commons to announce what she described as a "comprehensive review of higher education funding." However, the euphemistic language could not disguise the harsh political reality: Labour was not only abandoning its promise to abolish tuition fees but was also set to increase them for the first time in eight years.

This announcement sent shockwaves through the party's support base, affecting everyone from student unions to trade union headquarters. This was not merely a policy U-turn; it represented a significant departure from one of the ten pledges that had helped Starmer secure the Labour leadership in 2020. "Support the abolition of tuition fees" was a central promise clearly outlined in his campaign literature [leadership pledge].

By November 2024, Phillipson announced that the maximum tuition fee for universities in England would rise by 3.1 percent starting in the 2025-26 academic year, bringing the cost for full-time undergraduates to £9,535 [fee announcement]. The government reportedly planned annual increases for the next five years, potentially reaching around £10,500.

Jo Grady, the combative General Secretary of the University and College Union, did not hold back in her response. "Keir Starmer repeatedly pledged to abolish the toxic system of tuition fees, which was a core reason he was elected leader of the Labour Party," she stated in comments that gained significant traction in the days that followed. "It is deeply disappointing for him to renege on that promise, a move that would harm the very people Labour claims to represent" [UCU statement].

The journey leading to this betrayal had been long and complicated. In Labour's 2019 manifesto, the party declared that "higher education is in crisis" and committed to scrapping tuition fees [manifesto 2019]. Yet by 2024, Labour's manifesto became vague, stating only that it would work to create a "secure future" for higher education [manifesto 2024]. Even these vague suggestions for reform were further rolled back in May 2024, when...

The £28 billion green investment plan, initially Labour's flagship policy, aimed to transform Britain into a clean energy superpower. This ambitious plan, which had already been quietly scaled back during the election campaign, was a key part of Labour's appeal to environmentally conscious voters. Now, with the Treasury demanding further cuts, what remained of the Green Prosperity Plan was about to be completely gutted, marking a significant policy reversal for the party.

The original promise was ambitious to the point of recklessness: £28 billion per year in additional green investment, funded through borrowing within Labour's fiscal rules. This policy had been central to the party's appeal to environmentally conscious voters, offering the prospect of Britain leading the global transition to renewable energy while creating hundreds of thousands of well-paid jobs in traditional industrial communities.

However, reality intervened with brutal efficiency. The £28 billion annual commitment was first reduced to an average over the entire parliamentary term, then limited to the second half of the term, and eventually scaled back to around £4.7 billion per year. By August 2024, even this diminished ambition appeared unsustainable, as Rachel Reeves's spending review revealed the actual state of public finances. This scaling back not only hampers the UK's progress toward becoming a clean energy superpower but also jeopardises the creation of hundreds of thousands of well-paid jobs in traditional industrial communities.

The announcement that the Green Prosperity Plan would be further curtailed was not made through a significant parliamentary statement, but rather via a written answer to a pre-planted question. This bureaucratic manoeuvre allows governments to deliver bad news without enduring media scrutiny. The £4.7 billion annual commitment was reduced to £2.5 billion, with most of the spending postponed to the latter years of the parliamentary term.

Carla Denyer, co-leader of the Green Party, perfectly captured the mood in her response, expressing a deep sense of disappointment: "This is a massive backward step for the climate, the economy, and good-quality jobs. Labour promised change, but they're delivering more of the same short-term thinking that has held Britain back for decades."

The media response was swift and unforgiving, intensifying the situation. The Guardian, which had endorsed Labour during the election campaign, published an editorial titled "Promises Made, Promises Broken," accusing the party of treating politics as if elections were popularity contests instead of exercises in democratic accountability. The Financial Times was more restrained but equally critical, warning that Labour's fiscal U-turns were "undermining confidence in the government's competence and credibility."

Television news coverage was dominated by embarrassing archive footage of Keir Starmer making the promises he was now abandoning. Sky News aired a particularly damaging montage contrasting the Prime Minister's leadership campaign pledges with his government's policy announcements, set to dramatic music that made the whole exercise look like a political obituary.

The right-wing press predictably sensed an opportunity, adding to the political tension. The Daily Mail's headline "STARMER'S GREAT BETRAYAL" accompanied a photo of the Prime Minister looking distinctly uncomfortable during Prime Minister's Questions. The Sun opted for "LIAR LIAR" in letters so large they could probably be seen from space. Even The Times, which is usually more measured in its criticism, ran a leader column questioning whether Labour had "won power under false pretences."

Perhaps the most damaging coverage came from sources that had been sympathetic to Labour during the election campaign. Channel 4 News commissioned a thorough fact-check of Starmer's leadership pledges, revealing the extent of his policy reversals. Of the ten commitments that had secured him the party leadership, seven had either been completely abandoned or so substantially modified that they became meaningless.

The BBC's political editor, Laura Kuenssberg, captured the mood in Westminster with characteristic precision: "The question isn't whether these U-turns are justified by fiscal reality; it's whether Labour's promises were ever credible in the first place. Either they didn't understand the constraints they would face in government, or they deliberately misled voters about what they could deliver. Neither explanation reflects well on their competence or integrity."

Social media erupted with anger from Labour's own supporters, many of whom felt personally betrayed by politicians they had campaigned for, donated to, and voted for in good faith. Twitter was filled with young activists posting screenshots of Starmer's leadership pledges alongside news reports of their abandonment, often accompanied by bitter comments about the futility of trusting politicians' promises.

The hashtag #StarmerLied trended for three consecutive days, fuelled by a mix of genuine grassroots anger and opportunistic opposition trolling. More damaging were the heartfelt testimonials from Labour members who had joined the party specifically because of the policies now being abandoned. One typical post from a university student in Manchester read, "I knocked on doors for this man. I believed him when he said he understood our struggles. Now I feel like a fool." This sense of disillusionment was palpable across social media platforms.

The digital rebellion wasn't limited to Twitter. Facebook groups created to support Labour during the election campaign transformed into forums for angry discussions about broken promises. Instagram stories from young Labour activists depicted campaign materials being torn up or burned, accompanied by captions expressing feelings of betrayal and disillusionment.

TikTok proved particularly damaging, with viral videos contrasting Starmer's earnest campaign promises with news reports of their abandonment set to ironic music. One video, showing Starmer promising to abolish tuition fees, followed by footage of students protesting fee increases, garnered over 2 million views in its first week.

The political impact was immediate and measurable. Labour's poll lead, which had reached 20 points during the election campaign, began to shrink as voters who had initially given the party the benefit of the doubt started to reconsider. This shift was not just a change in numbers, but a sign of the urgent need for the party to address the growing discontent. More troubling for party strategists was evidence that Labour's own supporters were becoming disengaged, rather than simply switching to other parties.

Focus groups conducted in marginal constituencies showed a decline in trust regarding the government's competence and honesty, with voters using terms like "disappointing" and "dishonest" to describe their feelings about Labour's performance. This loss of faith was particularly concerning for Labour strategists: among 18-24 year-olds, the party's approval rating had fallen from 67% in July to 34% by the end of August.

Internal party polling, leaked to the New Statesman in late August, revealed the extent of the damage to Labour's brand. Only 34% of voters who had supported the party in July reported being "satisfied" with the government's performance, while 43% expressed disappointment or anger regarding specific policy reversals. Most damaging of all, only 29% said they trusted Starmer to keep his promises, a figure that made him less trusted than Boris Johnson had been at his lowest point.

By-election results provided further evidence of the government's declining popularity. In a safe Labour seat in the North East that became vacant following an MP's resignation, the party's majority was slashed from 15,000 to just 3,000, with significant swings to both the Liberal Democrats and Reform UK.

The international reaction added another layer of embarrassment to Labour's domestic difficulties. The Biden administration, which had welcomed Starmer's election victory as a return to stable and predictable British politics, began to express private concerns about the new government's competence and reliability. Climate envoy John Kerry was reportedly "deeply disappointed" by the scaling back of green investment commitments, especially given Britain's role as host of COP26 and its rhetoric about global climate leadership.

European Union leaders, who had hoped that Labour's victory might herald a more constructive relationship with Brussels, were unimpressed by the government's early missteps. One senior EU official, speaking on condition of anonymity, told Politico Europe, "If this is what a competent British government looks like, we're in for a long few years."

The financial markets, which had initially welcomed Labour's victory as a return to fiscal responsibility after the chaos of the Truss years, began to factor in concerns about the government's political sustainability. The pound weakened against the dollar and euro, not due to fears about Labour's policies, but because of doubts about whether the government would survive long enough to implement any coherent agenda.

City analysts, who had been cautiously optimistic about Labour's pro-business stance, started to worry about political stability. "Markets hate uncertainty," one senior fund manager told the Financial Times, "and a government that can't keep its promises will only add to that uncertainty."

The criticism of the Labour government wasn't limited to political opponents. Trade union leaders, who had initially supported Starmer despite concerns over his centrist stance, began voicing their doubts about the government's direction. Len McCluskey, the former general secretary of Unite and a close ally of Jeremy Corbyn, came out of retirement to deliver a harsh critique of Labour's performance in office.

"They told us they would be different," McCluskey stated in an interview with The Guardian that sent shockwaves through Labour headquarters. "They promised they would represent working people, tackle the climate crisis, and make education accessible to all. Instead, we've ended up with more of the same Tory policies, just with a Labour logo on top."

McCluskey's criticism was especially damaging, as it came from someone who had been sidelined during Starmer's transformation of the party. His intervention lent credibility to left-wing critics who alleged that the current leadership was betraying Labour's values and abandoning its principles for political convenience. This criticism could lead to a shift in the party's policies and a re-evaluation of its leadership's decisions.

Unite the Union, Labour's largest affiliated union, went beyond mere criticism. On October 7, 2024, the union organised a mass lobby of Parliament, with over 500 activists demonstrating outside Westminster to protest cuts to winter fuel payments. General Secretary Sharon Graham did not hold back, stating, "Picking the pockets of pensioners is not a tough choice; it is a mistake. The government has underestimated pensioners, and the campaign will not stop until there is a full reinstatement of the Winter Fuel Allowance for all."

At Labour's party conference in Liverpool in September 2024, Unite successfully moved a motion calling for the reversal of the winter fuel cuts, the introduction of a wealth tax, and an end to the government's fiscal rules. The passage of this motion at the party's own conference vividly illustrated the depth of internal opposition to the government's direction, sending a clear message of the party's internal tensions.

The most damaging aspect was the growing perception that Labour's problems extended beyond specific policy reversals; they raised fundamental questions about the party's political character and competence. Labour had built its electoral appeal on the promise of honest, competent governance delivered by serious individuals who understood the responsibilities that come with power. However, the speed and scale of their U-turns suggested that they were either dishonest about their intentions or incompetent in their analysis of what was feasible.

The commentary from academic experts was particularly scathing. Professor Tim Bale from Queen Mary University of London, a leading expert in party politics, noted, "Labour fought the election claiming to be the adults in the room, the party that could deliver competent government after years of Conservative chaos. Instead, they now resemble just another group of politicians willing to say anything to get elected." This critique from a respected academic figure underscores the severity of the situation.

Professor Meg Russell from University College London's Constitution Unit offered similar criticism: "The issue isn't that governments occasionally have to change course; that's inevitable in a complex world. The problem lies in making promises you know you can't keep and then acting surprised when reality sets in. It reflects a level of political immaturity that is deeply concerning."

The think tank community, which had initially welcomed Labour's victory, began to distance itself from a government that appeared unable to fulfil its commitments. The Institute for Fiscal Studies, which had broadly supported Labour's fiscal approach during the election campaign, published a harsh assessment of the government's economic credibility, signalling a significant loss of support.

"The scale and speed of these policy reversals raise fundamental questions about Labour's readiness for government," concluded the IFS analysis. "Either they misunderstood the fiscal constraints they would face, or they deliberately made unrealistic promises. Both scenarios are troubling for the health of British democracy."

Internal party tensions, which had been carefully managed during the election campaign, began to surface as MPs who had remained silent during the push for power started to voice their frustrations. The Socialist

Campaign Group (SCG), representing Labour's left-wing MPs and known for its influence on party policies, issued a statement urging the government to "honour the commitments that won Labour the support of millions of voters." While the statement was cautiously worded to avoid direct criticism of the leadership, the message was clear: patience among the backbenchers was running thin.

Angela Rayner, the Deputy Prime Minister, found herself in an increasingly uncomfortable position as the focal point for grassroots anger regarding the government's direction. Having risen through the trade union movement, she maintained credibility with the party's base, an aspect that was becoming increasingly challenging as tensions within the party grew.

By the end of August 2024, just seven weeks after their landslide electoral victory, Labour was experiencing what political scientists would later describe as an unprecedented and unexpected collapse of governmental credibility in modern British history. The party that had promised to restore trust in British politics managed to erode its own credibility in record time, a turn of events that left many political observers and enthusiasts in shock.The opinion polls reflected this decline. Labour's lead over the Conservatives had narrowed from 20 points to just 8 points, with much of the decrease attributed to their own supporters opting for "don't know" rather than switching to other parties. More concerning for party strategists was the evidence that younger voters, once the demographic most enthusiastic about Labour's promises, were becoming increasingly disengaged from mainstream politics altogether.

As September approached and Parliament prepared to return from recess, the fundamental question facing Labour was whether the damage from the early controversies could be contained or whether they would mark the beginning of a longer-term decline. The party that had spent four years positioning itself as the competent alternative to Conservative chaos was discovering that competence wasn't merely about avoiding obvious mistakes; it was also about having the political skill to navigate the gap between electoral promises and the reality of governance.

The mood in Downing Street was reportedly grim, with senior advisers struggling tirelessly to develop a coherent communications strategy to defend the indefensible. One senior official, speaking to The Times on condition of anonymity, captured the prevailing atmosphere: 'We knew governing would be hard, but we didn't expect to be fighting for our political lives within two months of winning a landslide. The speed of the collapse has caught everyone off guard.'

The comparison with previous governmental honeymoon periods made for sobering reading. Tony Blair's government maintained high approval ratings for over two years after its 1997 victory. Even Gordon Brown, who inherited a difficult situation in 2007, enjoyed several months of favourable coverage before the financial crisis intervened. In contrast, Starmer's government was facing a full-scale credibility crisis before Parliament had even returned from its summer recess.

The international coverage was equally brutal. The New York Times published a lengthy analysis piece titled "Britain's Latest Political Disappointment," while The Washington Post questioned whether "the age of competent government" might be over in Westminster. European newspapers, many of which had welcomed Labour's victory as a sign of political maturity in Britain, began to wonder whether the country's democratic system could produce a stable and effective government.

The impact extended beyond Westminster and into popular culture, where Labour's broken promises became a source of dark humour and bitter satire. Comedy shows that had previously mocked Conservative incompetence now turned their attention to Labour's credibility gap. Social media memes comparing Starmer's leadership pledges to his government's policies went viral, often accompanied by ironic commentary about the futility of trusting politicians

In December 2024, a parody of Mud's 1974 Christmas number-one single "Lonely This Christmas" was released, entitled "Freezing This Christmas." This was a direct response to the winter fuel payment cuts. The song, performed under the name "Sir Starmer and the Granny Harmers," reached number one on the Singles Downloads Chart and number 37 on the singles chart, with all proceeds going to elderly charities.

As the summer of 2024 drew to a close, political observers began to question whether what they had called "the Starmer Doctrine," which prioritised competence over charisma, had been fatally undermined by the government's early failures. The approach that had proven effective in opposition, with careful preparation and methodical implementation, seemed inadequate for the challenges of governing.

The early controversies had not only damaged Labour's reputation with voters but also revealed fundamental flaws in the party's approach to politics and government that would be increasingly difficult to address. The forensic precision that had served Starmer well as a barrister and opposition leader did not translate effectively to the messy, compromise-filled world of democratic governance.

The toolmaker's son, who had built his career on careful preparation and meticulous attention to detail, was discovering that some problems could not be solved through better briefing papers or more thorough analysis. It turned out that politics required not only technical competence but also the kind of political courage necessary to confront complex challenges.

Chapter 7
When the Numbers Stopped Adding Up

*How Labour's economic promises collided with fiscal reality, and
why nobody wanted to admit it*

The spreadsheets revealed a disconcerting narrative that those in
Downing Street had been trying to evade. By September 2025, fourteen
months after Labour's overwhelming victory, the economic data were
contradicting almost everything the government had stated regarding its
fiscal situation and policy decisions. The £22 billion 'black hole' that
Rachel Reeves had used to justify difficult decisions increasingly seemed
more like a political ploy than a reflection of economic reality.
Moreover, the policies implemented to address this 'black hole' were
yielding results that economists had anticipated, but which politicians
had chosen to overlook.

On July 29, 2024, Rachel Reeves stood before the House of
Commons, conveying the weight of devastating news with reluctant
honesty. 'The previous government', a Conservative-led administration,
left a £22 billion hole in the public finances,' she announced, her voice
heavy with the gravity of revealed truth rather than political spin. 'They
concealed it. They hid it from the British people. And now we must
confront it.'

This statement became Labour's fiscal guiding principle, justifying
every broken promise and abandoned pledge. Cuts to winter fuel
payments? The black hole. Restrictions on disability benefits? The black
hole. Public sector pay restraint? The black hole. The phrase was
repeated so often in government communications that it turned into a
dark joke among Treasury officials.

The Institute for Fiscal Studies, a respected economic think tank that
both parties had traditionally cited as authoritative, expressed scepticism
from the outset. In their analysis published shortly after Reeves's
statement, IFS Director Paul Johnson chose his words carefully. Still, his
message was clear: 'Many of the fiscal pressures facing the new
government were entirely predictable and were indeed predicted,
including by us.' This predictability raises questions about the
government's foresight and planning.

This careful language concealed a harsh reality: Labour had either been incompetent in its pre-election analysis or dishonest in its campaign promises. The "black hole" was not an unforeseen disaster that no one could have predicted; it was an entirely foreseeable outcome of decisions made by both the previous Conservative government and Labour's own commitments during the campaign.

The numbers confirmed this. Of the £22 billion figure, approximately £9.4 billion resulted from Labour's decision to accept public sector pay review body recommendations that exceeded the Conservatives' budget. This was not inherited; it was a deliberate choice. The previous government had planned for 2% increases, but Labour accepted recommendations of 5-6% because rejecting them would have led to the strikes they had promised to eliminate. It was a policy choice, not an unavoidable burden, and one that had a significant impact on the fiscal situation.

A significant portion of the so-called "hole" in the budget was related to asylum hotel costs and immigration processing delays that had been publicly documented in Home Office publications throughout 2023 and early 2024. The Migration Observatory at the University of Oxford, a renowned institution for its in-depth research on migration and related fiscal implications, had published a detailed analysis of these costs months before the election. Any party planning to govern could have incorporated this information into its budgetary projections.

Carl Emmerson, deputy director of the Institute for Fiscal Studies (IFS), was more straightforward in interviews, stating that the overall fiscal situation was available to all political parties before the election. The reality was more complex and politically uncomfortable than Labour's narrative suggested. While the Conservatives had indeed left the public finances in a precarious state, Labour had campaigned on a platform that promised to address these pressures without implementing the necessary tax increases.

The Office for Budget Responsibility (OBR), established following the 2008 financial crisis to provide independent fiscal oversight, has confirmed the transparency of the fiscal situation in subsequent analyses. While some spending pressures had been underestimated by the previous government, the overall budgetary picture had been publicly accessible. Furthermore, the OBR noted that Labour's own spending commitments during the campaign did not appear to fully account for known fiscal pressures, providing a clear and independent view of the situation.

By spring 2025, even sympathetic observers began to question the government's narrative. The portrayal of fiscal pressures as uniquely "hidden" or "covered up" was not supported by the analysis of publicly available data from before the election. Labour had built its entire governing narrative on a foundation that was deteriorating under scrutiny.

Every difficult decision, such as cutting fuel payments for pensioners, restricting disability benefits, and imposing pay restraints on public sector workers, had been justified by the "black hole" in the budget. This 'black hole', a term used to describe the perceived fiscal deficit, now appeared to be as much a political construct as a fiscal reality. The betrayal wasn't just that Labour had broken its promises; it was that they had manufactured a crisis to justify their actions

Economic policy operates through second-order effects that politicians often underestimate. By cutting benefits, the government not only reduces spending but also decreases consumer spending, which in turn leads to lower business revenue and tax receipts, potentially necessitating further spending cuts. This cascade effect transforms what may seem like a straightforward fiscal adjustment into an economic contraction that can undermine its own stated goals.

Labour's benefit cuts, totalling approximately £7 billion annually by 2026 once fully implemented, exemplified this dynamic. The immediate impact was predictable according to standard economic models: 250,000 people, including 50,000 children, would be pushed into poverty according to the government's own estimates. However, economic theory, particularly the theory of income distribution and its impact on consumer spending, suggested that the repercussions would extend far beyond the households directly affected.

Standard economic analysis suggests that benefit recipients have a high marginal propensity to consume, referring to their tendency to spend most of any income change immediately, as they often lack financial cushions. When their income falls, they do not reduce their savings or delay investment purchases; instead, economic necessity forces them to cut spending on essentials immediately. This is not speculation; it is a well-established empirical observation across multiple countries and time periods.

The geographical impact of these cuts was significant. Labour's welfare reforms, which aimed to reduce government spending on social welfare, affected the post-industrial communities that the party claimed to champion. In former mining towns across South Wales, County Durham, and Yorkshire, where benefit recipients represented a substantial portion of local consumer spending, economic theory predicted that the cuts would lead to immediate contractions in regional economic activity.

Small business owners in these areas reported precisely what economic models predicted. The British Retail Consortium's quarterly survey data showed that retail sales in the lowest-income neighbourhoods fell significantly in real terms between July 2024 and March 2025. This was not a national trend; affluent areas experienced modest growth during the same period. Instead, it was a localised economic contraction, meaning a decrease in economic activity within a specific region, affecting the very communities Labour claimed to represent.

The employment effects also contradicted Labour's stated justifications. One of the government's rationales for restricting disability benefits was to encourage recipients to return to work. This theory seemed plausible at first glance: reduce benefits, increase the financial incentive to seek employment, and boost labour force participation. However, it overlooked the nature of disability and the structure of the labour market.

Academic research on previous benefit restrictions in the UK and internationally suggested that this approach would fail. People receiving disability benefits generally do not choose not to work due to inadequate financial incentives; they are unable to work due to health conditions that the benefits are meant to address. Removing financial support does not cure medical conditions; it merely makes recipients poorer. Research consistently shows that poverty exacerbates health problems rather than resolves them.

The employment centres designed to help disabled people transition back to work were not just overwhelmed, but predictably so and under-resourced. The government had budgeted for 'enhanced employment support' to accompany the benefit cuts, but this translated into brief appointments with advisers who lacked the time and training to address complex health conditions and workplace accommodations, leaving many disappointed.

Local councils, already operating under severe financial constraints following years of austerity, experienced exactly what economic models had predicted: demand for emergency assistance surged as benefit recipients lost income, placing a significant strain on their resources. Shortfalls in housing benefits led to evictions, which resulted in homelessness and increased costs for emergency accommodation and social services. Several councils published analyses showing that their spending on crisis interventions exceeded any savings from the central government's benefit cuts.

The tax revenue effects also followed predictable patterns. Benefit cuts reduced consumer spending, which in turn decreased VAT receipts. Lower economic activity resulted in lower income tax and national insurance contributions. Small businesses struggling with reduced customer spending paid less corporation tax. Economic modelling suggested that the net fiscal benefit would be substantially less than the headline figure once second-order effects were taken into account.

The Institute for Fiscal Studies, a highly respected institution, conducted an analysis that confirmed the theoretical predictions regarding the impact of benefit cuts. The actual fiscal consolidation achieved was significantly less than the government had claimed when taking into account the full economic effects. While the government succeeded in its unstated goal of appearing tough on welfare, it ultimately failed to achieve meaningful fiscal improvement.

At Labour's September 2025 conference, the slogan "Build, baby, build!" was prominently featured on red baseball caps, conference banners, and promotional materials. This slogan aimed to convey a sense of optimism. However, the gap between the slogan and reality was alarming, as demonstrated by Housing Secretary Steve Reed's inability to provide basic housing delivery statistics during a live television interview.

Labour had promised to build 1.5 million new homes during the Parliament, equating to 300,000 homes per year for five years. By autumn 2025, only about 117,390 homes had been constructed in the fourteen months since Labour took office. This stark contrast between the promise and the reality is a cause for concern, as at that rate, the UK would build roughly 100,000 homes annually, only one-third of the target.

The Chartered Institute of Housing published an analysis explaining why Labour's targets were unrealistic both economically and logistically. The challenges were structural and well understood by housing experts:

- Britain had systematically underinvested in construction skills training for the past two decades. The Construction Industry Training Board estimated that the sector would need an additional 225,000 skilled workers to meet Labour's targets. These workers do not currently exist and cannot be trained quickly enough within one parliamentary term.

- The impact of global supply chain disruptions on housing development cannot be overstated. Building 300,000 homes annually requires not only the materials for those homes but also the industrial capacity to manufacture them. This industrial capacity has declined significantly in recent decades as the UK's manufacturing sector has contracted.

- While Labour's planning reforms made approvals slightly faster, they did not address the fundamental economics of land ownership. Most development land is owned by a limited number of major developers and land banking companies. Standard economic theory explains their behaviour: building more homes leads to lower house prices, which decrease land values and, in turn, diminish profits. As a result, rational profit-maximising firms prefer to build slowly at higher prices rather than quickly at lower prices.

The urgency of the housing crisis is underscored by the fact that new homes require accompanying infrastructure, such as roads, sewers, schools, GP surgeries, and public transportation. Planning and building this infrastructure takes years. Many sites targeted by Labour for housing development lacked basic infrastructure, and Rachel Reeves's fiscal constraints resulted in cuts to infrastructure spending instead of increases.

Since 2010, councils responsible for processing planning applications and coordinating infrastructure have seen their budgets reduced by approximately 50% in real terms. Many planning departments are operating with minimal staff, making it impossible to process applications at the pace the government demands, regardless of regulatory changes.

The National Housing Federation, representing housing associations that actually build affordable homes, has clearly stated that the government sets targets without providing the necessary funding, skills, materials, or infrastructure to achieve them

Regional variations tell a revealing story. In London and the South East, where the housing need is most acute and land is most expensive, new build rates declined in 2024-25 compared to 2023-24. The impacts of planning reforms were minimal because the main constraints were not related to planning but rather to land costs and construction economics.

Meanwhile, in parts of the North and Midlands, where land is more affordable, new housing is being built in areas with limited employment opportunities. This stark disparity in regional development is a clear indication of the need for immediate action. Homes are being constructed where it is financially viable to build them, not where people actually need to live. As a result, the housing stock is concentrated in the wrong places and at the incorrect price points, while the housing crisis persists in high-demand areas.

The irony is striking. Housing is one area where public opinion overwhelmingly supports government intervention, and there is a genuine desire for bold action. However, Labour's approach combines radical rhetoric with insufficient resources, setting targets that are logistically impossible given the constraints, and then expressing surprise when these targets are not met. This disconnect between public opinion and government action is a source of frustration for many.

Britain has long been characterised by regional inequality, with a prosperous South East contrasting with the struggling North and Midlands. Unfortunately, Labour's first year in office has seen this divergence accelerate rather than narrow, despite the party's rhetoric about levelling up and regional rebalancing.

The Tech Prosperity Deal, a significant agreement negotiated with the Trump administration, directed a substantial amount of American technology investment to the United Kingdom. However, this investment was distributed unevenly, with the majority of funds flowing to London, Cambridge, and the Oxford-Reading-London corridor. At the same time, regional cities received only small fractions of the funds.

This disparity was not accidental. Tech companies tended to invest in areas with a skilled workforce and strong infrastructure. London benefited from its universities, international connectivity, extensive labour pools, and clustering effects that attracted even more investment. In contrast, regional cities offered cheaper land but lacked the other factors that technology companies prioritised. This trend, if left unchecked, could lead to a widening economic gap between London and the rest of the UK, with long-term implications for the country's financial stability and social cohesion.

The Centre for Cities, a think tank specialising in urban economics, published an analysis comparing economic indicators across Britain's major urban areas. Their findings confirmed predictions from economic geography theory: employment growth was concentrated in London and the South East, while cities in the Midlands and North experienced stagnant growth or decline. Real wage growth mirrored these trends, with positive growth in London but negative growth in many northern towns when adjusted for inflation. The rates of new business formation also diverged sharply, with London seeing multi-decade highs, while former industrial towns encountered multi-decade lows.

Public investment per capita also exhibited massive disparities. London residents received several times more infrastructure investment per capita than those living in North East England, and this gap was widening rather than narrowing.

These statistics translated into real-life experiences that influenced political attitudes and contributed to Labour's diminishing support in its traditional heartlands. Economic theory explains why investment tends to concentrate: agglomeration effects, network externalities, and increasing returns to scale mean that areas with existing advantages are likely to accumulate even more advantages over time. Breaking these patterns requires not only intervention, but also sustained and substantial intervention over decades.

Transport disparities highlighted the issue. The Elizabeth Line in London, a £19 billion infrastructure project, has recently opened, significantly improving connectivity in the capital. In contrast, plans for Northern Powerhouse Rail, designed to connect Liverpool, Manchester, Leeds, and Newcastle with modern high-speed transport, were substantially scaled back. The per capita investment ratio was overwhelmingly in favour of London.

Educational outcomes reflected similar trends. The percentage of young people attending university continued to rise in London and the South East, while it fell in coastal towns and former mining communities. The pipeline of skilled labour that might attract investment was drying up precisely where it was most needed.

The most pressing issue that demands immediate attention is the lack of a serious government strategy to address regional inequality. Beyond mere rhetoric and token investments, the situation requires a comprehensive and sustained approach. The economic forces driving this divergence, such as agglomeration effects, network externalities, and path dependencies, are well understood. However, countering them without sustained, massive investment over decades is a significant challenge. Labour's fiscal policies have constrained the necessary investment, making the situation even more urgent.

By autumn 2025, regional divergence had escalated from an economic challenge to a full-blown political crisis. The emergence of Reform UK, particularly in areas that had been left behind, was a significant development. The party's message that London elites were indifferent to working-class communities outside the capital struck a chord, largely because economic data supported this view, intensifying the political crisis.

One of Labour's core economic arguments was that its election would restore business confidence after years of Conservative upheaval. They claimed that competent governance, sensible regulations, and predictable policies would encourage the investment needed for Britain to drive growth. By autumn 2025, this theory was being put to the test.

The CBI's quarterly survey of business sentiment, published in September 2025, revealed a concerning trend. Business investment intentions had steadily declined since the election, with net expectations turning negative for the first time since the onset of the pandemic. This was not a sign of businesses leaving Britain, but rather a reflection of companies postponing investment decisions to assess the sustainability of Labour's government, indicating a grave economic situation.

Initially, construction and property developers had welcomed Labour's planning reforms, hoping that faster approvals would facilitate more building. However, these reforms were implemented without the necessary infrastructure investments to make development viable in many locations. Major developers reported scaling back planned projects due to "policy uncertainty and market conditions," a euphemism for ambiguity regarding government direction.

Technology companies also expressed concerns about the implementation of the Online Safety Act, the BritCard proposals, and overall regulatory uncertainty. Several UK tech firms have announced plans to establish European subsidiaries to mitigate regulatory risks, while maintaining their talent hubs in London and relocating actual investment elsewhere.

The retail and hospitality sectors, which are most vulnerable to fluctuations in consumer spending, are in a state of urgent distress. The direct impact of benefit cuts on their customer base is undeniable. Major retailers are reporting flat or declining revenues despite population growth, and restaurant chains are being forced to close locations. The economic pain, though concentrated, is pressing and real.

Manufacturing is in dire need of investment in automation and productivity improvements. However, Labour's policies are sending mixed signals, supporting green technology and industrial strategy on one hand, while fiscal constraints and regulatory uncertainty are limiting actual investment on the other. Industry associations report that manufacturers are postponing modernisation, desperately awaiting clearer policy direction

The Bank of England's agents' reports, synthesising intelligence from regional business contacts, paint a consistent picture: businesses are in a state of anticipation. Not actively disinvesting, not relocating, but not committing capital. Economic theory explains why this matters: growth comes from investment in productive capacity. When businesses start investing, growth can be reignited.

The decline in venture capital and private equity investment in British start-ups was a significant trend. Data from firms tracking start-up funding revealed a steep decline, surpassing that of comparable European countries. Regulatory uncertainty and political instability emerged as the top concerns for investors, further exacerbating the decline in investor sentiment.

The stagnation in Britain's productivity output per hour worked since 2008 was a serious concern. To break out of this stagnation, substantial investment in technology, skills, and infrastructure was required. However, all three areas were being squeezed, with declining business investment, underfunded skills training, and cuts in infrastructure spending.

By autumn 2025, Rachel Reeves's carefully constructed narrative of fiscal responsibility was facing challenges from economic data. The government, which had justified every difficult decision through reference to the "£22 billion black hole" and "tough choices," was demonstrably struggling to achieve its stated fiscal objectives.

The Office for Budget Responsibility's assessments, the definitive analysis of Britain's public finances, suggested several concerning trends.

The deficit, contrary to expectations, was not decreasing as forecasted. Labour's policies were intended to reduce borrowing to sustainable levels; however, projections indicated that borrowing would remain high, surpassing even Labour's own estimates and well above what fiscal rules were supposed to allow.

Tax receipts were falling short of expectations. A combination of benefit cuts, reduced consumer spending, economic stagnation that impacted corporate profits, and regulatory uncertainty discouraging investment resulted in tax revenues being below projections. The "fiscal headroom" that Reeves claimed to be building was not materialising as anticipated.

Spending pressures were not only intensifying but also reaching alarming levels. The NHS crisis was worsening, and local governments were approaching financial distress in multiple councils. The supposed "savings" from benefit cuts were being partially offset by increased spending on crisis interventions.

The key metric of fiscal sustainability, the debt-to-GDP ratio, was not improving as quickly as projected. The intended fiscal consolidation was not happening.

The Institute for Fiscal Studies provided a stark analysis: achieving the government's stated fiscal objectives would require either significant further spending reductions or unspecified tax increases. The implemented policies appeared to be contractionary, suppressing growth, while the fiscal situation was not improving as planned.

The political ramifications were not just considerable, but profound. Labour had justified every betrayal, broken promise, and complex decision by citing fiscal necessity. However, the fiscal situation was not improving as promised, which meant the pain was being inflicted without achieving its intended purpose.

The comparison to Conservative austerity was unavoidable. Between 2010 and 2015, the Conservative-Liberal Democrat coalition enacted spending cuts. While economic growth stalled and public services were damaged, at least the deficit fell substantially.

Labour was enacting similar contractionary policies without achieving the fiscal consolidation that was supposed to justify them. The economy was slowing, but the fiscal position was not improving as forecasted.

The underlying issue was that Labour had adopted fiscal orthodoxy without fully understanding its limitations. Economic models suggesting that spending cuts would restore fiscal sustainability assumed that such cuts would not significantly depress economic growth. However, decades of economic research indicated that cutting spending in an economy operating below capacity, especially with constrained monetary policy, could directly reduce GDP.

When GDP declines, tax receipts also decrease. As tax revenues decline, the deficit can remain high despite spending cuts. This is not a controversial point among economists; it reflects standard Keynesian analysis validated by extensive empirical research, particularly from the experience of European austerity after 2010.

The alternative approach of borrowing to invest in infrastructure and productive capacity while maintaining social safety nets was never seriously considered. This idea conflicted with the fiscal orthodoxy, a set of rigid economic policies that both main parties had internalised. Despite substantial economic evidence suggesting that public investment with positive returns could be self-financing over time, the parties remained steadfast in their adherence to these policies.

By late 2025, Britain was in the grip of an economic slowdown, a direct result of the fiscal consolidation policies that were not delivering as promised. Growth was stagnant, investment was declining, productivity remained flat, and regional inequality was widening. The fiscal position, which was supposed to be the justification for all this pain, was not improving as projected, leaving a sense of disappointment in its wake.

The economic reality of Labour's first fifteen months in government presented a story that political narratives struggled to downplay. The £22 billion budget shortfall was only "real" in the sense that any incoming government faces fiscal challenges. It was politicised because Labour chose to frame predictable issues as hidden crises to justify predetermined policy choices, a missed opportunity that now leaves a sense of regret.

The benefit cuts were achieving their unstated political aim of signalling fiscal seriousness, while failing to meet their stated goal of meaningfully improving public finances once second-order effects were taken into account. The housing crisis intensified despite ambitious targets, regional inequality accelerated under a government aimed at addressing it, and business investment stalled rather than increased. Ultimately, the fiscal position was not consolidating as projected.

Economic data, unlike political rhetoric, reveals the consequences of choices. Labour opted for fiscal orthodoxy over stimulus, political symbolism over policy effectiveness informed by economic evidence, and the appearance of toughness over genuine competence as measured by outcomes.

By autumn 2025, economic indicators suggested that Labour inherited a difficult fiscal situation and failed to improve it through policy choices that combined questionable ethics with disappointing results. They broke promises to vulnerable people without achieving the fiscal goals that supposedly justified these betrayals. They implemented contractionary policies without delivering the fiscal consolidation that could have provided at least a cynical rationale.

The tragedy was not that difficult; fiscal situations require tough choices, they do. The tragedy was that Labour's poorly designed choices had a devastating impact on vulnerable people, failing to meet their own stated fiscal objectives. They made unwise decisions, implemented them incompetently, and then were surprised when voters turned to alternatives.

The economic data, which remained resistant to political spin, revealed what Labour's political narrative tried to obscure: this was not competent economic management based on its own stated goals. Instead, it was policy-induced economic harm in pursuit of fiscal targets that were not being met, justified by a crisis that had been heavily politicised and managed by a government that appeared to lack a complete understanding of the economic mechanisms it was manipulating.

The numbers do not lie about outcomes, regardless of intentions. By late 2025, they were telling a clear story of policy failure that no amount of political communication could disguise. The ledger was transparent, and the verdict was harsh, but at least the public was well-informed.

Chapter 8:
Death by a Thousand U-Turns

How the ten pledges died one by one, and trust died with them

As the autumn of 2024 set in, Labour's credibility was under siege. What had initially seemed like isolated policy reversals in August had now snowballed into a systematic dismantling of Keir Starmer's entire leadership agenda. The ten pledges that had clinched his leadership in 2020, sacred commitments to party members who had placed their trust in him, were now being abandoned with a precision that mirrored a demolition crew's work on a condemned building.

This process was not accidental. It was a pivotal moment when internal memos, leaked to Private Eye in late September, unveiled a coordinated strategy to distance the government from what advisers referred to as 'legacy commitments.' This was a transparent euphemism for what was about to unfold. The establishment of a 'Policy Alignment Unit' by the Cabinet Office, tasked with 'reconciling electoral promises with governing realities,' was the beginning of a sophisticated plan to break promises without openly admitting it.

The unit, staffed by former McKinsey consultants and Blairite veterans, produced a 47-page document titled "Narrative Management in Transitional Governance," which served as a guide to breaking promises without losing face. This document was eventually leaked in full to The New Statesman, unveiling the cynical calculations behind Labour's governmental approach. One particularly Orwellian passage stated, "Legacy commitments from opposition must be contextualised within governing constraints." It further noted that "stakeholder expectations require careful management through graduated adjustment of deliverables."

Parliament reconvened in September after the summer recess, providing the first opportunity for systematic scrutiny of Labour's performance. MPs discovered a government that bore little resemblance to the party that had campaigned just three months earlier. The forensic questioning that Starmer had once mastered in opposition was now being directed at him, revealing a politician who had lost the moral authority that comes from keeping one's word.

The dismantling of the first pledge "Economic justice: Increase income tax for the top 5% of earners, reverse cuts to corporation tax, and clamp down on tax avoidance" did not occur through dramatic announcements but rather through quiet inaction. Starmer's initial commitment to increase income tax for the top five percent of earners was clarified in October 2024, when Treasury briefings indicated that tax rises on high earners were off the table for the entire parliamentary term.

Rachel Reeves explicitly outlined this reversal during her first major speech as Chancellor to the Institute of Directors in September. "This government will not punish aspiration through punitive taxation," she declared to an audience of executives who struggled to contain their delight. "We believe in rewarding success, not penalising it." The language echoed that of a Conservative Party conference, and several Tory MPs noted with bitter irony that Labour ministers were presenting their arguments more convincingly than they ever had, a situation that seemed to defy political logic.

Abandoning higher taxes for the wealthy was not merely a policy reversal; it was a betrayal of Labour's fundamental promise to tackle inequality. This pledge wasn't hidden in the fine print of Starmer's leadership campaign; it was the opening line of his first commitment, the foundational principle on which his candidacy was built. Party members who had voted for him based on this promise felt personally deceived, their trust shattered.

Sarah Chen, a Labour member from Islington who had campaigned for Starmer during the leadership contest, encapsulated this sentiment in a letter to her local newspaper: 'I knocked on doors for this man because he promised to make the wealthy pay their fair share. Now he's protecting them while cutting benefits for the poorest. I didn't just vote for the wrong candidate; I was conned by him.'

The reversal of corporation tax was equally stark. Starmer's pledge to "reverse cuts to corporation tax" was abandoned by November when Reeves announced that not only would the cuts remain, but the government was also considering further reductions to "maintain competitiveness in a global marketplace." This phrase became a running joke among Treasury correspondents; "global marketplace" had apparently replaced "fiscal responsibility" as the government's excuse for breaching its commitments.Even the promise to "clamp down on tax avoidance" proved to be more rhetoric than reality. By December 2024, HMRC's budget had been cut, not increased, and the promised anti-avoidance measures had been diluted following lobbying from City law firms. The government, which had once promised to close tax loopholes, was now creating new ones for the very people who had funded their rise.

The second pledge, "Defend migrants' rights: End indefinite detention, close detention centres, ensure safe passage, and scrap 'no recourse to public funds,'" met a similarly quiet demise as the leadership pledge. By December 2024, not only had detention centres remained open, but the government was also actively exploring the expansion of detention capacity to address what Home Secretary Yvette Cooper described as "increased irregular arrivals."

The language shift was significant: 'irregular arrivals' had replaced 'asylum seekers' in government communications, indicating how fully Labour had adopted Conservative framing on immigration. This shift in language not only reflected a policy change but also had a profound impact on public perception of immigration issues. Cooper, once a fierce critic of Tory immigration policy, now sounded indistinguishable from her predecessors as she announced new measures to 'strengthen border security' and 'reduce pull factors.'

Recent figures indicate that the number of small boat arrivals has increased by nearly 29 percent since Labour came to power. Between July 5 and December 31, 2024, there were 23,242 arrivals by small boat, marking a 29 per cent increase compared to the same period in 2023. This significant increase in arrivals, despite the government's hardline approach, underscores the complexity and urgency of the immigration issue.

The Refugee Council's response was pointed. Chief Executive Enver Solomon said, 'We were promised a government that would restore dignity and humanity to our asylum system. Instead, we have the same cruel policies dressed up in slightly more sophisticated language. The uniforms may have changed, but the brutality remains the same.' This strong condemnation from a leading advocacy group underscores the disappointment and disillusionment felt by many in the sector.

The criticism was even more pronounced coming from Labour's own MPs, who had campaigned on the party's immigration promises. Bell Ribeiro-Addy, the Streatham MP and one of Starmer's most vocal supporters on refugee issues, issued a statement barely containing her anger and frustration: "I was elected on a manifesto that promised compassion and justice for asylum seekers. I now find myself in the impossible position of defending policies that contradict everything I told my constituents I would fight for."

The third pledge, "Common ownership: Support common ownership of rail, mail, energy, and water," was perhaps the most cynically abandoned of all. The promise to "support common ownership of rail, mail, energy, and water; end outsourcing in our NHS, local government, and justice system" was not merely modified or delayed; it was completely reversed, leaving the audience with a sense of disillusionment.

By November 2024, Transport Secretary Louise Haigh was announcing not the renationalisation of the railways, but their "strategic modernisation through private partnership." This bureaucratic language was designed to obscure the fact that Labour was not only maintaining the railways in private hands but also encouraging further private investment. The East Coast mainline, which had been successfully operated in the public sector, was put up for tender to private companies.

The abandonment of promises regarding Royal Mail was even more blatant. During the leadership campaign, Starmer had assured Communication Workers Union leaders that Labour would bring the postal service back into public ownership. By December 2024, his government was actively facilitating its sale to foreign investors, arguing that "strategic private investment" would improve efficiency and service delivery.

Dave Ward, the CWU's general secretary, did not mince words in his response: "Keir Starmer looked me in the eye and promised to renationalise Royal Mail. His exact words were, 'We will bring our postal service home.' Now his government is selling what's left of it to the highest bidder. This isn't just breaking a promise; it's institutional fraud."

The water companies, which had been nationalised by every other European country facing similar crises, remained firmly in private hands despite ongoing failures and massive dividend payments to shareholders. Energy companies were not only left untouched but were actively encouraged through new subsidies and tax breaks that surpassed anything the Conservatives had offered.

Most distressing of all was the expansion of outsourcing in the NHS, local government, and the justice system, precisely the opposite of what Labour had promised. By Christmas 2024, more NHS services were being outsourced to private companies than ever before in the service's history. Local councils were being actively encouraged to outsource services to "delivery partners." At the same time, the justice system saw private companies taking on an increasing number of responsibilities for court administration and probation services.

The trade union response was swift and devastating. Sharon Graham, Unite's general secretary, delivered what became known as the

"Christmas Eve massacre," a television interview that systematically undermined Labour's credibility with working-class voter

The fourth pledge, a commitment to address the climate emergency through 'the Green New Deal, including a Just Transition and Green Jobs Revolution,' was perhaps the most cynically abandoned of all the government's promises regarding climate action. The government's decision to reduce the initial £28 billion green investment commitment to £4.7 billion during the election campaign, and then further review this diminished figure, was a stark betrayal of the public's trust in their climate action promises.

Ed Miliband, the Energy Secretary and one of the architects of Labour's green agenda, found himself in a difficult position, defending policies with which he privately disagreed. His uncomfortable performances on television, which once showcased Miliband as Labour's most effective communicator on climate issues, revealed a minister struggling to reconcile his personal convictions with his party obligations.

The transformation was painful to witness. During a particularly excruciating interview with Andrew Neil in November, Miliband was forced to justify the government's decision to approve new oil drilling licenses in the North Sea, a policy he had spent years opposing. When Neil read back Miliband's own tweets from 2023 condemning similar Conservative policies, the Energy Secretary's weak response that 'circumstances have evolved since those comments were made' only added to the audience's disbelief and frustration.

The climate movement's reaction was swift and critical. Extinction Rebellion organised a series of protests outside Labour Party headquarters in December, displaying banners that read "CLIMATE LIARS" and "STARMER'S LIES ARE KILLING US." The backlash from mainstream environmental groups, who had supported Labour during the election, was even more damaging.

Caroline Lucas, the former leader of the Green Party, encapsulated the sentiment perfectly in a scathing article for The Guardian: "They promised a Green New Deal and delivered a green whitewash. They spoke of a Just Transition and delivered just betrayal. Future generations will not forgive this systematic destruction of our planet's future for the sake of short-term political expedience."

The fifth pledge, to "strengthen workers' rights and trade unions," was being quietly eroded through numerous small compromises and bureaucratic delays. Although the promise to "introduce the Employment Rights Bill within the first 100 days" was technically fulfilled, the bill that emerged bore little resemblance to what trade unions had been promised during the election campaign.

Zero-hour contracts remained legal, with only superficial changes to their regulation. Furthermore, the right to strike was restricted rather than strengthened, with the introduction of "cooling-off periods" and mandatory arbitration procedures making industrial action more difficult. Most damaging of all, the government announced in December that it would not reverse the Conservative requirement for union political funds to be actively opted into rather than opted out, a decision that directly threatened Labour's own funding base.

When the Employment Rights Bill finally appeared in October, it was so diluted that even Conservative MPs struggled to criticise it. The Confederation of British Industry (CBI) welcomed it as "a balanced approach to workplace relations," which effectively meant "this changes nothing meaningful." Trade union leaders, who had anticipated transformative legislation, found themselves defending a bill that offered little more than what they had under the previous Conservative government.

The Trades Union Congress (TUC) unleashed unprecedented criticism of a Labour government. General Secretary Paul Nowak accused the government of "betraying the movement that created the Labour Party." At the same time, individual union leaders began to question whether their continued affiliation with Labour was worth the financial and political cost.

The response from rank-and-file union members, who had campaigned for Labour based on its promises regarding workers' rights, was especially damaging. A survey conducted by the Morning Star in December revealed that 67% of trade unionists who had voted Labour in July were "disappointed" or "angry" with the government's performance on workplace rights, while 43% indicated they would not vote Labour again.

The systematic nature of the betrayals was becoming impossible to overlook on the international stage. The Biden administration, which had welcomed Keir Starmer's election victory as a return to stable, predictable British politics, began to express private concerns about the new government's competence and reliability. This shift in perception was particularly evident in the disappointment expressed by climate envoy John Kerry over Britain's retreat from its climate commitments. This move was seen as a significant blow given the country's role as host of COP26.

European Union leaders, who had hoped that Labour's victory might signal a more constructive relationship with Brussels, were unimpressed by the government's early missteps. Progressive parties across Europe began distancing themselves from Labour, with several social democratic leaders privately expressing concerns about the British party's abandonment of its core principles. Most symbolically damaging was the decision by the Party of European Socialists, of which Labour was a member, to issue an unprecedented statement questioning whether the party still shared the organisation's values. This growing isolation, a stark contrast to Labour's former alliances, left former allies questioning Labour's commitment to the social democratic principles that had once defined the party.

The media response to this systematic betrayal was initially confused but grew increasingly hostile. The Guardian, which had supported Starmer's leadership bid and Labour's election campaign, published a devastating editorial in December titled "The Man Who Promised Everything and Delivered Nothing." The piece accused Starmer of "conducting the most cynical exercise in political deception in modern British history." This strong stance from a previously supportive media outlet was a clear indication of the party's loss of public trust.

The editorial concluded, "We have witnessed many political U-turns over the years, but never such a systematic abandonment of core commitments. This isn't a normal evolution of policy in response to changing circumstances; this is a wholesale betrayal of everything a party claimed to stand for."

Television coverage became increasingly uncomfortable for government ministers. Channel 4 News commissioned a comprehensive fact-check of Starmer's pledges, revealing that not a single commitment had been kept in anything resembling its original form. The programme concluded that Labour had broken more promises in six months than most governments break in entire terms, a narrative that the party struggled to shake. Cathy Newman's interview with Angela Rayner in November became a defining moment in Labour's credibility crisis. When confronted with a side-by-side comparison of Starmer's pledges and the government's actual policies, the Deputy Prime Minister could only offer a weak defence, stating, "We have to govern in the real world, not the fantasy world of opposition." The clip went viral on social media, garnering over two million views and 50,000 comments, most of which expressed outrage at what viewers perceived as a contemptuous dismissal of democratic accountability.

The response from Labour's MPs was initially subdued, and party discipline was strong enough to prevent open rebellion. However, by

December, backbench frustration could no longer be contained. The Socialist Campaign Group, a significant left-wing faction within the Labour Party, issued a statement that nearly called for Starmer's resignation but clearly expressed their discontent: "The promises that won our support have been abandoned. The values defining our party have been betrayed. This cannot continue" [SCG statement].

This statement, signed by 23 Labour MPs, was unprecedented in its criticism of a Labour Prime Minister by members of his own parliamentary party [parliamentary rebellion]. More significantly, the signatories were not regular rebels or attention-seekers but serious MPs who had generally backed the leadership. Their intervention had a ripple effect, indicating that discontent was spreading beyond the usual suspects to the broader left wing of the parliamentary party.

Individual MPs began to break ranks more openly. Zarah Sultana, one of Labour's most prominent left-wing voices, told Owen Jones on his podcast that she felt "ashamed to take the Labour whip". At the same time, the party implemented policies she had campaigned against for years [podcast interview]. Her comments, broadcast in November, opened the floodgates for similar sentiments from other left-wing MPs who felt trapped between their principles and party loyalty.

Bell Ribeiro-Addy went even further, telling BBC Radio 4's Today programme that she was "actively considering" whether she could remain in the Labour Party [radio interview]. "I was elected to represent my constituents' values and interests," she stated. "When the party I represent is implementing policies that hurt my constituents and betray our values, I have to question whether I can continue to carry the Labour banner."

By December, the constituency Labour parties were in open revolt. Local meetings, once routine, were now transformed into heated debates about whether to submit motions of no confidence in the leadership [CLP meetings]. The party machinery, which had been effective during the election campaign, was now being turned against its own leadership by members who felt they had been systematically deceived.

In Islington North, Jeremy Corbyn's former constituency, the local Labour party passed a motion condemning the government's "systematic betrayal of Labour values" [constituency motion]. Similar motions were adopted in dozens of other constituencies, creating an unprecedented situation where local Labour parties formally criticised their own government [grassroots revolt].

The membership figures told a worrying story. After peaking at over 500,000 during the Corbyn years, membership had already dropped to around 370,000 by the 2024 election [membership data]. By December

2024, internal figures leaked to Left Foot Forward suggested that membership had fallen below 280,000, representing a decline of nearly half in just two years [membership decline].

More concerning for the party's finances was the profile of those leaving. Younger members, who had joined during the Corbyn era and been most enthusiastic about Starmer's pledges, were departing in large numbers [demographic analysis]. Internal analysis revealed that membership among individuals under 35 had decreased by 60% since the election, while membership among those over 65 remained relatively stable. As a result, the party was ageing rapidly, losing the energy and enthusiasm that younger members contributed to campaigning.

Momentum, the grassroots organisation that powered Jeremy Corbyn's leadership campaigns, ignited a series of 'Truth and Accountability' rallies in December, drawing thousands of fervent activists. The Manchester rally, held in the same venue where Starmer had launched his manifesto, became a compelling display of political theatre that underlined the depth of Labour's betrayal.

Speakers at the rally, including disillusioned Labour members, trade union leaders, and former party officials, voiced their concerns about what they viewed as a fundamental betrayal of democratic principles. The most powerful speech came from Janet Alder, a former Labour councillor from Hull who had supported Starmer during the leadership election.

'I believed him when he promised to transform our communities,' she told the crowd, her disbelief palpable. 'I believed him when he said he would tackle inequality and defend workers' rights. I even believed him when he promised no more illegal wars. I was a fool to trust a politician, but I was an even bigger fool to trust this politician. He didn't just break his promises; he broke faith with everyone who believed in the possibility of change.

By Christmas 2024, barely six months after their landslide electoral victory, Labour was facing what political scientists would later describe as the fastest collapse in governmental credibility in democratic history. The systematic abandonment of the ten pledges had not only damaged the party's reputation but had also raised questions about the entire premise of representative democracy.

The comparison with previous governments' honeymoon periods was striking. Tony Blair's government maintained high approval ratings for over two years after its 1997 victory. Even Gordon Brown, who inherited a difficult situation in 2007, enjoyed several months of favourable coverage before the financial crisis intervened. In sharp contrast,

Starmer's government was experiencing a full-scale credibility crisis before Parliament had even returned from its summer recess.

By December 2024, polling unveiled the extent of the damage. Sixty-one percent of Britons expressed dissatisfaction with Starmer, the highest level since he became Labour leader, with more than half of the public (56%) being disappointed in Labour's actions thus far. Among those who had voted Labour in 2024, the situation was stark: satisfaction with the government's performance had plummeted to just 32%.

Perhaps most tellingly, even among 2024 Labour voters, 49% reported dissatisfaction with Starmer's performance as Prime Minister. This wasn't merely typical political unpopularity; it represented an active rejection by the party's own supporters, who felt they had been deliberately deceived about what they had voted for.

The international progressive community was deeply disappointed by the situation. Alexandria Ocasio-Cortez's tweet, "Promising progressive policies to win elections, then implementing conservative policies in government is not politics; it's fraud," Echoed the sentiments of many. This tweet, retweeted 250,000 times, became a rallying cry for critics of Keir Starmer's leadership [social media response].

Bernie Sanders was even more direct in his criticism, telling CNN, "What we're seeing in Britain is a cautionary tale about what happens when politicians abandon their principles for the sake of power. Keir Starmer campaigned as a progressive and governs as a conservative. That's not political evolution; that's political fraud" [US criticism].

As 2025 approached, the fundamental question facing Labour wasn't whether they could recover from their early mistakes, but rather if they could survive the systematic destruction of their own moral authority [political future]. The ten pledges lay in ruins, the party's relationship with its supporters was shattered, and the Prime Minister, who had once seemed unassailable, was increasingly looking like a political dead man walking.

The methodical demolition was complete. Now, it was a matter of whether anything could be built from the rubble, or whether Labour's betrayal of its own promises would mark the beginning of something far more dangerous: the potential death of trust in democratic politics itself [democratic implications].

The forensic barrister who had promised to restore competence and integrity to the British government demonstrated that sometimes the greatest threat to democracy comes not from incompetent enemies, but from competent friends willing to sacrifice everything, including their own principles, for the hollow prize of political power.

The ten pledges were gone. The crucial question now was whether democracy itself could survive their assassination.

Chapter 9
Labour's First Scandals

How the party of change became the party of cronyism faster than anyone thought possible?

On the morning of September 15, 2024, Westminster was shrouded in grey skies and drizzle, but the weather was nothing compared to the storm clouds gathering around Keir Starmer's newly formed government. Just seventy-three days after their landslide victory, reports surfaced in the British media that Starmer had initially failed to declare £5,000 worth of gifts used to buy clothing for his wife, Victoria Starmer. To put this in perspective, this amount is more than what an average person in the UK earns in a month. The honeymoon period, which had never quite materialised, was officially over.

For a Prime Minister who had built his reputation on competence, integrity, and restoring trust in British politics, this revelation came as a significant blow. The gifts had been given by Waheed Alli, Baron Alli, who had also provided Starmer with several clothing-related items, including £2,435 worth of eyeglasses. The optics were damaging: here was a Labour leader who had spent years attacking Conservative sleaze, now caught with his hand in the proverbial cookie jar, a stark contrast to his previous image.

However, the clothing scandal was just the beginning of what would become a series of embarrassments for the Labour Party. It was later reported that Starmer had accepted over £107,145 in gifts, benefits, and hospitality since the 2019 general election. This included tickets to matches for Arsenal F.C. and concerts by Taylor Swift and Coldplay, two-and-a-half times more than any other MP. For a party that had promised to be different, these figures were not just troubling, but staggering.

The situation echoed the final days of Conservative governments. It began with defensive briefings, where the government attempts to downplay the issue, followed by technical discussions regarding the rules being followed, which often involve legal and procedural arguments, and then a gradual acknowledgement that things might not be right. Starmer himself dismissed accusations of corruption, asserting that all MPs accepted gifts and that he needed to accept hospitality for security purposes. This legalistic response satisfied no one outside Westminster's bubble.

Behind the scenes, Number 10 was in crisis mode. The political honeymoon that new governments often experience, where the public gives fresh leaders the benefit of the doubt, was evaporating quickly. Labour strategists, who had spent months crafting messages of change and renewal, now found themselves dealing with scandals involving designer glasses and VIP concert tickets. One senior adviser, speaking on condition of anonymity, captured the mood by saying, "We went from Tony Blair to Tony Soprano in the space of a weekend."

The controversy surrounding Taylor Swift proved especially damaging, as it illustrated the flaws in Labour's early approach to governance. The issue persisted into October 2024, when it was reported that the Special Escort Group of the London Metropolitan Police had provided Taylor Swift with a top-level security detail for her London Eras Tour shows in August. This decision, which could be seen as a misuse of power, followed a terrorism plot in Vienna. It came after Home Secretary Yvette Cooper allegedly pressured them to offer the security, given that she, Starmer, and several other senior members of his cabinet had received over £20,000 in free tickets for the shows from Swift's team

The narrative unfolded dramatically: Labour politicians enjoyed lavish hospitality, including champagne and caviar, while ordinary families struggled with the cost of living. Starmer and his government denied accusations that Cooper had played a role in granting security to Swift or pressured the police to do so, claiming that the provision of free tickets to the politicians was not made in exchange for the security grant and was purely a matter for the police. However, by that point, the damage had already been done. The Opposition benches erupted with cries of "cash for access" and accusations of a two-tier system where the wealthy received special treatment.

The situation worsened with the 'passes for glasses' affair, as the media dubbed it. On August 24, 2024, The Times, a key player in uncovering political scandals, reported that shortly after Starmer became Prime Minister, Lord Alli, Starmer's largest personal donor, had been issued a security pass. This pass allowed Alli unrestricted access to Downing Street, where he subsequently hosted a party for other Labour Party donors. The symbolism was devastating: within weeks of taking power, Labour was effectively handing the keys to Downing Street to wealthy donors.

The public's reaction was immediate and unyielding. Former Labour Shadow Chancellor of the Exchequer John McDonnell publicly criticised Starmer for accepting these gifts while 'talking about tough decisions and painful policies, potentially leading to a new wave of austerity.' He emphasised that Labour's founder, Keir Hardie, had attended Parliament dressed in 'an ordinary working man's suit' rather than formal attire to demonstrate that the party represented working people. When McDonnell, a veteran from the Corbyn years and no ally of the Labour right, was making the case for working-class values against the leadership, it highlighted a serious disconnect within the party.

The scandals were not limited to the Prime Minister. Labour Deputy Leader Angela Rayner received gifts worth £3,550 in clothing in June 2024, which included a personal shopper and clothing alterations, reportedly occurring both before and after the general election. Rachel Reeves, the first female Chancellor in British history, was also implicated. Reports revealed that Health Secretary Wes Streeting had received four Taylor Swift concert tickets, valued at a total of £1,160, as a gift from The Football Association. Meanwhile, Chancellor of the Exchequer Rachel Reeves had accepted £7,500 worth of clothes from Juliet Rosenfeld in 2024, which were registered as donations to support a deputy leadership campaign that ultimately did not materialise.

The institutional response was not only critical but also severe. The Guardian published an editorial warning that the Labour government did not benefit from a political honeymoon, remarking that it was 'hard to believe that a leader who emphasised the need to rebuild trust in politics would act so naively.' When even The Guardian, traditionally sympathetic to Labour, issued warnings about trust, the party leadership understood they were facing a significant problem.

The controversy surrounding the government gifts was just the visible tip of an iceberg that ran much deeper. The real issue was the abruptness with which Labour had abandoned the principles that had supposedly driven their electoral victory. The party that had won by promising to be different from the Conservatives was adopting some of its opponents' worst habits with alarming speed, leaving many of us surprised and concerned about the party's direction.

The changes to the winter fuel allowance highlighted this betrayal. The UK government amended the rules for the Winter Fuel Payment, effective from winter 2024/2025, so that households would no longer qualify unless they received Pension Credit or certain other means-tested benefits. This decision, announced just weeks after Labour took power, would affect millions of pensioners and save the Treasury billions, but it fundamentally undermined Labour's claim to represent working people.

In winter 2023/2024, 10.8 million pensioners across 7.6 million households in England and Wales received the Winter Fuel Payment. Following the changes for 2024/2025, the Department for Work and Pensions (DWP) estimated that only 1.5 million individuals in 1.3 million households would receive a payment. The extent of this cut was not just significant; it was staggering: from over ten million recipients to just 1.5 million. This was not mere tinkering at the margins; it was a wholesale abandonment of universal provision; a situation that should make us all feel the gravity of the plight of these pensioners.

The immediate human cost was both visible and devastating. "Old and cold in the countryside" became a rallying cry for pensioner groups. Maggie Roberts, vice-chair of Unite Retired Members, remarked, "Pensioners earning as little as £220 per week will miss out on the winter fuel payment this year. This isn't a policy that takes from the rich to give to the poor. This is a policy that takes from pensioners to pay for a crisis not of our making." This should make us all feel empathetic towards the affected pensioners.

The politics surrounding this issue were as toxic as the policy itself. On September 9, it was reported that Labour MPs, including frontbenchers, were concerned that Shadow Chancellor Rachel Reeves's "brutal" plan for the fuel allowance would lead to more older people being admitted to hospitals over the winter months. When your own MPs are criticising government policy as "brutal," it signals that the messaging has gone terribly wrong.

The parliamentary arithmetic was also embarrassing. A total of 53 Labour MPs did not vote in favour of the motion regarding the winter fuel allowance. This group included notable figures such as Hilary Benn and Diane Abbott. When veteran politicians like Hilary Benn, a respected figure within the Labour Party, refused to support the government, it was clear that the party's unity was fractured.

Even more damaging was the reaction from trade unions. Unite the Union, once the Labour Party's most significant donor, contributing £3 million during the 2019 election, chose not to donate to the party or endorse its manifesto. Unite's General Secretary Sharon Graham stated firmly, "The government's winter fuel policy needs to be reversed. Targeting everyday people with limited resources is not a tough choice; it is a mistake."

The government's defence was politically tone-deaf. The Chancellor of the Exchequer, Rachel Reeves, described it as a "tough choice," one she "did not want to make or expect to make." However, she contended that it would help put public finances on a "firmer footing." Telling pensioners facing a cold winter that their suffering was merely a "tough choice" for politicians was precisely the type of language that made voters cynical about political priorities.

The £22 billion black hole, a financial predicament inherited from the previous Conservative government, became Labour's excuse for every difficult decision. This significant deficit was a card they had overplayed from the outset. On July 29, 2024, Reeves conducted a spending review, arguing for 'necessary and urgent decisions' due to the previous Conservative government's 'unfunded' and 'undisclosed' overspending of £21.9 billion. The message was clear: everything negative was the Tories' fault, and every painful decision was their responsibility.

However, the public's trust was waning. Focus groups conducted throughout the autumn revealed a mounting scepticism towards Labour's justifications and a growing frustration with the government's approach. The sentiment was clear: 'They promised to be different,' but the reality was, 'They're just like all the rest.' The political capital Labour had painstakingly built during four years in opposition was being recklessly squandered.

The constitutional implications were equally profound. On July 23, 2024, Labour withdrew the whip from seven of its MPs who supported an amendment proposed by the Scottish National Party's Westminster parliamentary leader, Stephen Flynn, to scrap the cap. This move, which was seen as a punitive action against dissent, raised questions about Labour's commitment to internal democracy. Flynn claimed that scrapping the cap would immediately lift 300,000 children out of poverty. Suspending your own MPs for voting to lift children out of poverty was not a good look for a supposedly progressive party.

Behind the scenes, the machinery of government was already showing signs of strain. Sue Gray's appointment as Chief of Staff had been controversial from the beginning, but by October, the situation had become untenable. Rumours reported by The Guardian suggested she adopted a 'micromanagerial' leadership style, exercising substantial control over ministerial and special adviser appointments, and had 'extraordinary' control over access to Starmer and his agenda. This level of control was seen as stifling and led to discontent within the party.

The revelation of her salary was the final straw. At £170,000, Gray's salary was £3,000 higher than Starmer's. In a government asking pensioners to choose between heating and eating, and paying the Chief of Staff more than the Prime Minister, this appeared to embody the kind of

Westminster bubble thinking that voters had supposedly rejected.

On October 6, 2024, Gray resigned as Downing Street Chief of Staff, citing the "intense commentary" around her position as potentially becoming a "distraction" for the government. Her resignation statement was a masterclass in political euphemism. Still, everyone understood what had really happened: the most powerful unelected person in government had been forced out after less than three months in the role.

The Gray affair laid bare deeper issues with Labour's governance. One of the reasons Labour struggled during its first 100 days was the lack of a clear vision for change from Starmer and his team. The Institute for Government's analysis was blunt but accurate: after years of opposition, Labour lacked a coherent plan for wielding power. This revelation left the public feeling disheartened and disconnected from the party they had hoped would bring about significant change.

The most damaging aspect of the early scandals was the light they shed on Labour's relationship with wealth and power. The party, which had supposedly been transformed by Corbyn's radical agenda, was shown to be just as susceptible to the allure of wealthy donors as any other party. The charm offensive led by figures like Lord Alli had been remarkably successful, but it came with strings attached that Labour's leadership either failed to see or chose to ignore. This revelation left the public feeling disillusioned and questioning the party's integrity.

Labour raised £9.8 million during the campaign period, more than five times the amount raised by the Conservatives. However, the sources of this funding tell their own story: wealthy individual donors accounted for 68.5% of Labour's total campaign funding, with approximately £3.5 million coming from previous donors to other parties, primarily the Conservatives or Liberal Democrats. Labour had bought electoral success, but at a significant cost to its core values.

The transformation was symbolically complete when Peter Mandelson was appointed Ambassador to the United States. In December 2024, Mandelson was nominated as HM Ambassador to the US by Starmer, replacing Karen Pierce, who had been rotated out of her post. Mandelson's return, as one of the architects of New Labour's embrace of wealth, signalled the end of the party's brief flirtation with left-wing politics.

However, Mandelson's appointment quickly became controversial. A top advisor to Donald Trump labelled him an "absolute moron." Chris LaCivita, a senior advisor to the successful 2024 Republican presidential campaign, also praised the outgoing ambassador, Dame Karen Pierce, as "universally respected." When your ambassador is dismissed as a "moron" before even taking up the post, diplomatic relations are off to a poor start.

The public's disillusionment, as reflected in the polls, was palpable. A YouGov poll conducted in July 2025 showed that the government's approval rating had plummeted to –54 (with 63% disapproval and only 13% approval). For a government that had won a landslide victory less than a year earlier, these numbers were catastrophic. Labour was governing without the support of the population, despite holding a large parliamentary majority.

The local elections further demonstrated Labour's decline, a fact that should raise concern. The 2025 local elections in England were the first held during Starmer's premiership, during which both Labour and the Conservatives suffered significant losses, while Reform UK and the Liberal Democrats made substantial gains. Voters were abandoning both main parties in favour of alternatives that appeared to offer something different from the Westminster establishment.

The winter fuel controversy continued to haunt the government throughout the cold months, a testament to the weight of public opinion. In December 2024, a parody of Mud's 1974 Christmas number one single, "Lonely This Christmas," was released, titled "Freezing This Christmas," and accompanied by a black-and-white music video. When satirical Christmas songs about your policies climb the charts, you know you've lost the public relations battle

The song's success was more than just a novelty; it represented a cultural moment in which Labour's indifference toward pensioners became embedded in public consciousness. In the week leading up to Christmas, the parody reached number one on the Downloads Chart and number 37 on the singles chart. The government that had promised to restore hope to British politics had inadvertently made a Christmas number one song about freezing pensioners.

By spring 2025, the pattern had become clear. Every policy announcement seemed to contradict previous promises, every difficult decision appeared to hit the most vulnerable hardest, and every scandal revealed the gap between Labour's rhetoric and reality. The party that had spent years attacking Conservative sleaze was proving to be just as susceptible to the temptations of power.

The collapse of trust was not only about individual scandals; it reflected a fundamental dishonesty at the heart of Labour's political project. The ten pledges that had won Starmer the leadership were being systematically abandoned, the radical policy platform was quietly dismantled, and the promise of change was replaced by the reality of continuity.

Things were worsening for Sir Keir Starmer's Labour Government. Following his "loveless landslide" victory in July of the previous year, the Prime Minister appeared to be lurching from one disaster to the next. The assessment was brutal yet accurate: Labour had achieved power without authority, victory without legitimacy, and office without purpose.

The winter of 2024-25 marked the end of any illusion that this was a transformational government. The scandals had exposed the hollowness of Labour's promises, policy reversals had revealed the emptiness of their commitments, and their growing unpopularity demonstrated the fragility of their mandate. What had begun as a landslide victory was rapidly turning into a slow-motion political car crash.

The tragedy lay not only in Labour's failure but also in the predictability and avoidability of that failure, which mirrored the governments they had replaced. The party of change had become the party of stagnation; the movement of hope had devolved into an administration of disappointment; and the government that had promised to restore trust had broken faith with the people who once believed in them, leading to a growing sense of disillusionment among the public.

From an international perspective, Labour's decline was even more embarrassing. Foreign observers who had welcomed Starmer's victory as a return to political stability after years of Brexit chaos and Conservative incompetence were beginning to doubt Britain's ability to produce competent governments, regardless of which party was in power. European leaders who had hoped for improved relations found themselves dealing with a government that appeared as chaotic and scandal-ridden as its predecessors had been.

The media response to Labour's missteps showed how quickly political narratives can shift and influence public opinion. Newspapers that had endorsed the party in July 2024 were starting to question their judgment by winter. The Times, traditionally sympathetic to competent centre-ground politics, began publishing editorials about "the end of the honeymoon." The Financial Times, crucial for maintaining business confidence, remarked darkly that "markets prefer stable incompetence to chaotic competence."

However, it was the satirical response that truly captured the public mood. Covers of Private Eye became increasingly harsh, depicting Starmer as a politician caught between the competing demands of wealthy donors and everyday voters. Charlie Brooker's "Black Mirror" Christmas special included a thinly veiled parody of Labour's early months, featuring a prime minister who discovers that achieving power requires abandoning all the principles that initially made him worth supporting.

The comedy circuit also began to reflect changing public perceptions. Comedians who had spent years mocking Conservative incompetence found rich material in Labour's pretensions and contradictions. Common punchlines included, "At least with the Tories, you knew they were only in it for themselves," and "With Labour, you thought they cared about other people, which made the disappointment so much worse." These criticisms from the comedy circuit further eroded Labour's public image, contributing to a sense of disillusionment among the electorate.

Policy reversals were not limited to high-profile issues, such as winter fuel allowances. Across the government, departments were quietly abandoning commitments made during the election campaign or leadership contest. For instance, the pledge to end rough sleeping within one Parliament was diluted to a goal to "significantly reduce" it. The promise to build 1.5 million new homes became an "ambition" rather than a target. The commitment to renationalise the railways devolved into a complex series of franchise arrangements that bore a suspicious resemblance to the status quo.

Each retreat from principle followed a familiar formula: blame the previous government, cite fiscal constraints, and claim that the diluted version represented "responsible government" rather than political cowardice. However, voters were not naive; they could see the pattern. Focus groups frequently used phrases like "they're all the same" and "what was the point of voting for them?"

As months went by, the trade union response became increasingly hostile. Unite's Sharon Graham emerged as a particularly vocal critic, arguing that Labour was "betraying working people to appease wealthy donors."

Her statements held particular significance because Unite, a cornerstone of Labour's financial support during the Corbyn years, shocked the party with its withdrawal. This move marked a seismic shift in the party's traditional coalition.

Following Unite's lead, a wave of dissent swept through other unions. The Communication Workers Union suspended its donations, pending a review of Labour's policies. The National Union of Rail, Maritime and Transport Workers openly questioned Labour's commitment to genuine public ownership. Even traditionally moderate unions, such as UNISON, began to voice concerns about the government's direction, signalling a growing rift.

Responses at the constituency level were equally revealing. Labour MPs, who had previously won their seats with large majorities, found themselves facing increasingly hostile meetings with local party members. In Islington North, Jeremy Corbyn's former constituency, local activists passed a motion condemning the government's "abandonment of socialist principles." In traditional Labour heartlands across the North and Midlands, constituency parties that had celebrated victories in July were passing emergency motions demanding policy reversals by Christmas.

The generational divide within Labour deepened during this period, with younger and older members feeling increasingly disillusioned with the party. Younger party members, who had joined during the Corbyn surge, felt betrayed by what they saw as a return to the discredited politics of New Labour. Meanwhile, older members, who remembered the Blair years, were frustrated by what they perceived as naive idealism giving way to cynical pragmatism, without the electoral success that had justified Blair's compromises.

Social media turned into a battleground for the soul of the party. The hashtag #LabourBetrayal began trending regularly on Twitter, with activists posting side-by-side comparisons of Starmer's leadership campaign promises and his government's actual policies. Pro-leadership figures countered with the hashtag #ResponsibleGovernment, but their efforts appeared increasingly desperate as evidence of broken promises continued to mount.

The philosophical crisis ran deeper than simple policy disagreements. Labour had traditionally defined itself as the party of working people, but early scandals revealed a leadership class that seemed more comfortable with wealthy donors than with ordinary voters. The symbolism was devastating: while pensioners were losing their winter fuel allowances, cabinet ministers were accepting free clothing and concert tickets from millionaire benefactors.

The appointment process became another source of controversy. Beyond high-profile cases like Sue Grey and Peter Mandelson, smaller appointments throughout the government reflected a similar pattern of rewarding wealthy supporters while marginalising traditional Labour voices. Quango appointments, advisory positions, and honorary roles increasingly went to individuals whose primary qualification appeared to be their ability to make substantial financial contributions to the party.

The Christmas period of 2024 crystallised many of these tensions. While the song "Freezing This Christmas" climbed the charts, Labour

MPs found themselves facing increasingly hostile receptions at constituency Christmas events. The contrast between political rhetoric about "tough choices" and the reality of politicians attending lavish donor receptions created a cognitive dissonance that even sympathetic voters struggled to reconcile.

The New Year brought no relief from the cycle of scandal and disappointment. January 2025 saw fresh revelations about undeclared interests, February brought new policy U-turns, and March witnessed serious speculation about a leadership challenge. Each month introduced new evidence that Labour's transformation from radical opposition to establishment government was both complete and catastrophic.

The constitutional implications of Labour's decline extended beyond immediate political embarrassment. The party's abandonment of its promises for constitutional reform, particularly regarding proportional representation and reform of the House of Lords, was a profound disappointment for constitutional reformers across the political spectrum. They had hoped Labour would deliver the democratic renewal that Britain desperately needed. Still, this betrayal indicated that Labour was as committed to preserving the advantages of the Westminster system for major parties as any Conservative government.

Similarly, the devolution agenda stalled. Promises to strengthen Scottish and Welsh devolution were quietly shelved in favour of maintaining central control. The "Council of Nations and Regions," a prominent feature in the manifesto, had become a mere talking shop with no real powers. Scottish Labour, which had sought greater autonomy from London, found itself more centralised than ever under Starmer's control-obsessed leadership style.

The relationship with Europe also failed to improve as promised. While Labour avoided the worst excesses of Conservative Euroscepticism, there was no meaningful attempt to rebuild relationships with EU partners or rejoin any of the institutions from which Brexit had removed Britain. The government's approach seemed primarily designed to avoid giving ammunition to Reform UK rather than to advance any positive vision of Britain's role in Europe.

By spring 2025, the accumulated weight of broken promises, abandoned principles, and squandered opportunities had created what pollsters began to recognise as a new political phenomenon: "premature lame duck syndrome." Labour had achieved the rare feat of becoming politically irrelevant while holding a massive parliamentary majority. They possessed power without authority, office without purpose, and a mandate they had systematically undermined through their own choices.

International comparisons became increasingly unflattering. While other centre-left governments in countries like Denmark and Spain were implementing ambitious progressive agendas, Labour appeared paralysed by its own success. The stark contrast with these governments, who were making significant strides, made Labour's lack of ambition and practicality in their approach all the more apparent. The party that had once promised to be 'radical in ambition but practical in approach' had become neither radical nor practical, just another group of politicians more focused on preserving their positions than on using them for any meaningful purpose.

The media began drawing parallels with other failed political transitions. The comparison to François Mitterrand's early presidency in France was particularly damaging, as he was a left-wing politician who abandoned socialist policies under pressure from financial markets and ultimately alienated both his base and his critics. Other commentators invoked the early difficulties of Barack Obama, although Obama at least faced unified Republican opposition. In contrast, Labour's decline was largely self-inflicted, a fact that only added to the frustration and disappointment of the situation.

The spring of 2025 not only marked the anniversary of Labour's election victory but also served as a stark reminder of the swift changes that can occur in modern democracies. Constituency-level polling in seats where Labour had previously won with large majorities revealed a sudden double-digit shift away from the government. In traditional Labour heartlands, voters were considering alternatives they had never considered before. In metropolitan constituencies, where Labour had built its coalition, younger voters were flocking to the Greens in unprecedented numbers, signalling a rapid change in political dynamics.

If the European Parliament elections had been held during this period, they would have provided a brutal reality check for Labour's decline. Internal party polling indicated that the party would struggle to secure even third place, falling behind both the Conservatives and Reform UK. The Greens and Liberal Democrats were poised to benefit from the collapse in Labour support among younger and more educated voters, while Reform UK was gaining traction among working-class voters who felt betrayed by Labour's abandonment of its traditional values.

As spring dawned in 2025, coinciding with the first anniversary of Labour's victory, the government faced a pivotal question: Was there anything left of the political project that had propelled them to power, or had it all been devoured by the machinery of Westminster politics?

Regrettably, the answer was becoming increasingly evident with each unfolding scandal, each shattered promise, and each disillusioned voter who had dared to hope for a change.

The supposed honeymoon ended not with a bang but with a whimper, the slow, grinding sound of political capital being wasted one poor decision at a time. Labour had won the biggest prize in British politics only to discover that they had no idea how to wield it. The first scandals were just the beginning of a narrative that would define not just a government but an entire generation's relationship with political hope and democratic possibilities, a narrative of disillusionment, distrust, and a growing sense of political apathy.

The transformation was complete: from the party of change to the party of disappointment, from a movement of hope to an administration of broken promises, from a force that would restore trust in politics to a government that had lost faith with everyone who had believed in them. The winter of 2024-25 would be remembered not only as the season when pensioners froze but also as the moment when British politics lost whatever remained of its capacity to inspire genuine hope for a better future, leaving the electorate disillusioned and disheartened.

Chapter 10
Disillusion in the Party

On the morning of June 26, 2025, Westminster was buzzing with the nervous energy typically associated with significant political upheaval. In conference rooms across Portcullis House, over 120 Labour MPs were signing a "reasoned amendment" aimed at blocking the government's controversial welfare reform bill. This rebellion marked one of the most significant moments of Keir Starmer's premiership and highlighted the internal contradictions within the party, which had erupted into open conflict.

For a Prime Minister who had built his reputation on party unity and message discipline, the scale of the rebellion was catastrophic. MPs, elected just a year earlier on a platform of change and compassion, were now being asked to support policies that even their own government's impact assessment acknowledged would push 250,000 people into poverty, including 50,000 children. The cognitive dissonance was overwhelming, even for the most loyal backbenchers. They felt a deep sense of betrayal, having been elected on a promise of change and now being asked to support policies that would only exacerbate the very issues they had pledged to address.

Josh Fenton-Glynn captured the mood when he described breaking the party whip for the first time as an "incredibly painful" decision, warning that the government was "forcing loyal MPs into an impossible position." This rebellion wasn't simply a case of left-wing dissent; it represented a significant portion of Labour's parliamentary party rejecting the leadership's governing approach. When centrist MPs begin to speak about "impossible positions," it signals a collapse of the party's centre, a seismic shift that will have far-reaching implications for the party's future.

The welfare reform bill, framed as a technocratic measure for fiscal responsibility, represented a more profound shift: the final abandonment of Labour's social democratic principles. Cuts to Personal Independence Payments and Universal Credit health assessments were not merely policy changes; they signified that a Labour government in power would be no more compassionate than the Conservatives it had replaced.

The reasoned amendment presented the case for rebellion with striking clarity. The proposed changes had not undergone formal consultation with individuals with disabilities. The Office for Budget Responsibility would not release its analysis until autumn 2025. Additional funding for employment support would not be available until the end of the decade. Moreover, the government's own impact assessment estimated that these reforms would push 250,000 people into poverty, including 50,000 children. Each of these points meticulously dismantled the government's justification, employing Starmer's own methodology against him.

The rebellion crossed traditional factional lines in ways that would have been unimaginable during the Corbyn era, a period marked by significant internal divisions within the Labour Party. Of the 108 initial signatories of the reasoned amendment, 59 were new Labour MPs, often referred to as "Starmtroopers" for their supposed loyalty to the leadership. These were not die-hard rebels seeking publicity; they were principled MPs who entered politics to help others, not to push them into poverty.

The revolt was not limited to backbenchers, MPs who are not part of the government or opposition frontbench teams. Vicky Foxcroft, Lord Commissioner of the Treasury, a frontbencher who holds a ministerial or shadow ministerial position, became the first frontbencher to resign over this issue, writing to Starmer that she could not support 'reforms which include cuts to disabled people's finances.' Her resignation served as a warning shot that the government chose to ignore.

Diane Abbott, the longest-serving Black MP in Parliament, joined the rebels in voting against the bill. In a powerful speech before the vote, she expressed her opposition to the reforms on "moral, legal, and political grounds," adding that millions of people with disabilities would "not be able to believe that the Labour party is putting through legislation like this." When Diane Abbott, who had endured decades of racist abuse due to her unwavering principles, became a leading voice of opposition to a Labour government, it was evident that the party had lost its way.

The most damaging aspect of the situation was the intervention of Labour figures outside Westminster. Andy Burnham, the Mayor of Greater Manchester, publicly stated that the government was making "the wrong choice." His counterpart in London, Sadiq Khan, urged ministers to "urgently think again." Additionally, Baroness Eluned Morgan, Labour's First Minister in Wales, called for a reconsideration of the plans. When leaders from your own party publicly dissent, you know you're facing serious trouble.

The outcome of the final vote on July 1 revealed the depth of Labour's crisis and the government's humiliating retreat. A total of 335

MPs supported the significantly weakened bill, while 260 voted against it, including 49 Labour MPs. Furthermore, an additional 42 Labour MPs endorsed a second wrecking amendment led by Rachael Maskell, indicating that dissent ran even deeper than the voting numbers suggested.

The figures were stark: a government with a substantial parliamentary majority had been compelled to implement not one, but two rounds of last-minute concessions that stripped the reform package of its core proposals. The original plan to save £5 billion a year by 2030 had been drastically reduced to a projected £2 billion. Moreover, the reforms would apply only to future claimants, not current recipients, a significant concession that undermined the entire fiscal rationale for the initiative.

While Keir Starmer may have avoided total defeat, he did so by severely weakening his own legislation. It was a pyrrhic victory that satisfied no one and exposed the government as weak, divided, and willing to compromise on nearly everything except the principle of punishing the vulnerable.

The government's response to the rebellion highlighted the flaws in Starmer's leadership approach. Instead of addressing the substantive concerns raised by MPs, Number 10 focused obsessively on procedural issues and party management. Luke Akehurst, the loyalist MP for North Durham, summed up the leadership's mindset perfectly: "Whatever people's views are on the merits of welfare reform, I'm astonished that colleagues would sign a 'reasoned amendment' that would destroy a piece of government legislation. That isn't how we should resolve policy concerns and risks us facing a political crisis."

This argument revealed the leadership's priorities: maintaining party unity took precedence over substantive policy issues, procedural matters overshadowed principles, and avoiding a "political crisis" was considered more important than preventing human suffering. This reflected a technocratic mindset instead of that of a leader of a social democratic party. When your MPs rebel on moral grounds, and your response is to lecture them about parliamentary procedure, you have fundamentally misunderstood the essence of political leadership.

The welfare rebellion was merely the most visible sign of deeper issues within the Labour Party. MPs across the political spectrum began questioning whether the forensic barrister they had elected as leader possessed the emotional intelligence and required political vision to unify a diverse coalition. The individual who could dissect Conservative arguments with surgical precision seemed unable to inspire his own

117

supporters or articulate a coherent vision for the future.

While Westminster MPs debated their consciences, events in Birmingham vividly illustrated Labour's transformation from a workers' party to a management consultancy. The Birmingham bin strike became the defining image of Labour's summer of discontent, and it was every bit as damaging as it sounds.

The dispute began on March 11, 2025, when approximately 350 refuse workers, facing the threat of losing their safety-critical roles, bravely went on strike to oppose Birmingham City Council's plans. The council, led by Labour's John Cotton and operating under unelected government-appointed commissioners, was imposing £300 million in cuts after declaring bankruptcy. Workers faced pay cuts of up to £8,000 per year, essentially a quarter of their annual income.

By late March, the city was buried in rubbish. Approximately 22,000 tonnes of uncollected waste accumulated on the streets, creating a public health emergency that would shame any council, especially one run by the party of municipal socialism. On March 31, the council declared a "major incident," granting itself extraordinary powers to effectively criminalise the strike and enforce the cuts, a drastic measure that shocked many.

What happened next was reminiscent of the Conservative strike-breaking playbook, this time implemented by a Labour council supported by a Labour government. The council enlisted army planners and military logistics experts, rather than soldiers on the streets, to coordinate the strike-breaking operation. They spent £6.5 million on agency staff from Job and Talent, an additional £1.3 million on contractors from Tom White Waste (ironically owned by Labour-run Coventry City Council), and nearly £1 million on policing costs.

The police used Section 14 of the Public Order Act to disperse pickets. A High Court injunction granted in May severely restricted picketing, confining workers to designated zones. The images that emerged were politically damaging: in Britain's second city, governed by Labour at both local and national levels, basic services were failing while the party employed the full force of the state against its own traditional supporters.

Sharon Graham, General Secretary of Unite, harshly criticised the government's delayed involvement in the dispute. "It's taken them a huge amount of time to get involved," she said. "I've been urging them to do that for weeks, and now they are. They don't seem to understand the basics of what's going on here. These workers are being asked to lose £8,000 of their pay, which is essentially a quarter of their income."

118

The symbolism of the situation was both devastating and undeniable. While Birmingham's bin workers faced losing £8,000 a year, Cabinet ministers were accepting designer clothing, luxury accommodations, and concert tickets from millionaire benefactors. The contrast between the treatment of low-paid workers and the privileges enjoyed by the political class could not have been starker.

It was a stark portrayal of the rift between Labour and the working class. Angela Rayner, the Deputy Prime Minister and a former care worker, a role that should have given her a unique understanding of the workers' plight, instead sided with the council. She urged the workers to accept what she termed as 'a significantly improved offer,' a proposal that had been overwhelmingly rejected in April. Her intervention, perceived as insensitive and offensive by union members, led to the unprecedented decision by Unite's policy conference to suspend her membership on July 11.

The public sector strikes that erupted during the spring and summer of 2025 posed a severe test to Starmer's leadership, unlike any parliamentary rebellion that had come before. Teachers, NHS workers, civil servants, and university staff were all either engaging in or threatening industrial action over pay, job cuts, and working conditions. This surge of strikes threatened to plunge the UK into chaos, affecting schools, hospitals, and public services nationwide. For a Prime Minister who had pledged to rejuvenate Britain's public services, it was a political catastrophe of significant proportions.

The irony was bitter and obvious: Labour had come to power promising to end the strikes that had plagued the final years of Conservative rule, but within a year, they were facing even more widespread industrial action from their traditional supporters. This unexpected turn of events, coupled with the bitter irony of the situation, put Labour in a difficult and unanticipated position. Starmer's public sector pay increases for 2024-2025, totalling almost £10 billion, had been intended to keep union discontent at bay. However, the settlements that had brought peace in 2024 proved inadequate against the inflationary pressures and accumulated grievances of 2025.

The government's response revealed the fundamental contradictions in Labour's approach. Number 10 flatly stated that there was no extra money for NHS and teacher pay rises, even as independent pay review bodies recommended increases that exceeded the government's budgeted amounts. When asked about potential pay awards, Starmer's responses were characteristically evasive: "The Pay Review Body sets out the recommendations, and then in due course, the government will respond to that. Last year, we accepted the recommendations, and that meant a pay rise."

However, the unions stood united and resolute. Sharon Graham of Unite, in a firm tone, warned that chaos could "absolutely" spread across the country. Having already withdrawn Unite's financial support from Labour over the winter fuel cuts, she was now positioning herself as the leader of a powerful and organised resistance to the government's pay restraint.

The healthcare strikes, a force to be reckoned with, posed a significant threat to the government's credibility. In July 2025, approximately 50,000 resident doctors (formerly known as junior doctors) launched a five-day strike from July 25 to July 30, marking the first national doctors' strike since the Labour Party came to power.

The mandate for action was decisive. In a ballot that closed on July 7, 90% of voting British Medical Association (BMA) members supported the strikes, with a turnout of 55.32%. Out of an electorate of 53,766 eligible doctors, 26,766 voted yes, granting the BMA a six-month mandate for industrial action lasting from July 21, 2025, to January 7, 2026.

The doctors' case was compelling. They were demanding a 29.2% pay increase to restore wages in real terms to 2008 levels before more than fifteen years of erosion under both Conservative and Labour governments. After settling the previous round of strikes in September 2024 with what was supposed to be "a journey towards pay restoration," the government was now offering only a 5.4% increase plus a £1,000 consolidated payment. This proposal was inadequate.

The government's response revealed a growing authoritarianism in Starmer's approach to industrial relations. Sir Jim Mackey, NHS England's CEO (who would soon oversee its abolition), insisted on a "much more resistant" approach. He criticised previous strikes for being "net positive" for doctors because some were able to earn back lost wages through overtime to address backlogs. His solution was to pressure hospitals to keep as many routine operations running as possible during strikes, putting patients in danger with skeletal staff in Accident and Emergency units.

This strategy was morally questionable and politically disastrous. By jeopardising patient safety to win a propaganda battle against striking doctors, the government was using tactics that would have made Conservative health secretaries blush. The party that had spent years denouncing Tory attempts to break strikes was now employing similar methods against healthcare workers struggling to make ends meet.

The nursing unions were equally defiant. The Royal College of Nursing, GMB, and Unite all reported strong opposition to the 3.6% pay offer for 2025-26 in consultative ballots. The GMB reported a 67% rejection rate among NHS members, while Unite's rejection rate was a staggering 89%. These were not marginal victories for union militants; they were overwhelming repudiations of government policy by the very workers Labour claimed to represent.

The educational sector is currently in a state of urgency. Daniel Kebede, the general secretary of the National Education Union (NEU), has issued a stark warning that a new wave of teacher strikes could disrupt schools as early as September 2025. At the union's annual conference in Harrogate in April, he emphasised the need for immediate action: if the School Teachers' Review Body's pay recommendation does not exceed inflation, is not fully funded, and does not address the recruitment and retention crisis, then the union is prepared to take industrial action

The numbers paint a grim picture. The Department for Education (DfE) has put forward a meagre 2.8% pay rise for 2025-26, suggesting that schools should find 'efficiencies' to fund part of it. The DfE has since admitted that schools would be able to afford less than half of this inadequate increase. Meanwhile, the Office for Budget Responsibility has projected average wage growth across the broader economy at 3.7%, indicating that teachers would be left significantly behind.

An indicative online ballot conducted in March found that 84% of NEU members were willing to take strike action. However, the turnout of 47.2% was just short of the 50% legal threshold required for formal industrial action, creating anxiety among government officials who understood the implications of widespread teacher strikes for parents and for Labour's electoral prospects.

As spring turned to summer, Kebede's tone became increasingly confrontational. "After 14 years of Conservative austerity, we expect better from a Labour government," he told delegates in Harrogate. "The government claims it would be indefensible for the NEU to take industrial action. Well, I say to this government that it is indefensible for a Labour government to cut school funding. Cuts hurt kids."

He cautioned that if Labour MPs failed to secure an improved, fully funded pay rise, they would "pay a high political price." The union would campaign in constituencies if necessary, marking an unprecedented threat from a union that had traditionally been one of Labour's closest allies in the education sector.

Meanwhile, sixth-form college teachers were already on strike, having staged multiple walkouts since November 2024 due to a two-tier pay system introduced by the Labour government. Teachers in academised sixth form colleges received the full 5.5% pay award, while those in non-academised colleges received only 3.5%. Kebede described the government's decision to differentiate between institutions performing identical work as "baffling" and fundamentally undermining the existing national collective bargaining arrangements.

More than 2,000 NEU members from 32 colleges participated in repeated strike actions throughout the academic year, with their colleagues in NASUWT also joining the industrial action. At rallies outside the Department for Education and at the Leeds constituency office of Chancellor Rachel Reeves, teachers chanted, "What do we want? Fair pay. When do we want it? Now!" They jeered at mentions of Education Secretary Bridget Phillipson and Skills Minister Jacqui Smith.

"That's something even the Tories didn't try to do," one teacher told journalists. "We just expected better from a Labour government. No Labour government worthy of the name should implement actions like this. It must be by design, and it's just really sickening."

One of the most damaging aspects of the industrial disputes was what they revealed about Starmer's character and leadership style. Throughout the spring and summer of 2025, as crisis after crisis engulfed his government, the Prime Minister remained notably detached from the human drama unfolding around him. While previous Labour leaders might have rolled up their sleeves and engaged directly in the messy business of industrial negotiations, Starmer opted to maintain a distance that his critics increasingly described as cold and managerial.

This detachment was evident in the government's approach to NHS reform. On 13 March 2025, Starmer announced the abolition of NHS England in a speech intended to signal a new era of efficiency and accountability. This move was presented as "the biggest decentralisation of power in the history of our National Health Service" and "the final nail in the coffin" of the Conservatives' disastrous 2012 reorganisation.

Health Secretary Wes Streeting informed MPs that NHS England's 15,300 staff and the Department of Health and Social Care's 3,300 employees would see their numbers slashed by 50%, resulting in the loss of approximately 9,000 jobs and an annual savings of around £500 million. Sir Jim Mackey, known for his ability to "turn around organisations, balance the books, and drive up productivity," was appointed to lead the transformation team through a two-year transition period.

The timing of this announcement was abysmal. NHS England CEO

Amanda Pritchard had stepped down in February 2025, creating a leadership void just as the government was demanding significant workforce reductions. Local Integrated Care Boards were instructed to cut their running costs by 50% by the third quarter of 2025–26, while trusts were told to reduce their corporate services budgets back to pre-pandemic levels.

The reform was presented in typically technocratic terms: efficiency savings, streamlined management, and reduced bureaucracy. However, critics perceived something more troubling: a government more focused on organisational charts than on improving patient outcomes, even as doctors and nurses were leaving their positions due to pay and working conditions. This approach, more concerned with paperwork than patient care, is a cause for concern for the entire public sector.

Professor Dame Til Wykes, head of the School of Mental Health and Psychological Sciences at King's College London, challenged the narrative: "The problems within the NHS are mostly due to a lack of funding, not management. With the demise of NHS England, the government may regret having full responsibility for all arising issues; they will have no one to blame except themselves."

The criticism was particularly stinging because it cut to the core of Starmer's political persona. Here was a leader skilled at identifying problems and assigning blame but seemingly unable to take responsibility for finding solutions. The forensic mind that had made him an effective opposition politician was proving inadequate to the complex challenges of governing a fractured society and a demoralised public sector. The weight of this criticism is palpable in the political landscape.

While doctors, nurses, and patients needed investment and support, they were instead receiving structural reorganisation and management consultancy. The announced job losses of 9,000 revealed with brutal insensitivity just weeks before Christmas bonuses targeted not "fat cat executives" but those responsible for organising vaccination programs, children's dental health projects, and other essential services. This stark contrast is an apparent injustice to those working tirelessly in the public sector.

The international context amplified Labour's domestic challenges, making them even more embarrassing. While the government claimed it could not afford a 3.6% pay rise for nurses or adequate support for teachers, Keir Starmer was committing Britain to costly overseas ventures.

By March 2025, the Prime Minister's office had confirmed the UK's support for United States airstrikes in Yemen, justified as 'routine allied

123

air-to-air refuelling.' This stark contrast highlighted the government's willingness to fund foreign military interventions, while claiming a lack of resources for British pensioners and healthcare workers, the backbone of the nation.

The trade disputes with Donald Trump's America added another layer of humiliation. In April 2025, Trump announced sweeping tariffs on foreign imports, imposing a 10% levy on imports from the United Kingdom. Starmer's response combined harsh rhetoric with immediate capitulation, a pattern that also characterised his approach to domestic policy.

The UK's response to Trump's metal tariffs was not one of strength, but of acquiescence. Instead of standing up for its sovereignty, the UK simply agreed. Rachel Reeves stated that discussions were 'ongoing' regarding a potential reduction of the UK's Digital Services Tax to prevent further trade disputes with the United States. The idea of cutting taxes for American tech giants while refusing to raise pay for British teachers was not only politically toxic but also a worrying sign of the government's priorities.

The cumulative effect of these actions painted a picture of Starmer as a leader who was tough on the weak but weak on the strong. He could suspend his own MPs for voting to lift children out of poverty, yet he could not stand up to American presidents or wealthy donors. He could cut benefits for disabled individuals, but he couldn't find money for the healthcare workers sustaining the NHS. The forensic barrister who had spent years exposing Conservative hypocrisy was now revealing his own inconsistencies, ones that were even more damaging because they came as a surprise from a Labour government

The psychological strain on Labour MPs became increasingly evident as the summer progressed. These were politicians who had entered Parliament believing they were joining a movement for social justice, only to discover they were expected to vote for policies that contradicted everything they professed to believe in. This cognitive dissonance was unsustainable, leading to increasingly contentious parliamentary meetings and anguished private conversations with journalists.

The atmosphere within the parliamentary Labour Party was toxic in ways that veteran MPs had not experienced since the darkest days of the 1980s. However, there was a crucial difference. In the 1980s, the divisions were ideological, with left versus right, moderates versus radicals, and competing visions of socialism. Now, the divisions were moral: MPs who retained their principles versus those who had abandoned them for the sake of their careers. This represented a more fundamental and perhaps irreparable split.

For many MPs, the breaking point did not come with any single policy but rather through an accumulation of betrayals. The winter fuel cuts were troubling. The Alli scandal was embarrassing. The welfare reforms were unconscionable. Together, these issues painted a picture of a government that had completely lost its moral compass, leaving the MPs deeply disillusioned.

These MPs had campaigned on doorsteps promising change, and now they were being asked to defend the indefensible. They had knocked on doors in their constituencies, explaining why Labour deserved another chance, why this time would be different, and why voters should trust them to restore decency to British politics. Now, they found themselves voting to push disabled people into poverty while their leader accepted designer suits from millionaire donors, a situation that left them in a profound moral dilemma.

As summer progressed, the whips' office struggled to maintain party discipline. Traditional methods of managing the party promises of advancement, threats of demotion, and appeals to loyalty were losing effectiveness. MPs who had nothing to lose, having already given up on ministerial ambitions, were increasingly willing to rebel. Those in marginal seats were calculating that voting with their conscience might be better for their electoral prospects than defending unpopular government policies.

The local election results in May 2025 provided concrete evidence of Labour's declining support among its traditional base. These local elections in England represented the first major electoral test of Starmer's premiership, and the results were disastrous. Both Labour and the Conservatives suffered significant losses, while Reform UK and the Liberal Democrats made substantial gains.

The message was brutally clear: voters were abandoning both establishment parties in favour of alternatives that seemed to offer something different from the Westminster consensus. Longtime Labour strongholds in working-class constituencies were now shifting their support to Reform UK, while middle-class urban areas were moving their support to the Greens or the Liberal Democrats. The coalition that had delivered Labour's landslide victory in 2024 was fragmenting, with various demographic groups fleeing in different directions.

Party officials attempted to downplay the results, suggesting that such turbulence is inevitable for any government. However, the scale of the losses and the direction of change indicated a different story. This wasn't merely a matter of mid-term unpopularity; it was a fundamental rejection of Labour's approach to governing. The party was not only losing votes; it was losing the trust of communities that had sustained it for over a century

In constituencies where Labour had governed unchallenged since the party's founding, Reform UK was becoming a competitive force. In areas where Labour MPs had enjoyed comfortable majorities, the Greens were mounting serious challenges from the left. In regions where Labour had always been the natural opposition to Conservative power, the Liberal Democrats were establishing themselves as credible alternatives.

The most damaging aspect of Labour's crisis was the response from the trade union movement to the government's perceived betrayals. The unions, which had been Labour's steadfast partners since the party's inception in 1900, providing funding, organisational support, and working-class legitimacy, were now facing a crisis of their own. The historic alliance, a cornerstone of Labour's identity, was under severe strain, possibly facing a terminal decline, marking the end of an era.

The Communication Workers Union suspended its donations pending a review of Labour's policies. The National Union of Rail, Maritime, and Transport Workers questioned whether Labour's approach to railway renationalisation represented genuine public ownership or was merely "privatisation by another name." Even traditionally moderate unions were beginning to doubt whether their longstanding alliance with Labour was still beneficial.

Sharon Graham's Unite union became the focal point for resistance against Labour's shift to the right. Her blend of working-class authenticity and tactical intelligence made her a formidable opponent for a government struggling with credibility issues. Unite's withdrawal of financial support in the autumn of 2024, initially viewed as an anomaly, began to be mirrored by other unions. The party's funding model, which had relied on union donations for over a century, was starting to crumble.

The unions' grievances extended beyond specific policies; they reflected a deeper sense of betrayal. These organisations had supported Labour through difficult times, maintained their affiliation during the New Labour years when the party's commitment to working-class interests was in question, and worked tirelessly to secure an electoral victory in 2024. In return, they expected a government that would at least attempt to improve the lives of workers. Instead, they were met with pay restraint disguised as fiscal responsibility, strike-breaking tactics reminiscent of those employed by Margaret Thatcher, and lectures about the need for "difficult decisions." When Unite's conference voted to suspend Angela Rayner's membership in July, it was not merely a protest against one minister's handling of a specific dispute; it signified a declaration that the traditional relationship between Labour and organised labour had come to an end.

The party membership was declining at an alarming rate, surpassing even the exodus during the Corbyn era. Constituency Labour Parties that had celebrated victory in July 2024 were now struggling to maintain a quorum at meetings as disillusioned members drifted away or joined alternative parties. The energy and enthusiasm that had fueled Labour's election campaign had evaporated, replaced by a pervasive sense of cynicism and despair that threatened the party's long-term viability.

This membership decline had practical implications beyond the immediate loss of subscriptions. These were the activists who delivered leaflets, knocked on doors, and staffed phone banks during election campaigns. Without them, Labour's celebrated ground game, often cited as an advantage over the Conservatives, would be severely compromised in future elections. The party was hollowing out from within, losing the volunteer base that had always been its secret weapon, a loss that would be keenly felt in the upcoming political battles.

Social media became a battleground for competing narratives about Labour's direction. The hashtag #LabourBetrayal trended regularly throughout spring and summer 2025, with former supporters explaining eloquently why they could no longer support a party that had forsaken its principles. Pro-government MPs and activists fought back with #ResponsibleGovernment hashtags, but their arguments appeared increasingly flimsy as evidence of broken promises accumulated.

The tone of online discourse reflected deeper issues. While previous internal Labour debates had consisted of passionate yet familial disagreements within a shared political tradition, the arguments in 2025 felt more like a divorce. Former members did not just disagree with current policy; they actively disavowed any connection to what Labour had become. The language of betrayal, abandonment, and treachery dominated discussions, suggesting an irreparable rift rather than a temporary disagreement.

The summer of 2025 marked the end of any pretence that Labour still resembled a social democratic party, aside from its name. The government's decision to implement welfare cuts, reducing support for the most vulnerable, and impose pay restraint, limiting wage increases for public sector workers, revealed its willingness to punish the vulnerable in pursuit of fiscal targets dictated by the same economic orthodoxy that had led to austerity. This was a stark departure from the party's traditional commitment to social welfare and equality. The strikes exposed authoritarian tendencies that previous Labour leaders would have recognised as contrary to the party's core values.

By August 2025, as Parliament rose for the summer recess, the transformation was complete. The party that had promised to bring hope to British politics had instead become a source of despair for millions who had believed in its promises. What was once a movement that inspired genuine enthusiasm had devolved into a technocratic exercise in managing decline. The government, which had vowed to rebuild trust, had systematically eroded faith in the prospect of progressive politics.

The forensic barrister who expertly challenged Conservative arguments proved unable to create a coherent alternative vision. The leader who had promised to restore competence to British governance presided over a series of self-inflicted crises that made his predecessors look statesmanlike by comparison. The leader who vowed to unite his party instead fractured it in ways that could prove irreparable.

As summer 2025 came to an end, Labour faced a critical question: was there anything left of the social democratic tradition that had originally founded the party, or had it been wholly consumed by the technocratic managerialism embodied by Starmer? This style of leadership, which prioritised administrative efficiency over ideological principles, was seen as a departure from the party's historical commitment to social justice. The strikes, rebellions, and resignations suggested a clear answer to everyone except the leadership itself.

Disillusion within the party was not merely about broken promises or policy failures; it concerned a fundamental loss of faith in the potential for democratic socialism in Britain. When your own MPs rebel against welfare cuts, traditional union allies withdraw their support and suspend ministers' memberships, party members leave in droves, and voters abandon you for alternatives on both the left and right, you haven't just lost political support; you've lost a significant part of your moral authority.

The tragedy of Labour's transformation was that it was unnecessary, avoidable, and destructive to everything the party had historically represented. The forensic barrister who vowed to restore integrity to British politics systematically undermined the integrity of his own movement. The leader who promised to change the country transformed his party beyond recognition, and not for the better.

The summer of 2025 would be remembered not as the season when Labour found its footing in government, but as the moment it lost its soul. The strikes, rebellions, and resignations were symptoms of a deeper issue: the complete abandonment of social democratic values by a leadership that confused technocratic competence for political wisdom.

The party of Keir Hardie, Clement Attlee, and Aneurin Bevan, the party that created the National Health Service, built council housing, and stood up for working people when no one else would, had become something unrecognisable and perhaps irredeemable. As Labour MPs returned to their constituencies that August, they were haunted by one question: Could the damage be reversed? Could the party find its way back to its founding principles, or was the transformation so complete that recovery was impossible?

The greatest tragedy was that it didn't have to be this way. Labour had won a historic mandate for change, an opportunity to reshape British society that comes along perhaps once in a generation. Instead of seizing that moment, Starmer's government squandered it on technocratic reforms, fiscal orthodoxy, and betrayals of the very people who had put them in power.

The forensic barrister had won the case but lost the cause, captured the government but destroyed the movement, achieved power but abandoned purpose. As the summer of disillusion gave way to autumn uncertainty, one thing became clear: The Labour Party that had won 411 seats in July 2024 no longer existed in any meaningful sense. What remained was a hollow institution, merely going through the motions of social democratic politics while systematically dismantling the values and commitments that had given those politics meaning.

Chapter 11
Labour's Descent into Sleaze

How the party that promised to "clean up politics" became more toxic than the governments they replaced

By September 2025, the pattern was unmistakable and troubling: each month brought new revelations, resignations, and growing concerns about whether Labour still had the moral authority to govern. What had begun as isolated controversies over designer glasses and concert tickets had evolved into something far more serious, a systematic collapse of ethical standards that made the sleaze-ridden Conservative governments of the previous decade look almost quaint by comparison.

The sixteen major scandals that engulfed Starmer's government between July 2024 and September 2025 were not merely political embarrassments; they represented a fundamental breach of trust with voters who had chosen Labour specifically because of their promise to restore integrity to British politics. Each resignation, each policy reversal, and every new revelation chipped away at the government's credibility, leading public polling to show that a staggering 75 percent of the British population now viewed all politicians as "just the same" in terms of corruption and sleaze. This figure, representing a significant majority of the population, underscores the widespread disillusionment with the political establishment.

The tragic irony was that this was precisely what Keir Starmer had vowed to prevent. During the 2024 election campaign, Labour's manifesto explicitly accused the Conservatives and the SNP of failing to "uphold the standards expected in public life." The party had made "serving the country" a key theme, positioning itself as the moral alternative to years of Tory corruption and incompetence. Millions voted for Labour precisely because Starmer had promised to "turn the page" and take decisive action to clean up public life. However, the stark contrast between these promises and the reality of Labour's governance left the electorate feeling deeply betrayed.

Instead, within fourteen months of taking power, Labour had accumulated more scandals per month in office than any government in modern British history. This rapid and alarming cascade of ethical failures, policy reversals, and ministerial departures created a narrative of chaos and corruption that undermined the government's authority more completely than any single catastrophic event could have achieved.

October 2024: The Gray Exodus

The first significant crack in Labour's facade appeared just three months after their landslide victory, when Sue Gray, the woman who had been instrumental in bringing down Boris Johnson over Partygate, was forced to resign as Starmer's chief of staff. The irony was palpable: the civil servant who had exposed Conservative corruption was herself embroiled in controversy over her handling of Labour's freebies scandal, a twist that no one had seen coming.

Gray's resignation came after months of criticism over multiple fronts that revealed the chaotic nature of Starmer's operation. Her mishandling of the gifts controversy that had dominated Labour's early months, and the revelations about friction within Number 10, where Gray's micro-managerial style had created a toxic atmosphere, all pointed to a disarrayed and directionless leadership.

But perhaps most damaging was the revelation that Gray was being paid £170,000 per year, £3,000 more than the Prime Minister's own salary. In a government that was cutting winter fuel payments for pensioners and demanding pay restraint from public sector workers, the symbolism was staggering. Here was the most powerful unelected person in government, earning more than the person who was supposed to be running the country, a fact that left many in shock and disbelief.

The appointment of Morgan McSweeney as Gray's replacement only added to the sense of dysfunction. McSweeney, previously head of political strategy, was seen as Starmer's enforcer, a party loyalist whose primary qualification was his willingness to suppress dissent rather than provide independent advice. The message was clear: Starmer valued loyalty over competence, political calculation over ethical guidance.

Gray was initially offered a face-saving role as the Prime Minister's envoy for the regions and nations, but even this consolation prize never materialised. The position that was supposed to demonstrate that Gray retained the Prime Minister's confidence simply evaporated, leaving her with nothing but a peerage in the House of Lords the traditional graveyard for failed political careers. The woman who had once been described as "the most powerful person you've never heard of" disappeared into obscurity, taking with her any pretence that Labour operated according to higher ethical standards than their predecessors.

October 2024: The Amesbury Assault

If Gray's resignation revealed the dysfunction at the heart of government, Mike Amesbury's arrest exposed something even more troubling: the casual violence that seemed to lurk beneath Labour's supposedly civilised exterior. The footage that emerged, showing Amesbury apparently punching a constituent, was not just shocking; it also shattered the perceived image of Labour politicians and the people they claimed to represent.

The incident was captured on mobile phone footage that quickly went viral, depicting the MP for Runcorn and Helsby in a street altercation that escalated to physical violence. For a party that had spent years criticising Conservative politicians for their behaviour, these images were not just devastating, but they were a stark contrast to the values Labour claimed to uphold. Here was a Labour MP literally attacking a member of the public, the very people he was supposed to serve.

Amesbury's subsequent guilty plea to assault charges confirmed what the footage suggested: this was not a case of mistaken identity or misunderstood circumstances. This was a serving MP who had lost control and resorted to violence against a constituent. The suspended custodial sentence he received was almost beside the point; the damage to Labour's reputation was immediate and lasting. The Labour Party's response to this incident, including the suspension of Amesbury and the subsequent investigation, demonstrated a commitment to accountability and a recognition of the seriousness of the issue.

The political consequences were equally severe. When Amesbury finally resigned his seat in March 2025, it triggered a by-election in Runcorn and Helsby, resulting in a narrow victory for Reform UK over Labour. The symbolism was striking: a seat that Labour had held comfortably was lost to Nigel Farage's populist movement because of the behaviour of a Labour politician who had forgotten the fundamental principle that public servants serve the public, not the other way around. The loss was not just a numerical defeat, but a blow to the party's integrity.

The Amesbury affair also highlighted Labour's broader problems with candidate selection and discipline. This was not merely a case of someone making a single mistake under pressure; the footage indicated a pattern of aggressive behaviour that should have been identified and addressed long before it escalated to criminal charges. The fact that

Amesbury was allowed to represent the party for months after the incident pointed to deeper issues within Labour's internal accountability mechanisms.

November 2024: Haigh's Fraud Conviction

Louise Haigh's resignation as Transport Secretary marked a significant scandal, revealing that senior Labour politicians had not been entirely honest about their backgrounds while seeking high office. Haigh's admission of having pleaded guilty to fraud by false representation in 2014 was not just embarrassing; it was a serious breach of the trust voters place in their representatives, and it had profound implications for the Labour Party.

The details of Haigh's conviction were particularly damaging, as they illustrated a pattern of deception that spanned from her original crime to her appointment in the Cabinet. The fraud charge arose from an investigation by her former employer, Aviva, regarding a missing work phone that Haigh claimed had been stolen. When the phone later appeared in her possession, she was charged and convicted of making false representations to obtain financial gain.

Haigh's failure to fully disclose this conviction when she was appointed to the Cabinet raised serious questions about her integrity as well as the vetting processes employed by Keir Starmer. How could someone with a criminal record for dishonesty have been appointed as the youngest member of the Cabinet? What did this say about Labour's commitment to the higher standards they had vowed to uphold?

Her resignation made her the first minister to leave Starmer's Cabinet, setting a precedent that would be followed by others in the months to come. More importantly, it established a recurring pattern that defined Labour's approach to managing scandals: initial denials, followed by reluctant admissions and belated resignations that came too late to mitigate the political fallout.

The Transport brief was one of Labour's most significant challenges, with promises to renationalise the railways and improve public transport central to their election platform. Haigh's departure meant that these critical policies were now tainted in the public's perception by associations with criminality and deception. It served as a perfect metaphor for how the personal failings of its politicians were undermining Labour's broader political project.

January 2025: The Siddiq Corruption Web

Tulip Siddiq's alleged involvement in the significant corruption scandal surrounding her aunt, former Bangladeshi Prime Minister Sheikh Hasina, has sent shockwaves through the political landscape. This represents one of the most serious breaches of ministerial standards during Labour's brief time in power. The scale of the allegations, involving the embezzlement of up to £3.9 billion from a £10 billion nuclear power project, is staggering. However, equally damaging is what this case reveals about Labour's approach to conflicts of interest and international corruption.

The core allegation is that Siddiq was linked to a corrupt agreement with Russia in 2013, which involved [specific details of the corrupt deal]. This agreement resulted in substantial financial losses for the people of Bangladesh. As Economic Secretary to the Treasury and City Minister, ironically, the government's anti-corruption minister Siddiq was meant to lead the fight against the very financial crimes that now implicate her family. The hypocrisy is astonishing: the official responsible for combating corruption in Britain was herself entangled in one of the largest corruption scandals in South Asian history.

The revelation that Siddiq had lived in London flats associated with allies of her aunt's regime deepened the scandal. These were not distant family ties that could be dismissed as irrelevant; they involved direct financial benefits received from a network now facing charges of corruption and human rights abuses, including allegations of crimes against humanity. The person tasked with cleaning up Britain's financial system had been profiting from one of the most corrupt regimes in the world. This situation could have profound implications for the UK's economic system.

The most damaging aspect was the indication that Siddiq had not been fully transparent about these connections when appointed to her ministerial role. The suggestion that she failed to completely disclose her family's involvement in Bangladeshi politics raised serious concerns about her honesty and judgment. Either she deliberately concealed critical information from her appointments panel, or she failed to recognise the apparent conflicts of interest created by her family ties.

The fact that Sir Laurie Magnus, the Prime Minister's ethics adviser, concluded that Siddiq technically had not breached the Ministerial Code only complicates the situation further. As the individual responsible for interpreting and enforcing the Ministerial Code, Magnus's conclusion was significant. This was a precise instance where the letter of the rules had been followed, yet their spirit had been entirely violated. Siddiq's eventual resignation in January 2025 was accompanied by her insistence that she had "provided all relevant information" when appointed, leaving voters to question whether Labour's ethical standards were so low that massive international corruption scandals could be deemed irrelevant to ministerial appointments

February 2025: Reeves's Résumé Inflation

Rachel Reeves's CV controversies, though seemingly minor in the grand scheme of Labour's issues, struck a chord with the public. They highlighted a significant breach of trust, a departure from the basic honesty voters expect from their representatives. As Britain's first female Chancellor, Reeves was seen as a beacon of Labour's promise of competent and trustworthy governance. However, her embellished LinkedIn profile shattered this perception, revealing a casual relationship with the truth, much like many of her colleagues

The specific details of Reeves's deceptions were particularly damaging, as they directly related to her professional qualifications for one of the most critical roles in government. Her claim of being an economist who had 'led major projects' at the Bank of England was simply false; she had worked in junior analytical roles that did not reflect the senior positions she alleged to have held. Similarly, her assertions about her experience at HBOS were misleading, suggesting a level of responsibility and expertise she had never possessed. This revelation left many in disbelief.

The timing of these revelations was unfortunate, as Reeves was in the process of establishing credibility with financial markets and international partners who needed to trust Britain's economic management. How could foreign investors have confidence in a Chancellor who could not accurately represent her own professional background? How could the public trust someone who had seemingly inflated her qualifications for years? More importantly, how could Reeves effectively manage Britain's finances when her credibility was in question?

Reeves's eventual apology and the amendment of her LinkedIn profile did little to address the fundamental question of her character raised by these deceptions. This was not a case of minor inaccuracies or different interpretations of the same facts; it was a deliberate misrepresentation of her professional experience aimed at advancing her political career. The individual who was supposed to be managing Britain's finances had engaged in the kind of résumé fraud that would lead to termination in most junior positions, let alone in senior government roles.

The broader implications were even more concerning. If Reeves was willing to lie about her professional background, what else might she misrepresent? Her handling of economic policy, her relationships with donors, and her promises to voters were all now viewed in a different light due to the revelation that she had spent years projecting a false version of her career to the British public. This cast a shadow of doubt on her every action and statement.

February 2025: Gwynne's Vile Messages

Andrew Gwynne's dismissal as a health minister was one of the most shocking scandals within the Labour Party, revealing a disturbing level of casual bigotry and indifference among its members. The private WhatsApp messages that led to his sacking were not only politically damaging but also morally repugnant, challenging fundamental beliefs about Labour's values and character.

The content of Gwynne's messages was alarming in its cruelty. His wish for a pensioner's death simply because they did not vote Labour demonstrated a disturbing level of political hatred that contradicted any claim to serve the public interest. Additionally, his comment that a constituent's name "sounds too Jewish" exposed antisemitic prejudices that the Labour Party had purportedly purged during the Corbyn era. These were not offhand remarks made under stress; they were considered communications shared with other local party members who seemingly saw no issue with such language.

The fact that these messages were sent in a WhatsApp group with other Labour activists indicated that Gwynne's views were not isolated incidents but part of a broader culture of intolerance within the party. How many other Labour politicians held similar views? How many other private conversations contained equally offensive remarks? This scandal raised questions that extended beyond the shortcomings of one minister to the character of the entire party.

Gwynne's role as a health minister made his dismissal even more significant. Here was a public official responsible for healthcare policy expressing death wishes for elderly voters who had exercised their democratic rights to vote for different parties. The hypocrisy was staggering; a politician tasked with protecting public health was privately celebrating the potential deaths of individuals whose only "fault" was voting differently than he preferred.

The swift nature of Gwynne's dismissal was one of the few positive outcomes of this situation, suggesting that some standards still existed within Labour's ranks. However, the damage had already been done voters could see that beneath Labour's public commitment to tolerance and inclusion lay private attitudes often indistinguishable from the worst examples of political extremism.

February 2025: The Aid Betrayal

Anneliese Dodds's resignation over Labour's U-turn on international aid funding represents a different type of scandal, not one of personal corruption or criminal behaviour, but a systematic betrayal of the election promises that had convinced voters to trust Labour with power. The decision to reduce overseas aid from 0.5 per cent to 0.3 per cent of GDP was not merely a policy reversal; it fundamentally undermined Labour's supposed commitment to international solidarity and moral leadership.

This broken promise was particularly egregious because it involved one of Labour's most specific and measurable commitments. During the election campaign, the party pledged to raise international aid to 0.7 percent of GDP "as soon as finances allowed." Instead, they chose to cut it further, redirecting funds towards defence spending in a move that resembled Conservative foreign policy more than the progressive internationalism Labour had promised.

Dodds's resignation highlighted the ethical dimensions of this betrayal. As International Development Minister, she was responsible for implementing policies she had publicly advocated during the election campaign. Her departure indicated that she could not, in good conscience, oversee the dismantling of Britain's aid program, choosing personal integrity over political advancement. This reflected poorly on her colleagues, who remained in their positions.

The policy itself was particularly damaging to Britain's international reputation at a time when global challenges demanded enhanced cooperation rather than reduced engagement. Issues such as climate change, global poverty, and international development are areas where British leadership could genuinely make a difference. However, Labour's aid cuts suggested a retreat into narrow nationalism, mirroring the policies they had criticised in their Conservative predecessors.

The timing of the cuts was also politically unwise, especially as Labour was asking for sacrifices from pensioners, public sector workers, and benefit recipients while apparently finding money for increased military spending. The message was clear: Labour would cut aid for the world's poorest people while maintaining funding for weapons and warfare. This priority structure revealed values that were markedly different from those the party claimed to represent during the election campaign.

April 2025: The Norris Nightmare

Dan Norris's arrest on suspicion of rape, child sex offences, child abduction, and misconduct in public office marked a low point in Labour's history of scandals. The seriousness of these allegations went beyond typical political concerns and raised fundamental questions about public safety and child protection. While Norris was entitled to the presumption of innocence until proven guilty, the nature of the charges prompted immediate scrutiny of Labour's vetting procedures and their duty of care.

The range of allegations was particularly alarming, leaving many in shock and disbelief. This was not just a single incident or an isolated mistake; the charges indicated a pattern of alleged criminal behaviour involving multiple serious offences. The inclusion of child-related charges made the case especially sensitive, raising concerns about whether any warning signs had been missed or overlooked by party officials.

Norris's immediate suspension from the Labour Party and his ban from the parliamentary estate were appropriate responses. However, these actions also highlighted the potential damage such allegations could inflict on the party's reputation. An MP elected under Labour's banner was now facing some of the most serious charges imaginable. The connection between Labour and these allegations would inevitably be damaging, regardless of the ultimate outcome of the legal proceedings, a fact that was not lost on the party's members and supporters.

The situation also underscored broader issues regarding the safeguarding procedures that political parties use to vet their candidates and members. What background checks were conducted before Norris was selected as a candidate? What ongoing monitoring was in place to identify potential issues before they escalated to criminal charges? The apparent lack of effective safeguarding mechanisms, a failure on the part of the Labour Party, reflected poorly on its organisational competence and its commitment to protecting vulnerable individuals.

Perhaps most troubling was the silence from other Labour politicians regarding the allegations. While legal constraints limited what could be said about ongoing criminal proceedings, the complete absence of any expression of concern for potential victims or commitment to improving safeguarding procedures suggested that the party was more focused on protecting its own reputation than on addressing profound issues of child protection and public safety. A more transparent and accountable response from the party would have been more reassuring to the public and would have demonstrated a genuine commitment to addressing the issues at hand.

June 2025: The Winter Fuel Flip-Flop

Labour's decision to reverse its stance on the winter fuel payment became one of the most politically damaging policy shifts for the party. This move highlighted broken promises and a lack of compassion for vulnerable individuals, ultimately undermining their credibility regarding both economic competence and social empathy.

At the outset, the decision to reduce payments for millions of pensioners sparked significant controversy, drawing attention to the issue and engaging the public. However, the subsequent reversal painted the government as both cruel and incompetent. The cuts, announced shortly after the election, faced intense backlash from charities, opposition parties, and even Labour's own MPs. The plan to means-test winter fuel payments, restricting them to the poorest pensioners, was framed as a necessary response to the economic situation Labour inherited from the Conservatives. Unfortunately, this policy had cruel consequences, forcing millions of elderly individuals to choose between heating their homes and affording food during the coldest months of the year.

The reversal, announced nearly a year later, proved to be even more damaging than the initial decision had been. The plan to restore payments for all pensioners with annual incomes of £35,000 or less was presented as a compassionate response to changing circumstances. However, this raised serious questions: Why hadn't these factors been considered before the cuts were made? If the payments were essential for the welfare of pensioners, why were they initially cut? Conversely, if they were deemed unnecessary, why restore them at all?

The timing of the U-turn was particularly suspect, occurring just as polling indicated a significant decline in Labour's support among older voters and in light of mounting by-election losses. The strategic timing of the reversal sheds light on the government's political calculations and its acknowledgement of the electoral consequences of its neglect of elderly citizens.

The broader implications for Labour's economic credibility were severe. The winter fuel payment saga revealed a government that made significant spending decisions without adequate analysis, implemented policies without considering their effects, and then reversed its stance when the political fallout became too great to bear. This was not the competent economic management Labour had promised; somewhat, it resembled the chaotic policymaking that characterised the worst periods of Conservative government.

June 2025: The Grooming Gangs Capitulation

Labour's eventual acceptance of all 12 recommendations from Baroness Casey's audit, along with the initiation of a statutory national inquiry into group-based child sexual abuse, represents a significant and embarrassing capitulation that exposes the government's weakness under persistent pressure. After months of insisting that no inquiry was necessary, Keir Starmer was compelled to reverse his stance, making him appear reactive rather than decisive. This delay in action has potentially prolonged the suffering of the victims, adding a human cost to Labour's political missteps

The government's initial resistance to calls for an inquiry was not just politically tone-deaf, but also morally questionable. When serious allegations of institutional failures in protecting children from sexual abuse were raised, the government's first instinct was to resist scrutiny instead of welcoming it. This behaviour did not reflect the confidence of true leaders in their institutions; instead, it suggested a fear of what an inquiry might reveal, highlighting the government's apprehension and lack of transparency.

The sustained pressure from various sources, including tech billionaire Elon Musk, ultimately compelled the government to take action, causing significant embarrassment. A British Prime Minister found himself being lectured on child protection by a foreign business leader while seemingly ignoring concerns from domestic charities, victims' groups, and opposition politicians. The optics were dreadful: Labour appeared more responsive to criticism from American billionaires than to the needs of British children, exposing the government's vulnerability to external influence.

While the eventual launch of the inquiry was presented as evidence of Labour's commitment to child protection, it actually underscored their earlier failures in judgment and leadership. A government genuinely dedicated to protecting children would have welcomed calls for increased scrutiny from the start, rather than resisting them for months before capitulating under pressure. This pattern of behaviour raises concerns about how Labour might handle future child protection issues and whether their decisions will be based on genuine concern or political expediency.

The delay in launching the inquiry also raised questions about Labour's priorities and competence. If the institutional failures in child protection warranted a statutory inquiry in June 2025, why had they not been considered severe enough in the preceding months? What had changed, apart from the political pressure Labour faced? The answers suggested a government more driven by political calculations than by genuine concern for vulnerable children.

July 2025: The Benefits Retreat

Labour's unexpected last-minute decision to reverse its plans for tightening eligibility for Personal Independence Payment (PIP) was a stark revelation of the government's weakness and lack of authority. The sudden abandonment of these reforms just hours before a vote in the House of Commons was not only a significant policy U-turn but also a public acknowledgement that the government could not secure the confidence of its own MPs on a key policy issue.

The scale of the rebellion that led to this reversal was unprecedented in modern British politics. Over 100 Labour MPs, a significant number, publicly demanded a reassessment of the proposals, representing more than a quarter of the parliamentary party. This was not merely a small faction causing trouble; it was a broad coalition of MPs struggling to reconcile the proposed cuts with their values and election promises.

The last-minute nature of the retreat added to the embarrassment, creating a sense of political tension and drama. Instead of conducting proper consultations and garnering support for their proposals, Labour pushed ahead with cuts they knew were controversial, only to abandon them when the political fallout became too severe. Presenting the decision to delay finalisation of the changes until after a review of the welfare system as principled policy-making instead appeared more like desperate damage control.

The fact that 47 Labour MPs still rebelled against the diluted legislation revealed the depth of discontent within the parliamentary party. Even after significant concessions, nearly one in eight Labour MPs refused to support their own government's welfare policies. This was not a typical political disagreement; it marked a fundamental breakdown in the relationship between the leadership and its MPs.

The broader implications for Labour's authority were devastating. If the government could not secure support for its welfare policies, a supposedly core area of Labour's expertise, what policies could it effectively implement? This retreat on benefits showcased a government that was weak, divided, and unable to undertake the decisive action that effective governance requires.

August 2025: Ali's Landlord Hypocrisy

Rushanara Ali's resignation as the homelessness minister highlighted a significant hypocrisy within the Labour Party, where politicians publicly advocated for progressive values while privately pursuing personal gain. Ali's decision to evict tenants and then re-list her property at a higher rent was not only morally questionable but also directly contradicted the principles outlined in Labour's own Renters' Rights Bill.

The specifics of Ali's behaviour were particularly damaging, as they showcased blatant hypocrisy. As the homelessness minister, she was responsible for implementing policies aimed at protecting vulnerable tenants from exploitation by landlords. Yet, she was engaging in the very type of exploitative behaviour that her department's policies were designed to prevent. The stark contradiction between her public role and private actions was staggering, leaving the public with a sense of betrayal.

What made the scandal even more troubling was the fact that Ali's actions would have been illegal under Labour's forthcoming legislation, the Renters' Rights Bill. This bill, which was a cornerstone of Labour's housing policy, explicitly prohibited landlords from ending tenancies to sell properties and subsequently re-listing them at higher rents, precisely what Ali had done. She was, in effect, enforcing policies that would have criminalised her own conduct as a private landlord.

Ali's assertion that she had "at all times" complied with "all legal requirements" and taken her responsibilities "seriously" only exacerbated the situation. This suggestion that legal compliance was a sufficient justification for her actions, which violated the spirit of her ministerial duties, demonstrated a profound misunderstanding of the higher standards expected of public servants. Just because something was legal did not make it morally acceptable for someone in her position.

The accusations of hypocrisy from charities and advocacy groups were particularly damaging, especially since these organisations should

142

have been Labour's natural allies. These were groups that worked with homeless people every day, yet they condemned a Labour minister for actions that contributed to the housing crisis she was meant to address. The symbolism was striking: even Labour's own supporters recognised that the party's actions contradicted its rhetoric, tarnishing its reputation.

September 2025: Rayner's Tax Scandal

Angela Rayner's resignation as Deputy Prime Minister, a seismic event in the wake of Labour's series of scandals, marked a watershed moment. It removed from the government one of the few politicians who had genuine working-class credibility and popular appeal. Her departure, triggered by tax issues related to a property purchase in Hove, was not merely another ministerial resignation; it represented the loss of Labour's most authentic connection to its traditional voter base.

The specific tax issue that led to Rayner's resignation was both profound and symbolic. Her failure to pay £40,000 in stamp duty when acquiring a property was not just a financial misstep, but a revelation of a casual attitude toward financial responsibilities that had characterised many of her colleagues. More importantly, it highlighted that even Labour's most prominent working-class representative had been drawn into the property speculation and tax avoidance typical of Britain's wealthy elite.

The conclusion by Sir Laurie Magnus that Rayner had breached the Ministerial Code was particularly significant, as it was the first time a senior Labour minister had been found in violation of governmental standards by the party's ethics adviser. Previous resignations often occurred before formal investigations were completed, allowing ministers to claim they were leaving for personal reasons rather than due to ethical failures. In Rayner's case, however, she was definitively found to have breached the standards expected of public servants.

The appointment of David Lammy as deputy prime minister in Rayner's place marked a significant shift in Labour's transformation. It was a shift from a party rooted in working-class communities to one dominated by metropolitan professionals. While Lammy possesses undeniable talent, he represents a very different constituency and political tradition than Rayner. His elevation symbolised Labour's shift from being a party of working people to one primarily serving the educated middle class

Perhaps most damaging was the initiation of a deputy leadership contest to fill Rayner's position. Observing Labour politicians vying for position while their government faltered only reinforced perceptions of a party more focused on internal power struggles than on serving the public interest. This leadership contest became a distraction from governance at the very moment when effective leadership was most necessary.

September 2025: The Mandelson-Epstein Connection

The sudden dismissal of Peter Mandelson as the UK Ambassador to the United States, a decision triggered by his association with convicted paedophile Jeffrey Epstein, sent shockwaves through the political landscape. The newly unearthed documents revealed Mandelson's unwavering support for Epstein, even going as far as to call him 'my best pal' and advising him to challenge his conviction for child sexual offences. These findings hinted at a connection that was far from the norm in diplomatic or business circles.

The discovery of a letter from the 2003' birthday book' and emails from 2008 painted a picture of a relationship that endured long after Epstein's conviction and public disgrace. This was not a mere professional or distant connection; it was a personal friendship, one that Mandelson chose to maintain despite being fully aware of Epstein's heinous crimes. The language used in the correspondence, particularly the term 'best pal,' revealed a level of intimacy that was deeply troubling, given the circumstances.

The timing of Mandelson's support for Epstein only served to amplify the shock of the revelations. His encouragement for Epstein to challenge his conviction suggested a belief that the charges were unjust or excessive. This was not a case of maintaining polite relations with a disgraced former associate; it was active support for a convicted paedophile from someone who would later hold a significant public office, a fact that is deeply disturbing and inappropriate.

Keir Starmer's initial defence of Mandelson, followed by his eventual dismissal once the full extent of the correspondence became known, highlighted the chaotic response of Labour to ethical crises. The Prime Minister's claim that he was unaware of the details of Mandelson's relationship with Epstein raised serious questions about the vetting procedures for senior appointments. How could someone with such compromising connections have been appointed to one of Britain's most critical diplomatic roles?

The broader impact on Labour's credibility was devastating. Here was a party that had pledged to restore integrity to public life, yet it appointed someone with documented ties to one of the most notorious sex offenders in recent history. Moreover, Mandelson's appointment had been controversial from the outset, due to his previous resignations from government and questionable business connections, which made the eventual revelations even more damaging.

The Sixteen Scandals: A Systematic Failure

By September 2025, the evidence was undeniable: Labour had not only failed to fulfil its promises of an ethical government, but it had also systematically violated every principle it claimed to represent. The sixteen major scandals that plagued the government fell into different categories of failure, yet they shared common themes that highlighted fundamental issues with Labour's approach to power.

The first category involved apparent corruption and conflicts of interest, including the Siddiq Bangladesh connections, the Alli access scandal, and various property and financial irregularities affecting multiple ministers. The Siddiq Bangladesh connections refer to undeclared UK properties linked to her aunt Sheikh Hasina's regime, a disputed land plot in Dhaka, and ongoing corruption probes in Bangladesh, which Siddiq denies as politically motivated. The Alli access scandal, on the other hand, involved These were not minor oversights or technical breaches of obscure rules; they were serious violations of fundamental ethical principles that any competent government should have anticipated and prevented.

The second category included criminal behaviour and personal misconduct: The Amesbury assault, the Norris allegations, the Haigh fraud conviction, and the Gwynne offensive messages. These incidents exposed a party that had failed to properly vet its candidates and members, allowing individuals with significant character flaws to gain positions of considerable responsibility

The third category consisted of policy incompetence and broken promises, including the winter fuel U-turns, benefit cuts, aid reductions, and delays in the grooming gang's inquiry. These issues demonstrated a government making significant decisions without proper consideration, implementing policies without grasping their consequences, and later reversing course when faced with unbearable political costs, leaving the public frustrated and disappointed.

The fourth category involved fundamental dishonesty regarding qualifications and backgrounds, as evidenced by the Reeves CV embellishments and other misrepresentations that emerged about ministers' professional experiences. These cases revealed a culture in which truth was optional and personal advancement took precedence over public service, a betrayal of the public's trust.

The cumulative effect of these scandals was the destruction of any remaining public confidence in Labour's ability to govern. Polling consistently showed that a majority of British voters considered the Labour government to be "sleazy," with many respondents indicating they saw no meaningful difference between Labour and Conservative standards of behaviour. The party that had come to power promising to be different had become indistinguishable from the governments they had displaced.

By the summer of 2025, Labour's relationship with the media had shifted from cautious support to outright hostility. The very newspapers that had endorsed Starmer's leadership campaign or remained neutral during the 2024 election were now running front-page investigations into government corruption and incompetence. This transformation was remarkable in its speed and comprehensiveness.

The Times, which had traditionally maintained a reasonably balanced approach toward Labour governments, began publishing editorials about the 'worrying amateurishness and dysfunction' within Starmer's top team. The criticisms were not limited to individual scandals; they reflected a systematic failure of governance. The 'worrying amateurishness and dysfunction' within Starmer's top team was evident in [specific examples of the team's amateurishness and dysfunction]. When The Times, the newspaper of record for Britain's establishment, began questioning the competence of a sitting government, the political damage was severe.

The Guardian, Labour's traditional media ally, was perhaps even more damaging in its criticism because of its historical loyalty to the party. The paper's editorials warning about Labour's failure to uphold its promises carried particular weight, as they could not be dismissed as partisan attacks from hostile publications. When The Guardian criticised Labour's ethical standards, it clearly signalled that the party had lost the confidence of its natural supporters.

The broadcast media were equally critical, with BBC political programs regularly discussing whether Labour could survive the series of scandals engulfing the government. The tone of the coverage shifted from cautious optimism in Labour's early months to open scepticism about the government's competence and integrity. Even traditionally supportive commentators struggled to defend behaviour that seemed indefensible.

146

International media coverage was particularly damaging, as it undermined Britain's reputation for stable, competent governance. Publications like The Financial Times and the Wall Street Journal, crucial for maintaining investor confidence, began publishing analyses suggesting that Britain had reverted to the political chaos characteristic of the final years of Conservative rule. The message was clear: changing the governing party had not resolved Britain's underlying issues with political stability and ethical standards

The polling data tracking Labour's decline paints a picture of unprecedented political collapse. After enjoying a post-election honeymoon during which approval ratings briefly exceeded 50 per cent, Labour's support has plummeted to levels that now make it unelectable. By September 2025, multiple polls indicated that the party was trailing behind both the Conservatives and Reform UK, with some surveys predicting a loss of more than 200 seats if an election were held immediately

The speed of Labour's decline is historically unmatched. Typically, previous governments took years to lose public confidence, with support gradually slipping away as policies failed and scandals mounted. In contrast, Labour managed to ruin its reputation in just over a year, setting a record for the fastest collapse in public support since modern polling began.

Perhaps more damaging than the raw polling numbers is the qualitative data regarding public attitudes toward the government. Focus groups consistently revealed language that suggested not just disappointment, but genuine anger and feelings of betrayal. Voters who had placed their trust in Labour's promises of ethical renewal felt personally deceived by an avalanche of scandals. The phrase 'they're all the same' repeatedly emerged in voter interviews, indicating that Labour had not only damaged its own credibility but also eroded public faith in democratic politics as a whole, a trust that will be hard to rebuild.

The demographic breakdown of Labour's polling collapse is particularly alarming for the party's long-term prospects. They are haemorrhaging support across all age groups, but the decline is especially precipitous among older voters, who had been reassured by Keir Starmer's moderate positioning. The cuts to winter fuel payments have been particularly damaging to pensioners, creating a group of voters who feel deeply let down by policies that threaten their basic welfare.

Among younger voters, Labour's decline is driven more by disillusionment regarding the gap between progressive rhetoric and conservative policies. Cuts to aid and welfare restrictions, along with the government's general rightward shift, have alienated many activists and idealistic voters who initially supported Labour as an alternative to Conservative insensitivity. As a result, the party is losing voters from both ends of the political spectrum, leaving them with a shrinking base of committed supporters.

Labour's scandals did not occur in a political vacuum; instead, they created opportunities for opposition parties to capitalise on the government's weaknesses and incompetence. None capitalised more effectively than Reform UK, Nigel Farage's populist movement that spent months positioning itself as the authentic voice of ordinary people against a corrupt political establishment.

The victory in the Runcorn and Helsby by-election in March 2025 marked a significant turning point for Reform, demonstrating its ability to wrest seats from Labour in traditionally working-class constituencies. The victory was narrow by just six votes, but it underscored that Reform's anti-establishment message resonated with voters who felt abandoned by mainstream politics. The symbolism was powerful: a seat lost due to Labour's corruption was won by a party that promised to cleanse the political swamp.

Reform's surge in polling throughout 2025 was built on a straightforward yet effective message: all established parties were corrupt, incompetent, and out of touch with the concerns of ordinary people. Labour's scandals provided perfect ammunition for this narrative, allowing Reform to present itself as the clean alternative to a political class that had lost all moral authority. Each new scandal involving Labour drove more voters toward Reform's anti-establishment message.

The specific nature of Labour's scandals directly played into Reform's strengths as a populist movement. The sight of politicians accepting free clothes while cutting benefits for disabled people, or residing in flats linked to international corruption while lecturing ordinary voters about public service, exemplifies the elite hypocrisy that populist movements thrive on. Reform did not need to fabricate grievances against the political establishment; Labour was providing them for free.

Perhaps most importantly, Labour's scandals allowed Reform to position itself as the party of ordinary decency in contrast to political corruption. While Farage's personal history of financial irregularities and controversial statements could have been problematic, they seemed less significant in comparison to the systematic ethical failures of a sitting government. By late 2025, Reform was regularly polling ahead of both Labour and the Conservatives, suggesting a complete realignment of

British politics around populist versus establishment themes.

The cascade of Labour's scandals raised fundamental questions about Britain's constitutional arrangements and democratic accountability. The traditional assumption that political parties would uphold basic ethical standards had been undermined by systematic failures that revealed weaknesses in the UK's regulatory framework. When a governing party is unwilling or unable to police its own members, what mechanisms exist to protect democratic integrity?

The role of the Prime Minister's ethics adviser became a focal point of constitutional debate. Sir Laurie Magnus had identified several ministers in breach of the Ministerial Code, but his powers were limited to making recommendations rather than enforcing consequences. The fact that ministers could ignore his findings or delay their implementation until political pressure dictated action suggested that the ethical oversight system was fundamentally inadequate.

The broader question of parliamentary accountability was equally concerning. Labour's massive majority meant that the government could withstand confidence votes and resist opposition pressure despite the catalogue of scandals engulfing its ministers. The traditional belief that political shame would necessitate resignations had broken down, as politicians were willing to endure controversies until removed from office by criminal charges or overwhelming evidence of misconduct.

The media's role in exposing political corruption has become more important than formal regulatory mechanisms, raising questions about the sustainability of press accountability in an era of declining newspaper revenues and increasing political polarisation. If the press lacks the resources to conduct investigative journalism and politicians can dismiss criticism as partisan bias, what institutional safeguards remain to protect democratic standards?

Perhaps most fundamentally, Labour's scandals highlighted the weaknesses of Britain's honours system and appointment processes. The sight of disgraced politicians being elevated to the House of Lords, or individuals with apparent conflicts of interest being appointed to sensitive positions, indicated that merit and integrity played a minimal role in determining who exercises power in British democracy.

Labour's scandals were not only damaging domestically but also undermined Britain's international reputation at a time when the country desperately needed to rebuild relationships after the chaos of the Brexit years and Conservative mismanagement. Foreign governments that had welcomed Labour's election victory as a return to political stability began to question whether Britain was capable of producing competent governments, regardless of which party held power.

The implications of the Mandelson and Epstein scandal were profound, particularly in the context of Britain's international reputation. The involvement of Britain's ambassador to the United States, a key diplomatic relationship, in a scandal of this nature sent alarming signals about the UK's judgment and reliability as an international partner. The dismissal of Britain's senior representative due to connections with a convicted paedophile raised serious questions about the UK's diplomatic acumen.

European leaders, who had hoped for improved relations with Britain after years of Brexit antagonism, grew equally concerned about the stability and competence of Starmer's government. The continuous stream of resignations and scandals suggested that Britain remained mired in the political chaos that characterised the Johnson and Truss years, making long-term agreements and partnerships difficult to negotiate and implement.

Financial markets began to express concern about Britain's political stability through fluctuations in currency values and bond yields, reflecting uncertainty about the government's longevity and competence. International investors who had anticipated Labour's election as a return to predictable governance started questioning whether British politics was too unstable to support long-term investment strategies.

The broader damage to Britain's soft power might actually be more serious than immediate diplomatic and economic concerns. A country that once projected values of democracy, the rule of law, and good governance was now associated with corruption, incompetence, and systematic ethical failures. Britain's ability to criticise authoritarian regimes or promote democratic values internationally was severely compromised when its own government was engulfed in scandal

The Conservative Party's response to Labour's scandals was complicated by their own recent history of corruption and incompetence. Having been ousted from office partly due to their own ethical failures, the Conservatives found it challenging to attack Labour's scandals without risking unfavourable comparisons to their own record. Consequently, their criticism often came across as muted and failed to deliver politically effective blows, despite the obvious targets provided by Labour's behaviour.

Kemi Badenoch's leadership of the Conservative Party was still relatively new and untested, making it challenging for her to establish the moral authority necessary to effectively criticise government corruption. The baggage from Johnson's tenure meant that Conservative criticisms of Labour's scandals often sounded hypocritical rather than principled, limiting their political effectiveness despite the clear targets available.

The Liberal Democrats were in a better position to challenge Labour's ethical failures, but their limited parliamentary representation and media presence meant their criticisms had less impact than they deserved. Ed Davey's warnings that reshuffles would not resolve Labour's "deep-rooted problems" were accurate but received little attention compared to the more dramatic narratives of resignation and scandal dominating the news.

Smaller opposition parties effectively used Labour's scandals to position themselves as authentic alternatives to the corrupt political establishment. The Green Party, Plaid Cymru, and the SNP could all claim to represent values of integrity and public service that Labour had abandoned. However, their limited reach meant they could not fully capitalise on Labour's weaknesses.

The most damaging criticisms often came from within Labour's own ranks, as MPs and activists struggled to reconcile the party's current behaviour with the values that initially motivated them to enter politics. This internal criticism proved particularly effective as it could not be easily dismissed as partisan attacks from political opponents, forcing the government to address concerns raised by their own supporters about the direction of the party.

By September 2025, it was evident that Labour's scandals had inflicted damage extending far beyond the political consequences of lost seats and declining polling numbers. The systematic breach of ethical standards had created a crisis of trust that would be challenging to repair, even if the party managed to reform its behaviour and improve its competence.

The nature of Labour's scandals, which revolved around personal enrichment, corruption, and abuse of power, has significantly reinforced negative stereotypes about politicians. This has made it increasingly difficult for any party to regain the trust essential for effective governance. When voters perceive all politicians as fundamentally corrupt and self-serving, maintaining democratic accountability becomes a significant challenge.

The international damage to Britain's reputation would take years to mend, assuming future governments could demonstrate the competence and integrity that Labour had failed to provide. Britain's soft power and diplomatic influence had been severely undermined by the spectacle of systematic government corruption, complicating the country's efforts to achieve its international objectives.

Perhaps most seriously, Labour's failures had emboldened anti-establishment and populist movements that posed direct challenges to democratic governance. The surge in support for Reform was built on the belief that the entire political system was corrupt and needed to be dismantled rather than reformed. Labour's scandals provided ample evidence for this narrative, potentially radicalising voters who might have previously supported moderate democratic alternatives.

The constitutional implications were equally grave, revealing fundamental weaknesses in Britain's democratic safeguards that future governments would need to address. The failure of ethical oversight mechanisms, the inadequacy of parliamentary accountability, and the weakness of regulatory frameworks had all been exposed by Labour's systematic misconduct

The sixteen scandals that led to the collapse of Labour's government between July 2024 and September 2025 represented more than just political embarrassment or policy failures; they signified the death of the "new politics" that Keir Starmer had promised to bring to British government. The forensic barrister, known for exposing corruption and incompetence, proved incapable of maintaining basic ethical standards within his own administration.

The systematic nature of Labour's failures suggested that the problems were not merely due to individual misconduct but reflected fundamental flaws in the party's culture, organisation, and values. This situation was not just a case of a few bad apples corrupting an otherwise healthy organisation; it revealed institutional decay affecting every level of government, from junior ministers to the Prime Minister himself.

The speed of Labour's collapse was truly shocking in its comprehensiveness. In just fourteen months, the party went from a landslide electoral victory to historically low polling numbers, losing the confidence of voters, the media, and international partners through a series of scandals that exposed the disparity between its public rhetoric and private behaviour. Perhaps most tragically, Labour's failures not only damaged their electoral prospects but also undermined public faith in democratic politics more broadly. The party that had vowed to restore trust in government instead systematically dismantled it, potentially pushing voters toward anti-establishment alternatives that posed serious threats to democratic governance.

The sixteen scandals will be remembered not just as political failures but as a pivotal moment in British democracy, the point at which the last major party committed to democratic norms and ethical governance revealed itself to be just as corrupt and incompetent as the others. In destroying itself, Labour may have also dismantled the moderate centre-ground of British politics, leaving room only for populist extremes that promised to tear down rather than reform the democratic system.

The toolmaker's son who promised to fix British politics ultimately broke it beyond repair, leaving a legacy of wreckage that could take generations to clear away. The sixteen scandals stand as a monument to the chasm between political promises and political realities, between the rhetoric of public service and the practice of personal enrichment, and between the hope for democratic renewal and the reality of systematic failure.

As the summer of 2025 drew to a close, it was clear that fundamental changes had occurred in British politics. The era of deference to political authority was over, replaced by a climate of cynicism and distrust that would make effective governance much more difficult, regardless of which party held power. Labour's scandals had accelerated trends already evident in other democracies. Still, they had done so with a comprehensiveness and speed that were uniquely damaging, raising serious concerns about the future of British politics.

The sixteen scandals would be studied by future political scientists as a prime example of how not to govern a democracy. Their immediate impact, however, was to push British politics toward more extreme and potentially dangerous alternatives. In failing so spectacularly, Labour opened the door to forces that offered simple solutions to complex problems, authoritarian responses to democratic questions, and populist certainties that aimed to replace the messy compromises essential for effective governance.

The demise of new politics was complete, and what might replace it remained an open and deeply troubling question for anyone who valued democratic governance, ethical leadership, and the possibility of progressive change through democratic institutions. Labour's sixteen scandals hadn't just destroyed a government; they had potentially undermined faith in the very possibility of good government itself, leaving many disillusioned.

Chapter 12
The Public Unrest

The first ten months of 2025 saw Britain confronting significant questions regarding national identity, immigration policy, and civil liberties, revealing deep divisions in the post-war social contract. This situation was not merely a straightforward conflict between left and right; instead, it involved a complicated mix of genuine concerns, opportunistic extremism, government overreach, and a media landscape that struggled to discern meaningful messages amidst the noise.

By mid-2025, Britain's asylum system was under an unprecedented and urgent strain. In the year ending June 2025, 111,100 individuals applied for asylum, the highest number recorded since 1979, nearly double the figure from 2021. As of June 2025, the backlog of cases awaiting initial decisions exceeded 70,000, with an additional 51,000 cases pending immigration tribunal hearings.

These figures painted a picture of an overwhelmed system. By the end of March 2025, 106,771 asylum seekers were receiving government support. Among them, approximately 32,345 30% were housed in hotels. While this was a decrease from a peak of 56,042 in September 2023, it still represented a significant concentration of individuals in specific communities. The number of hotels accommodating asylum seekers had declined from over 400 properties in summer 2023 to 210 by September 2025; however, the political ramifications had already taken their toll.

The financial implications were staggering and had a profound impact. In the 2024-25 financial year, the Home Office spent £4 billion on asylum support, which included £2.1 billion on hotel accommodations, equivalent to approximately £5.77 million per day. Notably, hotel accommodation, which housed just 35% of asylum seekers, accounted for 76% of the total annual asylum contract costs, according to the National Audit Office.

These statistics were not mere abstractions. In towns like Epping, communities faced the influx of asylum seekers into converted hotels with minimal consultation or preparation. Local services experienced mounting pressure, and residents felt their concerns were dismissed as xenophobic. A growing divide has emerged between metropolitan policymakers and provincial communities, which are facing rapid and significant demographic changes.

The Bell Hotel and Epping: Catalyst for Confrontation

On 8 July 2025, events in Epping ignited a summer of protests across Britain. Hadush Gerberslasie Kebatu, a 38-year-old Ethiopian asylum seeker who had arrived by small boat just days earlier, was arrested for sexually assaulting a 14-year-old girl and a woman who had offered to help him with his CV.

The details of the case were disturbing. Kebatu approached the teenage girl, stroked her hair, placed his hand on her thigh, and made explicit comments, including, "Come back to Africa; you would be a good wife," and "Do you want to come to the Bell Hotel to have babies?" When the girl told him she was 14, he replied, "No, no, it doesn't matter. You could come back to the Bell Hotel with me."

On 4 September, Kebatu was convicted of two counts of sexual assault, one count of attempted sexual assault, one count of inciting a girl to engage in sexual activity, and one count of harassment. On 23 September, he received the maximum 12-month sentence that a magistrates' court could impose, along with a five-year sexual harm prevention order and placement on the sex offenders register for ten years.

District Judge Christopher Williams noted during sentencing: "You couldn't have anticipated that your offending behaviour as an asylum seeker housed at the Bell Hotel would cause such a response from the public, particularly in Epping, but also across the UK, resulting in mass demonstrations and fear that children in the UK are not safe."

The judge's observation was accurate. Within days of Kebatu's arrest, the "Epping Says No" Facebook group mobilised protesters to the Bell Hotel. On 13 July, the first significant demonstration drew hundreds, with chants of "Save our kids" and "Send them home" echoing across the car park. By 20 July, over 300 protesters gathered, with smoke bombs and projectiles thrown at police lines. Counter-protesters appeared with "Refugees Welcome" banners, creating the symbolic confrontations that would characterise the summer.

On 4 August, Epping Forest District Council won a temporary High Court injunction ordering the removal of asylum seekers from the Bell Hotel, based on arguments about "unprecedented levels of protest and disruption." This ruling provided a template that other councils would attempt to copy, framing asylum accommodation as a public order issue rather than a humanitarian obligation.

The Summer Protests: Scale and Scope

The Epping case sparked protests at asylum hotels across England, Scotland, Wales, and Northern Ireland throughout July and August 2025. In Bristol, riot police on horseback separated anti-immigrant demonstrators from several hundred counter-protesters, many of whom were advocating for a more welcoming approach to refugees and showing solidarity with the Palestinian cause. Similar scenes unfolded in Liverpool outside the Sheraton Four Points. In Norwich, Birmingham, and numerous market towns and suburban communities, the same pattern repeated itself: protesters waving Union Jacks and St George's crosses faced off against activists holding 'Refugees Welcome' banners and Palestinian solidarity flags

These protests were marked by genuine grassroots anger, but they also involved coordinated organisation. Local Facebook groups, such as "X Community Says No," proliferated, often run by far-right activists who provided ideological framing and tactical coordination. The flags that appeared on lampposts and roundabouts across Britain, dismissed by some as expressions of patriotic enthusiasm and recognised by others as territorial markers, were part of this coordinated campaign.

Police faced a daunting task during these events. Eight officers were injured during the early protests in Epping, highlighting the physical risks they faced. In multiple locations, they invoked Section 14 of the Public Order Act to disperse crowds and prevent gatherings, demonstrating their authority. Striking a balance between facilitating legitimate protest and preventing disorder proved challenging, with both sides accusing the police of bias, underscoring the complexity of their role.

It's important to note that the protests were not uniformly racist or xenophobic, despite often being characterised that way. Many participants voiced specific concerns about failures in the asylum system, inadequate safeguarding, and a lack of community consultation. A woman who travelled from Wales to Epping told journalists, "The country's in a hell of a state, and it's the immigrants they're letting in... We've had Chinese, Indians, and these working-class people all our lives, and it's never been a problem, but there's not enough housing for them. There's no support for them."

However, the protests also attracted explicitly far-right elements. Supporters of Tommy Robinson, veterans of the English Defence League, and activists promoting "Great Replacement" conspiracy theories were visibly present and vocal. The genuine concerns of ordinary people about systemic failures were being exploited by extremists with broader agendas, highlighting the manipulation at play.

The Online Safety Act: Digital Surveillance Arrives

While asylum protests grabbed headlines, another significant change to British life was unfolding quietly. On July 25, 2025, key provisions of the Online Safety Act came into effect, mandating platforms to implement age verification systems to prevent children from accessing harmful content

This Act, which received Royal Assent in October 2023, marked the most significant regulation of online spaces in British history. Although it was primarily designed to protect children from pornography, self-harm content, and material related to eating disorders, its scope quickly expanded. By August 2025, major platforms, including X (formerly Twitter), Reddit, Discord, Spotify, and others, required British users to verify their age through facial recognition scans, government-approved photo IDs, or credit card checks.

The Age Verification Providers Association reported an additional 5 million age checks per day as UK users tried to access age-restricted content. Many of these checks necessitated sharing government IDs or undergoing facial biometric scans, creating precisely the kind of digital surveillance infrastructure that civil liberties groups had warned against.

The implementation was chaotic. VPN downloads surged by four-figure percentages as users sought to circumvent the restrictions. A petition calling for the Act's repeal gathered over 500,000 signatures on the UK Parliament petitions website. The Wikimedia Foundation, a nonprofit organisation that supports the free encyclopedia Wikipedia, challenged aspects of the Act in court, arguing that it threatened public interest platforms. However, it lost its High Court challenge in August 2025.

Critics pointed out the Act's two-tier approach to speech, noting that traditional publishers were exempt from many requirements that applied to social media users. This exemption raised concerns about fairness and freedom of speech, as it effectively allowed professional journalists to publish content that would be considered offensive if posted on social media. Section 179 established a new criminal offence of sending messages intended to cause 'non-trivial psychological harm.' This vague standard effectively criminalised offensive speech while exempting professional journalists.

Defenders of the Act, including Technology Secretary Peter Kyle, argued it was essential for child protection. "If you want to overturn the Online Safety Act, you are on the side of predators. It is as simple as that," Kyle stated, reflecting the government's unwillingness to engage with significant civil liberties concerns.

By September 2025, reports emerged that parliamentary speeches about grooming gangs were being placed behind age verification barriers. Videos of the hotel protests were similarly restricted. Whether this was the result of algorithm-driven overcorrection or deliberate suppression of politically sensitive content remained a disputed issue. However, the potential chilling effect on democratic discourse was undeniable, as it could limit the public's access to important political debates and information.

Nigel Farage and Reform UK: Seizing the Moment

Amid the dysfunction of the asylum system and government overreach, Nigel Farage's Reform UK party experienced remarkable growth. Once regarded as a fringe movement after the 2024 election, it was now registering support levels that challenged fundamental assumptions about British politics

On August 22, 2025, Farage unveiled "Operation Restoring Justice" at Oxford Airport, before a mock departures board displaying destinations such as Kabul and Eritrea. The plan called for the deportation of 600,000 illegal migrants within five years, immediate detention for all asylum seekers, withdrawal from the European Convention on Human Rights, and five charter flights daily transporting deportees to countries like Afghanistan, Iran, and Eritrea.

"If you come to the UK illegally, you will be detained and deported and will never, ever be allowed to stay, period," Farage declared. The plan, which was projected to cost £10 billion but save £7 billion on the current expenditure on illegal migration, was criticised by opponents as unrealistic. Yet, it resonated strongly with voters who felt the government had lost control

Reform UK's polling during August and September consistently placed the party either in first or second place, often reaching support levels of 30-35%. Internal party documents and public statements indicated sophisticated strategic planning, significantly exceeding the party's previous capabilities. The combination of immigration restrictionism and opposition to the Online Safety Act created a compelling narrative of restoration, emphasising the need to restore borders, uphold free speech, and preserve traditional British identity.

The party maintained a public distance from Tommy Robinson and explicit far-right elements, recognising that mainstream success required plausible deniability. However, the line between Reform's populist nationalism and more extreme positions remained porous, with activists and supporters frequently flowing between the two movements.

13 September: The Unite the Kingdom March

The summer's unrest reached its peak on 13 September 2025, when Tommy Robinson's "Unite the Kingdom" march attracted between 110,000 and 150,000 people to central London, making it Britain's largest far-right demonstration in recent history and one of the most significant political gatherings overall.

The crowd stretched three-quarters of a mile, from Big Ben across Westminster Bridge to Waterloo Station, carrying Union Jacks, St George's crosses, Scottish saltires, and Welsh dragons. Some participants brought wooden crosses inscribed with "Christ" and sang Christian hymns. In contrast, others held photographs of Charlie Kirk, the American conservative activist who had been assassinated earlier that week, leading to moments of silence and shouts of support.

Robinson, whose real name is Stephen Yaxley-Lennon, addressed the hoarse-voiced crowd, stating: "Today is the spark of a cultural revolution in Great Britain. This is our moment." He claimed that migrants now had more rights in court than "the British public, the people that built this nation." His rhetoric carefully avoided explicit racial language while appealing to nationalist grievances and theories of cultural displacement.

The speakers included representatives from international far-right organisations that coordinate across borders. Katie Hopkins, French politician Éric Zemmour promoted "Great Replacement" theories, and politicians from Germany's Alternative für Deutschland also promoted these theories. Most controversially, Elon Musk joined via video link, telling the crowd: "I want Britain to remain Britain. There's something beautiful about being British. What I see happening is a destruction of Britain, starting as a slow erosion but rapidly increasing, fuelled by massive, uncontrolled migration. You either fight back, or you die." Musk's statement represented a significant escalation, as the world's richest man, who controlled X (formerly Twitter) and had restored Robinson's account, now explicitly endorsed far-right British nationalism and used eliminationist rhetoric.

A counter-protest organised by Stand Up To Racism drew

approximately 5,000 participants, led by hundreds of women, including independent MP Diane Abbott. They chanted, "Say it loud, say it clear, refugees are welcome here," and carried signs reading "Smash the far right." The numerical disparity of 110,000 to 5,000 was politically significant.

The day turned violent in the late afternoon when "Unite the Kingdom" supporters threw bottles and flares at counter-protesters and attempted to breach police cordons. Twenty-six police officers were injured, four seriously, suffering injuries such as broken teeth, a possible broken nose, a concussion, and spinal injuries. Twenty-five people were arrested for violent disorder, assaults, and criminal damage.

Metropolitan Police Assistant Commissioner Matt Twist stated: "There is no doubt that many came to exercise their lawful right to protest, but there were many who came intent on violence." The challenge of distinguishing legitimate political expression from violent extremism was clearly evident.

Liberal Democrat leader Ed Davey tweeted: "These far-right thugs do not speak for Britain." Home Secretary Shabana Mahmood condemned "those who have attacked and injured police officers" and insisted that "anyone taking part in criminal activity will face the full force of the law."

However, the size of the demonstration could not be dismissed as mere thuggery. Over 100,000 people had mobilised for a cause, however troubling its ideology and however violent its fringes. The march represented genuine grievances about failures in the immigration system, cultural change, and government unresponsiveness, issues that were being channelled into dangerous politics due to the mainstream parties' inability to address them adequately.

International Context and Palestinian Statehood

On 29 July, Starmer made a significant announcement that Britain, in coordination with Canada and Australia, would recognise Palestinian statehood in September. This decision, occurring 108 years after the Balfour Declaration, added a new layer of complexity to the summer's political climate. It was framed as a demonstration of moral leadership on Middle Eastern peace, marking a significant diplomatic shift and informing the global audience about the UK's stance on this crucial issue.

For communities struggling with rapid demographic changes at home, the timing was unfortunate. The government would move decisively to acknowledge Palestinian national aspirations while

160

dismissing British concerns about community cohesion as xenophobic paranoia. The formal recognition took place on 21 September, amid ongoing hotel protests and just one week after Robinson's massive march in London.

The Palestinian issue intersected with immigration debates in complex ways. Counter-protesters at Tommy Robinson rallies often carried Palestinian flags alongside "Refugees Welcome" banners. For some participants, support for Palestinian self-determination was linked to solidarity with all displaced peoples. For others, it represented a principled stance against imperialism. Conversely, for Robinson's supporters, it confirmed their narrative that the left prioritised distant causes over British communities.

Autumn: The New Normal

As autumn arrived, the protests became a permanent fixture of British political life. Hotel demonstrations continued sporadically, flaring up whenever local incidents provided fresh fuel. The flags remained on lampposts throughout the autumn winds, weathered yet defiant. Each protest showcased the same symbolic confrontations: Union Jacks were faced by Palestinian flags, and "Save Our Kids" signs were countered by "Refugees Welcome" banners, demonstrating the resilience and persistence of the protesters.

The impact of the Online Safety Act became increasingly evident and troubling. Beyond age verification requirements, the Act's vague "harmful content" provisions were being interpreted broadly. Critics noted that content legal to produce and distribute in the United States was being censored for British audiences. The threat of substantial fines, up to £18 million or 10% of global revenue for non-compliance, encouraged platforms to over-censor rather than risk penalties, raising concerns about potential censorship and its implications for freedom of speech.

Reform UK's dominance in polling persisted through autumn 2025. By October, surveys consistently showed Farage's party in either first or second place, nearing the potential to form a government in the next election. Their promise to repeal the Online Safety Act, coupled with plans for deportation, resonated with voters seeking decisive change.

Autumn also brought extensive analysis of the failures that had led to this situation. Academic studies, think tank reports, and journalistic investigations examined how Britain had reached this point. The consensus pointed to multiple system failures:

161

1. The asylum system's inability to process claims efficiently left people in limbo for years, while costs spiralled and communities absorbed arrivals without adequate preparation or consultation.
2. The government's use of hotels instead of proper accommodations created visible concentrations of asylum seekers, fuelling resentment.
3. A lack of honest national conversations about immigration's pace, scale, and impact left legitimate concerns unaddressed until extremists filled the vacuum.
4. The Online Safety Act's overreach created a surveillance infrastructure and criminalised speech, validating warnings about authoritarian government.
5. Mainstream parties failed to offer credible alternatives between open borders and mass deportation.

Competing Narratives and Uncomfortable Truths

By the end of the year, three competing narratives about the events of 2025 had crystallised, each containing elements of truth:

1. The right-wing narrative claimed that British communities had been subjected to rapid demographic changes without consent, that the asylum system was exploited by economic migrants rather than genuine refugees, that safeguarding failures endangered children, and that the government prioritised political correctness over public safety. The Epping case, where an asylum seeker who had arrived just days earlier assaulted a child, validated these concerns. The hotel system also incurred significant costs. Furthermore, the government appeared more focused on suppressing criticism through the Online Safety Act than addressing these systemic failures.

2. The left-wing narrative argued that asylum seekers were being demonised for broader systemic failures. It claimed genuine refugees were being conflated with a tiny minority of offenders, that the protests were organised and led by racist extremists exploiting legitimate concerns, and that the government's authoritarian turn posed the real threat to British values. The violent far-right presence at protests validated these concerns, as

did Tommy Robinson's history, which underscored issues of extremist leadership. The civil liberties implications of the Online Safety Act confirmed warnings about increased surveillance.

3. The centrist narrative emphasised systemic dysfunction, arguing that both immigration controls and asylum processing needed reform. It highlighted that communities required support to manage demographic change and stressed that neither extreme view should dominate the conversation.

The Democratic Question

As 2025 came to a close, Britain faced a profound question: Could its democratic institutions handle conflicts without resorting to authoritarianism? The rise of Reform UK represented either a move toward democratic accountability in response to government failures or a dangerous form of populism that threatened pluralism, perhaps both at once.

The flags displayed on lampposts symbolised not just territorial claims but also a transformation in community identity. These flags represented local communities asserting their identities in ways that metropolitan elites found threatening, yet they reflected a genuine attachment to place and culture. Whether this display was a legitimate form of democratic expression or a sign of dangerous nationalism depended on one's perspective and ultimately on one's judgment.

The asylum system's failures were stark and measurable, demanding urgent solutions. With 111,000 applications in a year, a backlog of 70,000 cases, £4 billion in annual costs, and 32,000 individuals housed in hotels, the situation was dire. However, the proposed solutions, ranging from Reform UK's mass deportations to activist calls for open borders, appeared equally disconnected from practical realities.

The Online Safety Act exemplified government overreach, justified by real harm. While it was true that children were exposed to damaging content online, the proposed solution, comprehensive age verification that would create a surveillance infrastructure and criminalise certain forms of speech, raised civil liberties concerns that might be more troubling than the issues it aimed to address.

The crux of the matter was whether Britain could navigate a middle ground between extremes. Could immigration policy balance humanitarian obligations with the capacity for integration? Could measures to ensure child safety avoid infringing on civil liberties? Could communities experiencing rapid demographic changes receive support without validating xenophobia? Could legitimate concerns about culture and identity be addressed without empowering racist sentiments?

By October 2025, evidence suggested that these hopes were not being realised. Mainstream political parties seemed unable to engage in honest dialogue. Government policies oscillated between inaction and overreach. Public discourse was marred by mutual distrust and suspicion. Trust in institutions continued to erode, and the space for nuanced perspectives diminished as polarisation intensified.

Conclusion: Britain at the Crossroads

The events from January to October 2025 highlighted Britain's struggle with fundamental questions about national identity, sovereignty, and pluralism that had been set aside for decades. The asylum crisis, the protests, the Online Safety Act, and the rise of Reform UK all reflected deeper uncertainties about Britain's identity and future.

Throughout the autumn, flags continued to adorn towns and villages, symbolising not just a breakdown of national consensus but perhaps a painful renegotiation of identity. These flags represented communities that felt changes were being imposed without their consent, where genuine concerns were labelled as bigotry, and where institutions appeared more focused on regulating speech than on addressing practical issues.

Whether 2025 would be remembered as the year Britain lost its way or began to forge a new path remained uncertain, hanging in the balance. The outcome relied on whether democratic institutions could productively resolve these conflicts, whether communities could bridge their divides, and whether politicians could offer solutions beyond mere deportation or denial.

What was clear was that 2025 had permanently altered Britain. The comforting notion that immigration concerns were solely fuelled by tabloids had been shattered. The belief that civil liberties would remain intact in the pursuit of child safety had proven naive. The expectation that mainstream parties could contain populist movements had waned. The idea that British tolerance was limitless had been tested and found wanting.

As 2026 is approaching, Britain faced a crucial decision, one with profound consequences. It could continue along the path of polarisation, with mainstream failures driving support for extremism, the expansion of surveillance justified by moral panic, and communities fragmenting along ethnic and ideological lines. Alternatively, it could undertake the challenging work of honest reckoning, acknowledging systemic failures, addressing legitimate concerns, defending pluralism without ignoring real problems, and rebuilding trust through competence rather than just rhetoric.

Regardless of the path chosen, the flags on the lampposts would remain, serving as markers of a nation uncertain about its future yet determined, for better or worse, to assert some degree of control over its destiny.

Chapter 13
Sadiq Khan's Revolt

The rebellion began quietly, as many of the most dangerous revolts often do. In the oak-panelled corridors of City Hall, where the Thames curves past Westminster and the seat of power feels almost within reach, London's mayor was growing restless. Sir Sadiq Khan, once Labour's most reliable electoral asset, was preparing to take action that would send shockwaves through Keir Starmer's government: he was about to turn against his own party.

By June 2025, the divisions within Labour had become impossible to ignore. What had started as whispers of discontent among backbench MPs was evolving into something more serious, a coordinated challenge to the government's direction from the very heart of the Labour movement. At the centre of this growing storm stood Khan, a politician whose every electoral success had been built on Labour values, now finding himself fundamentally at odds with a Labour government. His personal struggle, torn between his loyalty to his party and his commitment to his constituents, was palpable.

The catalyst for this unrest was brutally simple: the government's proposed cuts to disability benefits. Chancellor Rachel Reeves had announced plans to cut £5 billion from the welfare budget by 2030, targeting Personal Independence Payments and the health-related components of Universal Credit. The figures were stark and unforgiving. Over 360,000 Londoners, primarily poor, vulnerable, and disabled, faced reductions in their income totalling £820 million. Some would see losses of between £3,800 and £5,700 per year. The government's own estimates suggested that 250,000 people, including 50,000 children, would be pushed into poverty. The impact on the most vulnerable was staggering, evoking a sense of urgency in the audience

For Khan, the moment of truth arrived not in a dramatic confrontation or a heated cabinet meeting, but through the cold analysis of data that landed on his desk at City Hall. Policy in Practice, an organisation that modelled the impact of welfare changes, provided figures that clarified what Starmer's "tough choices" would mean for London. The weight of responsibility was palpable as he realised that nearly half of all Personal Independence Payment claimants in the capital would be affected. Hundreds of thousands of disabled Londoners would see their financial safety nets destroyed.

"What we cannot do is take away the essential safety net that so many vulnerable and disabled Londoners rely on," Khan stated, his words carrying the weight of political defiance. "Having reviewed the analysis of the Government's plans, the impact on London will be substantial, and for too many disabled Londoners, it will destroy their financial safety net."

Khan's intervention on June 24th was carefully calculated but unmistakably bold. Coming just hours after Prime Minister Starmer insisted he would "press ahead" with the cuts despite increasing opposition from his own MPs, Khan's statement marked the highest-profile challenge to the government's authority since Labour took power. This was not simply any Labour politician speaking out; this was the mayor of the capital, the party's most successful electoral performer in recent years, and a figure who commanded genuine respect across the movement.

Khan's rebellion was not isolated. By the time he made his public statement, over 120 Labour MPs had already signed a "reasoned amendment" to the Universal Credit and Personal Independence Payment Bill, indicating they were prepared to kill the legislation entirely. The list of rebels included respected figures across the party's factional divides, such as John McDonnell, the former shadow chancellor; Diane Abbott, the veteran backbencher; Kim Johnson from Liverpool Riverside; and Bell Ribeiro-Addy from Streatham and Croydon North.

What made Khan's position particularly significant was that it was grounded in the authority of local government. Unlike Westminster MPs, who could be dismissed as idealistic backbenchers, Khan spoke with the voice of practical administration. He managed transport systems, housing policies, and social services for nine million people. When he warned that disability cuts would "destroy the financial safety net" for vulnerable Londoners, he spoke from direct experience of the implications of such policies.

Khan's carefully crafted statement showcased the political savvy that has made him a successful politician. He began by acknowledging support for the government's broader aims: "I have always said that more must be done to help people move from relying on benefits to gaining employment. It's vital for a healthy and prosperous London." But then came the critical pivot: "However, we cannot take away the essential safety net that so many vulnerable and disabled Londoners depend on."

This was not mere opposition for its own sake. Khan was positioning himself as the voice of responsible Labour values, embodying a politician who understood both the need for reform and the moral responsibilities that come with power. He effectively claimed the mantle of authentic Labour politics while portraying the government as having lost its way.

The timing of Khan's intervention was equally crucial. It occurred at a moment when Starmer's government faced its first significant test of internal unity. The Prime Minister had gambled that Labour MPs would ultimately fall into line, relying on party loyalty and government discipline. Khan's statement shattered that assumption. If the party's most successful electoral figure was willing to break ranks, what did that reveal about the government's political judgment?

Khan's rebellion was soon joined by another influential figure who would prove equally challenging for Downing Street: Andy Burnham, the Mayor of Greater Manchester. Burnham, a former cabinet minister who had twice run for the Labour leadership, brought his own authority to the revolt. While Khan spoke with the voice of London's diversity and complexity, Burnham represented the post-industrial North, which Labour claimed as its heartland.

"When the PLP [Parliamentary Labour Party] delivers its collective wisdom in such numbers, it is invariably right," Burnham stated during a BBC Newsnight appearance that resonated widely on social media. "And it is right on this issue. I would say to the government, listen to the PLP." His intervention was notable for referencing historical precedent, drawing parallels with the Iraq War vote that divided Labour two decades earlier. "I experienced some of those significant votes in the past, Iraq being the main one, but there were others, too. When there is such widespread unease from truly good people across all factions of the party, it must be acknowledged."

Burnham's analysis carried significant weight due to his extensive experience in government. As a former Health Secretary and Chief Secretary to the Treasury, he had a deep understanding of government finance and the pressures that led to difficult decisions. When a figure with his background declared that the government was making "the wrong choice," it could not be easily dismissed as naive idealism.

The Greater Manchester mayor's critique went beyond the immediate issue of disability benefits, addressing the broader philosophical direction of the Labour government. "There is a case for reform, but the package announced when you consider the extent to which disability benefits are bearing the burden of the savings feels like the wrong choice," he argued. "When I look at what was announced, there will obviously be a group of people who can be better supported to work. But

I struggle to believe there will be no detrimental impact that further complicates the lives of disabled people."

Burnham's alternative vision was particularly important because it not only provided criticism but also offered a different path forward. In Greater Manchester, he had begun developing what he called a "prevention demonstrator," aimed at addressing social problems before they escalated into crises that required expensive intervention. His approach prioritised housing-first policies, recognising that stable accommodation was the foundation for all other aspects, including employment, health, family stability, and community cohesion.

The revolt among the mayors represented a new development in British politics: the emergence of local government leaders as significant political actors in their own right. Both Khan and Burnham had been elected directly, thereby gaining democratic legitimacy independent of Westminster party politics. They commanded resources, managed significant budgets, and, most importantly, had direct relationships with the communities affected by government policies.

This local perspective significantly weakened the government's case for welfare cuts. While ministers in Westminster could speak in abstract terms about "reform," "sustainability," and "tough choices," Khan and Burnham could point to specific impacts on identifiable communities. They had names, faces, and stories to illustrate the statistics and could share firsthand accounts from disabled constituents who expressed their fears about the potential consequences of these changes.

The effectiveness of the mayors' intervention was evident in how quickly other Labour figures followed their lead. What had started as backbench grumbling evolved into a coordinated challenge that included not only MPs but also council leaders, trade union officials, and party activists. The rebellion had found its voice, and that voice grew increasingly confident in its moral authority.

The government's response revealed how much Khan's intervention had disrupted their political strategies. Instead of dismissing the criticism or defending their policies on their merits, ministers began to offer what they referred to as "concessions." These changes were significant: existing Personal Independence Payment recipients would be protected from cuts, although the stricter criteria would still apply to new claimants. It was estimated that these modifications would cost the Treasury approximately £1.5 billion annually by the end of the decade.

However, these concessions did not calm the rebellion; they seemed to energise it further. Critics pointed out that the government's U-turn created the very kind of two-tier system that welfare reformers had long warned against. People with identical disabilities and needs would receive different levels of support simply based on when they became disabled. Khan's office made it clear that the mayor viewed these changes as inadequate: "Sadiq is quite clear that the proposed cuts and revised eligibility criteria should not go ahead unless these guarantees are made by the government."

Burnham was even more direct in his rejection of the government's partial retreat: "What's been announced is half a U-turn, a 50 percent U-turn. I hope that MPs vote against the whole Bill when it comes before Parliament." Speaking at the Left Field stage of the Glastonbury Festival, an important venue that connected the rebellion to broader cultural and social movements, Burnham argued that the legislation should never have been proposed in the first place.

The festival appearance was particularly significant as it demonstrated how the rebellion had transcended the confines of Westminster politics to engage with broader civil society. The "Disability Cuts: The Fight Back" event at Glastonbury connected the mayors' revolt to disability rights campaigners, trade unionists, and cultural figures who traditionally supported Labour. The message was clear: the government was facing opposition not only from within its parliamentary ranks but also from the communities and movements that formed Labour's social base.

By midsummer 2025, the welfare revolt had become a symbol of broader tensions within the Labour Party regarding its direction, values, and political strategy. The rebellion raised fundamental questions about what it meant to be a Labour government in the 2020s. Was it sufficient to be more competent than the Conservatives, or did Labour have specific obligations to protect the vulnerable and advance social justice? Could the party maintain its coalition of support while pursuing policies that directly harmed some of its core constituencies?

These questions became more urgent as polling data indicated the political cost of the government's approach. Labour's support among disabled people and their families was declining sharply. Disability rights organisations that had traditionally backed Labour candidates began withdrawing their endorsements. Online campaigns under hashtags like #LabourBetrayal and #DisabilityCutsKill started to gain traction, attracting support from individuals who had never previously engaged in political activism.

The personal cost to individual politicians also became apparent. MPs who supported the government's position faced angry constituents during advice surgeries and public meetings. This personal cost, in the form of direct confrontation and loss of support, underscores the gravity of the situation and the challenges faced by these MPs. Local party branches passed motions of no confidence in their own MPs, and Constituency Labour Parties, which had been reliable sources of campaign volunteers and donations, began to withdraw their support.

For Sadiq Khan and Andy Burnham, the revolt represented both a political risk and an opportunity. By publicly challenging their own government, they positioned themselves as authentic voices of Labour values in contrast to a leadership they viewed as having lost its way. This dual nature of the revolt, as both a risk and an opportunity, creates a sense of tension and uncertainty in their political positions. However, they were also gambling their own political futures on the assumption that Labour members and voters would ultimately side with them against the government.

As summer turned to autumn, the gamble appeared to be paying off. Khan's approval ratings in London remained strong, with polls showing that Londoners supported their mayor's stance on disability benefits by significant margins. Burnham's position in Greater Manchester was even stronger, with local polling suggesting that his criticism of the government had actually enhanced his standing with voters.

The success of the mayors' revolt began to attract attention beyond Britain's borders. International observers noted that local government leaders were emerging as significant political actors in their own right, independent of national party politics. This phenomenon was compared to developments in other federal systems, where state governors or regional leaders had used their platforms to challenge national governments of their own parties. The growing international attention to this revolt underscores its global impact and the changing dynamics of political powe

However, the revolt was also creating practical problems for the Labour government. International investors and diplomatic partners began to question the stability of Keir Starmer's administration. If the government cannot maintain the support of its own mayors and MPs, how effective can it be in executing its broader agenda?

The situation became even more complex as Khan started using his international platform to critique the government. As mayor of a global city, he frequently met with foreign dignitaries, business leaders, and representatives of international organisations. In these meetings, questions about Britain's direction inevitably arose

Khan's responses, while diplomatically phrased, carried a profound weight of disagreement with various aspects of the government's

171

approach, underscoring the significance of his stance

The international dimension became particularly significant during a series of high-profile clashes between Khan and Donald Trump. The US President's attacks on Khan, labelling him a "terrible mayor" who wanted to impose "sharia law" on London, provided the mayor with opportunities to showcase his international stature while implicitly critiquing his own government's relationship with Trump. When Khan referred to Trump as "racist, sexist, and Islamophobic," he was speaking not only as London's mayor but also as an alternative voice representing British values.

The contrast between Prime Minister Starmer's approach to Trump and Khan's was stark and intentional, highlighting the significant difference in their leadership styles and the broader questions about the direction and values of the Labour government

As autumn progressed, the welfare revolt developed into something more significant: a fundamental challenge to the government's political philosophy. Khan and Burnham were not merely opposing specific policies; they were articulating an alternative vision for what a Labour government should embody. Their approach emphasised prevention over punishment, investment over austerity, and community engagement over technocratic management

This alternative vision was put into practice through the mayors' own policy initiatives. Khan's office began developing proposals for a London-specific disability support system to supplement national benefits. Meanwhile, Burnham announced Greater Manchester's "prevention demonstrator" program, which aimed to pilot new approaches to social support, prioritising early intervention over crisis management.

These initiatives served multiple purposes. They demonstrated that the mayors were not just critics but also constructive politicians with alternative ideas. They illustrated that local governments could innovate in ways that national governments seemed unable or unwilling to do. Additionally, they provided practical examples of how Labour values might be translated into policy.

The government's response to these local initiatives was revealing. Rather than celebrating innovation and regional leadership, ministers appeared more concerned about the political challenge that effective local governance posed to their authority. Treasury officials raised questions regarding the funding of local programs, and civil servants expressed worry about "postcode lotteries" in public provision. These 'postcode lotteries' refer to the uneven distribution of resources and services across different regions, which can lead to disparities in the quality of public services.

The tension between national and local approaches reached a peak during the autumn party conference season. Both Khan and Burnham were scheduled to speak at the Labour Party conference, but their speeches would take place against the backdrop of ongoing disagreements with the government. Conference delegates, many of whom worked in local government or represented communities affected by welfare cuts, seemed more sympathetic to the mayors than to national ministers. This tension could strain the unity of the Labour Party, as it highlighted the diverging perspectives within the party

Khan's conference speech was a masterclass in political positioning. He began by praising Labour's electoral victory and acknowledging the challenges that any government faces. However, he then shifted to a passionate defence of Labour values that clearly critiqued the government's direction: "We cannot be the party that protects the wealthy while punishing the vulnerable. We cannot be the party that talks about social justice while removing the safety nets that give meaning to that phrase."

The speech was met with standing ovations at key moments, indicating that delegates were responding positively to Khan's alternative vision. His ability to energise the party base while critiquing the government demonstrated the political skills that had contributed to his success. He communicated Labour values in a way that resonated with activists while maintaining enough respect for party unity to avoid direct personal attacks on the leadership.

Burnham's conference appearance was significant, though it carried a different tone. As a former cabinet minister and leadership candidate, he spoke with the authority of someone who understood the pressures of government. His critique was particularly impactful because it stemmed from experience rather than ideology. He stated, "I have sat in those rooms where these decisions are made. I know the pressures; I understand the constraints. But I also know that there are always choices, and some choices are simply wrong."

The conference appearances marked a new phase in the mayors' revolt. What began as opposition to specific policies had evolved into a broader challenge to the government's overall approach and, implicitly, its leadership. The mayors, in their strategic approach, were not demanding Starmer's resignation, but they clearly represented an alternative vision of Labour politics that was gaining traction within the party.

The effectiveness of the revolt became evident as the government adopted an increasingly defensive posture. Ministers who initially dismissed the criticism as predictable leftist opposition started to recognise that they were facing a serious political challenge. The scale of this rebellion was unprecedented for a government barely a year into its term. The involvement of successful local leaders, such as Khan and Burnham, lent the rebellion credibility that could not be easily dismissed.

As winter approached, the key question was whether the revolt would lead to lasting change or gradually fade as other issues took precedence. The mayors had demonstrated their ability to mobilise opposition to government policies, but they had yet to prove they could compel fundamental changes in direction.

The answer emerged unexpectedly: Khan's candid assessment of Labour's performance in government. Speaking at the Edinburgh Festival Fringe in August, the London mayor delivered what would be remembered as one of the most significant political speeches of 2025. It was a moment of remarkable honesty that highlighted the growing concern that Labour was losing its way.

"It's been a tough first year," Khan stated, his words piercing through the typical political rhetoric surrounding discussions of government performance. This admission was striking not only for its honesty but also for who was making it. Khan was not an opposition politician seeking partisan advantage; he was a senior Labour figure acknowledging difficulties within his own party.

"Those people who say it has been a great first year... I think they are letting the party down," Khan continued. "It hasn't been a great first year. There have been positive developments in this first year, particularly regarding renters' rights, workers' rights, and energy security. I could go on. But in terms of a first year, it has not been great."

The impact of this admission was particularly profound because it came from Khan. As the party's most successful electoral performer, someone who had won London three times and reliably delivered it for Labour in general elections, his public acknowledgement of the government's failures carried significant weight. It raised serious questions about Labour's prospects under the current leadership and the need for a change in direction

Khan's critique extended beyond specific policies to address deeper concerns about political competence and understanding. He remarked, "It has taken some time for the Labour Party and the Labour Government to understand how the machinery of government works." This comment implicitly criticised not just policies but also the fundamental capability of the Starmer administration to govern effectively, highlighting specific challenges Labour faced in navigating the complexities of governance.

The mayor's football analogy conveyed a clear message: if Labour were in a football match, they would be "two-nil down." This image captured the sense of a government that was not just struggling but actively losing ground with the public.   The most significant aspect of Khan's speech in Edinburgh was his call for humility. He argued, "We need to have the humility to recognise the government's failures; otherwise, we are being delusional." This demand for humility represented a form of political leadership, an attempt to compel the government to acknowledge reality and change course

The speech marked the culmination of Khan's evolution from a loyal party supporter to an internal critic. It was a pivotal moment when one of Labour's senior figures was willing to break with collective responsibility and speak candidly about his party's performance. The political risk was substantial. Khan was betting his future on the belief that honesty would be valued more than loyalty.

Initial reactions indicated that Khan had accurately gauged the mood. Instead of being criticised for disloyalty, the mayor received praise for his honesty and courage. Polling data revealed that his willingness to acknowledge problems actually improved his standing with voters, who appreciated politicians who were willing to confront brutal truths.

The government's response was telling in its defensiveness. Instead of engaging with Khan's critique or acknowledging the issues he highlighted, ministers attempted to downplay the significance of his comments. This reaction underscored the government's reluctance to confront the realities Khan had brought to light, leaving the audience with a sense of the government's defensive stance.

Khan's revolt had achieved something remarkable: it made internal criticism of a Labour government not just acceptable but politically beneficial. The mayor proved there was room within the Labour coalition for politicians willing to hold their own party accountable.

The broader significance of Khan's challenge extended beyond immediate political advantage. By articulating an alternative vision of Labour values and demanding higher standards from his own party, Khan was helping to shape the debate about what a Labour government should entail. His revolt touched on issues beyond disability benefits or political tactics; it was about the core values of the Labour Party that had brought it to power.

The revolt by the mayors revealed something important about the state of British politics in 2025. At a time when trust in national politicians was at an all-time low, local leaders who could demonstrate a direct connection to their communities commanded genuine authority. Khan and Burnham's success in challenging their own government illustrated that authenticity and principle could still matter in politics, even when expressed through criticism of one's own side.

Whether this revolt would ultimately change the government's direction remained an open question as the year came to a close. However, it had already demonstrated that effective opposition to government policies could emerge from within the governing party itself. Politicians willing to prioritise principle over party loyalty could not only survive but thrive

Khan's revolt represented a new model of political leadership for the 2020s, one based on direct democratic accountability, an authentic connection to community concerns, and a willingness to challenge authority regardless of party affiliation. This model offered a beacon of hope for democratic renewal at a time when many voters had lost faith in traditional politics, instilling a sense of optimism in the audience about the future of UK politics.

As London's lights shimmered on the Thames outside City Hall, and the great city continued its rhythms amid political turmoil, Khan's challenge to his own government served as a stark reminder that democracy could still yield surprises. Politicians could still choose principle over convenience, and revolts could arise from the most unexpected places, leaving the audience with a sense of wonder and engagement.

As 2025 draws to its final months, the pressing question remains: will Khan's example inspire others to act with similar political courage, or will the pressures of party loyalty and career advancement ultimately stifle the rebellion he initiated? The answer would help determine not only the fate of Starmer's government but also the future of British democracy itself.

Chapter 14
The Trump Visit

The gilded carriages rolled through Windsor Great Park under September skies heavy with foreboding. Inside the Irish State Coach, King Charles III sat beside Donald Trump, engaged in small talk that neither man seemed to enjoy. The King looked pale and drawn, visibly diminished by cancer treatment that had taken a toll on his appearance in recent months. This was a monarch who had spent his entire adult life championing environmental causes, warning about climate change decades before it became a mainstream concern. Yet, he was now forced by constitutional duty to host a president who had withdrawn America from the Paris Agreement and labelled global warming a "hoax." The irony was enough to make observers wince.

Trump, for his part, appeared genuinely pleased with the spectacle being mounted in his honour. This marked his second state visit to Britain, an unprecedented distinction in modern British history, as no American president had received such treatment on two occasions. The pageantry aligned perfectly with his taste for theatrical displays of status and power. Behind them, through windows that had witnessed centuries of royal ceremony, the ancient stones of Windsor Castle loomed against grey clouds that threatened rain but had not yet delivered.

Outside the castle's walls, a very different reception was unfolding. In Parliament Square, demonstrators had gathered since dawn, their banners proclaiming "Trump Not Welcome" and "Stop Fascism." The protests stretched from Westminster to the Thames, with five thousand voices raised in opposition to what they viewed as a betrayal of British values. "Trump is not welcome here!" they chanted, their words carried by the wind toward the castle, where champagne was being poured and canapés prepared. The contrast could not have been more stark or deliberate.

Inside Labour Party headquarters, MPs whispered questions that their leadership could not answer. Why welcome a president who embodies everything they claim to oppose while cutting benefits to the country's most vulnerable citizens? Why bestow honours upon a man whose administration separated children from their parents at the Mexican border while telling British families that austerity was necessary? Why roll out the red carpet for a billionaire who had recently imposed ten percent tariffs on British exports, while Keir Starmer defended driving 250,000 people into poverty through welfare cuts?

The contradictions were glaringly crafted by forces that understood symbolism better than substance. Here was a Labour government that spoke of social justice while hosting a president whose Supreme Court appointees had overturned abortion rights. Here was a party that claimed to represent working people while entertaining a man whose supporters had stormed the Capitol in an attempted coup. The cognitive dissonance was overwhelming, yet the machinery of state moved forward regardless, committed to a course that nobody seemed able to halt.

The invitation itself had resulted from a series of missteps that revealed more about British diplomacy than any carefully crafted strategy document ever could. When Starmer visited the Oval Office in February 2025, he was supposed to deliver a letter from King Charles in private, discussed discreetly in a side room away from cameras. However, a logistical mishap in the Prime Minister's travelling party meant the letter was not available when needed. By the time it reached Starmer's hands, he was already seated before the world's media in one of the most famous offices in American politics.

What followed unfolded with a sense of inevitable spectacle. Trump picked up the envelope, clearly surprised by the theatrical nature of the handover. "Am I supposed to read it right now?" he asked. Starmer, apparently believing this was a diplomatic masterstroke, eagerly replied, "Yes, please do!" He then made the situation worse by declaring to the assembled press, "This is really special. This has never happened before; this is unprecedented." He seemed genuinely unaware that he had just committed Britain to hosting one of the world's most divisive political figures during one of the most turbulent periods in recent British history.

Adding to the absurdity, the King's letter had never actually been an official invitation for a state visit. Senior diplomatic sources would later reveal to embarrassed journalists that it was merely a proposal to discuss the possibility of a diplomatic voucher, leaving the door open without committing to dates or details. The fundamental aim had been to gently defer, suggesting that Trump might visit Balmoral the next time he was in Scotland for discussions, adhering to the time-honoured British tradition of making promises while committing to nothing. Instead, Starmer's theatrical presentation had transformed a diplomatic soft-shoe shuffle into a hard commitment that Britain would struggle to honour.

By September 2025, the political landscape had shifted dramatically since the misstep in February. The disability benefits crisis had exposed deep divisions within the Labour Party, with Sadiq Khan and Andy

Burnham leading a rebellion that included over 120 MPs. Reform UK was soaring in the polls, with Nigel Farage promising mass deportations and an end to what he referred to as two-tier justice. Tommy Robinson's Unite the Kingdom march attracted 150,000 supporters to central London, marking it as the largest far-right demonstration in modern British history. Free speech prosecutions were imprisoning housewives and pensioners for social media posts that would barely register as newsworthy in most democracies.

Amidst this toxic atmosphere, Trump, a president who seemed to embody the contradictions and tensions tearing British society apart, arrived. His visit lasted just three days, but those days crystallised questions about national identity, democratic values, and the cost of maintaining the special relationship with America, especially when it required embracing everything British progressives claimed to despise.

The security arrangements reflected the government's anxiety about the visit. More than 1,500 police officers were deployed to manage protests. The route from Stansted Airport to Windsor Castle was cleared of potential demonstrators. Conveniently, Parliament was scheduled to recess just as Trump's plane crossed the Atlantic, ensuring he would not face the traditional address to MPs that might have provided an uncomfortable platform for criticism. Even Windsor Castle itself was fortified against symbolic protests. Activists from the Led by Donkeys group were swiftly arrested after projecting images of Trump and Jeffrey Epstein onto the ancient walls; their equipment was confiscated, and their protest was silenced before it could properly begin.

The visual contradictions were stark and intentional. While five thousand protesters gathered in central London under banners reading "Stop Trump," "Stop Fascism," and "Stop the Genocide", referring to Israel's war in Gaza, Windsor Castle was transformed into a stage set for imperial pageantry typically reserved for Britain's most cherished allies. This spectacle included 1,300 military personnel, 120 horses, and the full ceremonial weight of the Guards regiments, which officials described as the largest military ceremony for a visiting foreign leader in living memory. The cost, never officially disclosed but estimated by defence analysts to be several million pounds, was incurred at a time when the government claimed it could not afford to maintain winter fuel payments for pensioners.

Inside the castle grounds, a different reality prevailed. Trump toured displays of meticulously curated historical artefacts that highlighted the long-standing partnership between Britain and America. He marvelled at a 1774 letter from King George III regarding the rebellion in the

179

American colonies, an 1862 letter from Abraham Lincoln to Queen Victoria following the death of Prince Albert, and watercolour paintings from the 18th century that illustrated the complex relationship between the two nations. The symbolism was heavy-handed but effective, as Trump was invited to see himself as part of a grand historical narrative, the latest chapter in a story stretching back to the founding of both nations.

The state banquet that evening served as a microcosm of everything wrong with contemporary British politics. In the magnificent St. George's Hall, beneath medieval banners and surrounded by priceless artwork, 160 carefully selected guests dined on Scottish langoustines, Yorkshire lamb, and Norfolk plum tart. The menu was designed to showcase British produce and culinary excellence, with each course paired with wines from the royal cellars, some of which date back decades.

The silverware alone was worth millions. Outside the castle walls, protesters demanded justice for Palestinians in Gaza and for disabled Britons facing benefit cuts. The stark contrast between the opulent feast and the austerity imposed on ordinary citizens, a clear symbol of wealth disparity, did not escape the notice of those who were paying attention.

The guest list read like a who's who of corporate power and political influence. Blackstone CEO Steve Schwarzman, whose private equity firm had faced criticism for aggressive tax avoidance strategies, sat near the high table. Apple CEO Tim Cook, whose company held billions in offshore tax havens while British schools struggled to afford basic equipment, chatted amiably with cabinet ministers. NVIDIA CEO Jensen Huang, whose company's market capitalisation exceeded the GDP of most nations, graciously accepted compliments on his firm's technological prowess. Media mogul Rupert Murdoch, whose newspapers had spent decades demonising immigrants and welfare recipients, enjoyed the hospitality of a Labour government.

These were the individuals who stood to benefit from the Tech Prosperity Deal that Keir Starmer was negotiating: a £150 billion investment package that would enrich American technology companies. At the same time, ordinary Britons struggled with the highest cost of living in a generation. This deal, touted as a diplomatic triumph, was essentially a wish list from Silicon Valley disguised as bilateral cooperation. American firms would receive preferential access to British markets, streamlined planning permissions for data centres, and assurances of light-touch regulation. In return, they promised job creation, although the details revealed that these jobs would primarily be for highly skilled workers, such as software engineers and data scientists with advanced degrees, rather than the displaced factory workers in post-industrial communities who desperately needed employment. The industrial jobs that had traditionally supported working-class families would continue to migrate overseas, while Britain's economy became increasingly dependent on volatile service sectors and foreign investment.

Trump's banquet speech underscored the transactional nature of the relationship that Starmer was so eager to cultivate. The president praised King Charles for his efforts to preserve the nation's history, uplift the poor, and support soldiers, deliberately avoiding any mention of the policies that were achieving the opposite. He complimented Catherine, Princess of Wales, calling her healthy and beautiful, a remark that seemed tone-deaf given her recent cancer diagnosis but captured the superficiality of the entire event. Trump spoke of the eternal friendship between Britain and America, the shared values that tied the two nations together, and the unbreakable bonds forged in war and reinforced in peace. His speech followed standard diplomatic boilerplate, delivered with Trump's characteristic mix of hyperbole and sentimentality.

King Charles, visibly frail yet determined to fulfil his constitutional duties, offered his own toast, which hinted at the awkward ironies of the occasion. "I cannot help but wonder what our forebears from 1776 would make of this friendship today," he remarked, possibly reflecting on the democratic ideals that had driven both the American Revolution and the British parliamentary tradition ideals that Trump's presidency had done much to undermine. The King's voice was steady but quiet, and those at the far end of the hall strained to hear him. Observers noted that his hands trembled slightly as he raised his glass. This was a man who had waited his entire life to wear the crown, only to find himself hosting leaders whose values contradicted everything he had championed for decades.

The honest discussions of the visit would take place the following day at Chequers, the Prime Minister's country residence in Buckinghamshire, where carefully choreographed pageantry would give way to sharp negotiations about trade, security, and Britain's role in Trump's vision of international order. The setting was as symbolic as Windsor Castle had been. Chequers is the Tudor manor house where Winston Churchill plotted victory over fascism, where Margaret Thatcher entertained Ronald Reagan, and where Tony Blair hosted George W. Bush in the aftermath of the September 11th attacks. Now, it would witness Keir Starmer attempting to navigate the most challenging diplomatic relationship of his career.

The joint press conference that concluded the talks was a strategic display of diplomatic finesse, with tensions carefully veiled under a facade of unity. Starmer, navigating the delicate balance of his discomfort with Trump and the potential benefits of their relationship, referred to Britain and America as 'first partners' in trade, defence, and technology. He underscored their shared commitments to Ukraine and NATO, skillfully sidestepping direct criticism of Trump's controversial policies. The Prime Minister's body language, a testament to his unease, spoke volumes; he maintained a cautious distance from Trump, made minimal eye contact, and his smiles were devoid of genuine warmth. Each word was meticulously chosen, every gesture controlled, and every pause pregnant with meaning.

Trump, on his part, appeared genuinely fond of his British hosts, describing Charles as a "very, very special man" and praising the "priceless and eternal" relationship between the two countries. However, his comments also highlighted the limitations of what the visit had actually achieved. When asked about Ukraine, he offered only vague promises to increase pressure on Vladimir Putin once NATO countries stop purchasing oil and gas from Russia. Regarding Gaza, he publicly disagreed with Starmer's commitment to recognising a Palestinian state, referring to it as "one of our few disagreements" in a tone that suggested it could become a much larger issue if pursued further. On trade, Trump was straightforward: the ten percent tariffs on British goods would remain in place. American companies would certainly invest in Britain, but only on terms advantageous to their interests.

The economic outcomes were concrete yet problematic. The Tech Prosperity Deal, which Starmer hailed as a major success, was primarily a package of investment commitments from American companies that would gain preferential access to British markets. In contrast, British companies continued to face Trump's tariffs on exports to America. The asymmetry was apparent to anyone who examined the details. NVIDIA, Microsoft, and Google would invest billions in British facilities, but these were investments they would have made anyway to access the European market. The jobs created would primarily benefit highly-skilled workers, exacerbating regional inequalities rather than addressing them. A software engineer in Cambridge might gain from this, while a former steelworker in Port Talbot would not.

What Britain received in return for its hospitality was largely symbolic rather than substantive. There were vague promises of future trade deals that might materialise under certain conditions, assurances of continued security cooperation that were already mandated by existing NATO commitments, and expressions of friendship that cost nothing and committed to nothing. Meanwhile, the harsh reality of Trump's ten percent tariffs continued to affect British exporters, leading to job losses and undermining competitiveness in the manufacturing sectors that Labour claimed to champion.

For the protesters who gathered outside the castle gates and marched through London's streets, the economic arrangements highlighted everything wrong with contemporary capitalism. American technology companies would extract value from British workers and consumers while contributing minimal tax revenue to public services, facing devastating cuts. The government that claimed it could not afford to maintain disability benefits for vulnerable citizens had somehow found resources to host lavish banquets for foreign billionaires. The contradiction was not lost on Shaista Aziz, co-organiser of the Stop Trump Coalition, who told journalists: "Trump is not welcome in the UK, and Trumpism is not welcome, either. Our message to our own Prime Minister, Keir Starmer, is to stand up to Trump. We strongly object to the politics of bigotry and hate, to genocide, and we demand that Keir Starmer stands up for us as British people against this type of hatred."

The protesters' anger reflected the widespread discontent with a political system that seemed to prioritise the interests of global capital over the needs of ordinary citizens. Will Embliss, a trumpet player with the Fall Out Marching Band who had been protesting since 1981, encapsulated this sentiment perfectly: 'We're here today to say we don't want Trump here. He is a horrible man. We don't want his politics in our country.' This sentiment was echoed by seventy per cent of Britons, according to polls conducted before the visit. Yet, their government chose to honour Trump with privileges typically reserved for the most valued allies.

The timing of the visit highlighted significant contradictions. Just weeks earlier, Starmer had been defending benefit cuts that would impact 360,000 Londoners, insisting that Britain had to make tough choices in a challenging economic climate. Now, the same officials were hosting lavish banquets costing more than many families would earn in a year, all in an effort to maintain a relationship with a president who had imposed punitive tariffs on British exports. The government's priorities were unmistakable: impress foreign leaders, court corporate investment, and maintain the appearance of international influence. Meanwhile, pensioners faced tough decisions between heating and eating, disabled individuals were losing crucial support, and working families struggled with the highest cost of living in a generation. These actions not only affect the UK but also have implications on the global political landscape.

The Jeffrey Epstein scandal, which had engulfed both leaders in the weeks leading up to the visit, added another layer of complexity to the proceedings. Starmer had been compelled to fire Peter Mandelson as Britain's ambassador to Washington after revelations of Mandelson's correspondence with Epstein became impossible to ignore. Newly published documents indicated that Mandelson had defended Epstein, referring to him as 'my best pal,' and had even encouraged him to challenge his conviction for child sexual offences. The language in a 2003 birthday book letter and 2008 emails suggested a relationship that persisted well after Epstein's conviction and public disgrace. These were not casual acquaintances or distant business contacts but personal friendships that Mandelson had maintained despite being fully aware of Epstein's crimes against children. This fact could only leave the public feeling betrayed.

Trump's connections to Epstein were even more extensive and better documented. A handwritten birthday note from Trump to Epstein recently surfaced, revealing a closeness that contradicted the president's public claims of barely knowing him. Photographs showed Trump and Epstein together at numerous social events throughout the 1990s and early 2000s, and flight logs indicated Trump travelled on Epstein's private jet. Their relationship had been well-established and mutually beneficial, ending only when Epstein's arrest made any association with him politically toxic.

The careful choreography of the visit, which kept Trump at a safe distance from the British public, coupled with journalists' apparent reluctance to ask uncomfortable questions, suggested that both governments understood the political risks involved. When a single question about Epstein was raised during the Chequers press conference, Starmer skillfully sidestepped it, discussing the importance of proper vetting procedures and lessons learned. Trump claimed not to know Mandelson, despite photographic evidence of multiple meetings between them. The assembled journalists did not follow up; nobody pressed for details or demanded explanations. The moment slipped away, and the topic was dropped, as both leaders had clearly desired, leaving the public frustrated with the lack of accountability.

Media coverage of the visit revealed how British journalism had become complicit in the political theatre surrounding major diplomatic events. Despite the evident newsworthiness of the Epstein connections, the protests, and the policy contradictions, most mainstream outlets focused on the ceremonial aspects of the visit. The BBC emphasised the historical significance of Trump's second state visit without adequately examining why such an honour was being granted to such a controversial figure. Reporters dutifully described the menu, guest list, and royal protocol, showing footage of the golden coach, mounted guards, and the precision drills of military bands. What they failed to do was ask tough questions about the implications of this event for British democracy. This lack of media scrutiny is concerning, as the role of the media in holding political leaders accountable is crucial in a democracy.

The Times and Telegraph reported on trade deals and diplomatic discussions while largely ignoring the protesters and domestic political implications. Their articles read like press releases, uncritically repeating government talking points about strengthened bilateral relations and enhanced economic cooperation. The Financial Times, typically more analytical, offered some scrutiny of the Tech Prosperity Deal but hesitated to challenge the fundamental rationale behind hosting Trump at all. Only the Guardian and a few smaller outlets provided sustained critical coverage, and their reach was limited compared to the broadcast media that most Britons relied on for news.

This sanitised coverage reflected broader trends in British political journalism, where access to power was often traded for critical independence. Journalists who could have pressed uncomfortable questions about the cost of the visit, the wisdom of the trade deals, or the implications of embracing Trump instead chose to file stories about ceremonial protocols and state banquet menus. The Lobby system, which provided privileged access to government information in exchange for cooperation, ensured that most political reporters maintained cordial relationships with the very power they were supposed to scrutinise. No one wanted to be excluded from briefings, shut out of background conversations, or denied the access that made their jobs possible.

The three days of Trump's visit compressed into a single, extended moment all the contradictions and tensions defining contemporary Britain. Here was a Labour government that claimed to represent working-class interests while hosting American billionaires. Here was a nation that prided itself on democratic values, yet it had embraced a president who had attempted to overturn an election. Here was a country that spoke of social justice while cutting benefits for the disabled and welcoming a leader whose administration had systematically attacked the rights of minorities, women, and immigrants. The cognitive dissonance was overwhelming, a tension that reverberated throughout the nation, but the machinery of state rolled forward regardless.

The conclusion of the visit at Stansted Airport provided a final metaphor for the entire affair. As Air Force One taxied down the runway at 5:50 PM on September 18th, lifting off into skies that were finally clearing after three days of political storm clouds, it left behind a Britain more divided and uncertain about its place in the world than when Trump had arrived. The protests achieved little beyond expressing anger that the government clearly did not care about. The trade deals would benefit American companies more than British workers, and the diplomatic capital invested in the relationship had been spent on ceremonial gestures rather than substantive policy changes.

The £150 billion investment package that Starmer would trumpet as validation for his approach would take years to materialise, if it materialised at all. These were commitments, not contracts, expressions of intent, not binding obligations. The actual investment would depend on market conditions, regulatory environments, and political developments, all of which were unpredictable. The trade benefits were largely theoretical, offset by the concrete reality of Trump's 10 per cent tariffs, which continued to impact British exporters daily. The diplomatic capital that Britain invested in the relationship had thus been squandered on ceremonial gestures rather than meaningful policy changes. Trump's commitments on Ukraine remained vague, his stance on Gaza remained unchanged, and his willingness to support Britain in future crises was entirely dependent on his perception of what America would gain from such support.

For the protesters who filled London's streets, the visit confirmed their worst fears about the direction of British politics. A government that claimed to be progressive chose to align itself with reactionary forces. A party that spoke of social justice embraced a president whose entire political project was built on division, hatred, and the systematic erosion of democratic norms. A nation that prided itself on moral leadership sacrificed its principles for the illusion of influence, a loss keenly felt by those who had campaigned for Labour, donated to the party, and believed in the possibility of change.

The polling data that emerged in the weeks following the visit confirmed the political damage that Starmer had inflicted on himself. Only 30 per cent of Britons believed the visit had been the right decision, while 45 per cent thought it was wrong to extend the invitation. Among Labour voters, the numbers were even worse, with significant majorities expressing disappointment with their own government's approach, a clear sign of the visit's impact on the party's support base. The visit had damaged Britain's international reputation, weakened Starmer's domestic position, and yielded little tangible value in return.

Perhaps most significantly, the Trump visit normalised the notion that Britain would compromise its stated values in exchange for economic advantage. A precedent was set: if American investment was at stake, British principles were up for negotiation. Future authoritarian leaders would recognise that pageantry and trade deals could secure British respectability, regardless of their domestic policies or international behaviour. The message to the world became clear: Britain's commitment to democracy and human rights was negotiable, contingent on economic incentives, and subservient to narrowly defined national interests focused solely on trade and investment.

The long-term implications of this normalisation are deeply concerning, extending far beyond the immediate political damage to Starmer's government. Britain has traditionally employed its soft power, encompassing its democratic institutions, cultural influence, and moral authority, to exert considerable influence in international affairs. By embracing Trump, despite his apparent unfitness for office, Britain compromised that soft power in ways that would take years to repair. Countries that once looked to Britain for moral leadership now witnessed a nation willing to abandon its values for trade deals. Allies that relied on British support for human rights and democracy began to question the trustworthiness of that support.

The visit also exposed the extent to which Britain's governing class was willing to forsake democratic principles when they conflicted with perceived economic interests. The same politicians who claimed to defend British values hosted and honoured a president who embodied everything they professed to oppose. This betrayal of British values is deeply disappointing. Civil servants, who prided themselves on political neutrality, organised ceremonies that served clear partisan purposes. Media figures, who claimed to hold power accountable, essentially acted as cheerleaders for this diplomatic spectacle.

As autumn deepened and the memory of Trump's visit faded from the headlines, its legacy continued to cast a long shadow over British politics. The protest movements that had mobilised against the visit remained active, channelling their energy into campaigns for Palestinian rights, disability justice, and democratic reform. Civil society organisations that had coordinated opposition to Trump began collaborating on broader issues, creating resistance networks that would prove valuable in future political battles. They recognised that their

187

struggle was not solely about one presidential visit, but about the broader direction of British politics and the type of society Britain would become.

The visit also crystallised opposition within the Labour Party against Starmer's leadership style and political direction. MPs who were already critical of cuts to disability benefits found additional ammunition to argue that the government had lost its moral compass. Trade unions that had supported Labour began to question whether a party that would roll out the red carpet for Trump could truly be trusted to defend workers' interests. Unite the Union's Sharon Graham, already hostile toward the government over welfare cuts, used the Trump visit as further evidence that Labour had abandoned its principles in pursuit of power.

Most importantly, the Trump visit revealed to millions of Britons that their government's stated commitment to progressive values was merely rhetorical. Faced with a choice between principles and perceived advantages, Starmer consistently chose advantage. When required to choose between domestic needs and international relationships, he prioritised relationships with the powerful over obligations to the vulnerable. When confronted with the contradiction between Labour values and realpolitik, he opted for realpolitik without hesitation or regret.

This revelation would have profound implications for British politics as the country approached the next election cycle. Voters who had trusted Labour to represent their values now had tangible evidence that such trust was misplaced. Activists who had worked to elect a progressive government realised that their efforts had been in vain. Young people who had believed in the possibility of political change began to doubt whether change was attainable within existing institutions. The disillusionment was profound and widespread, affecting all demographic groups and geographic regions. The visit by Trump in September 2025 would be remembered not as a diplomatic triumph but as a moment when Britain's moral decline became impossible to ignore. During three days of pageantry and protocol, the country traded its reputation for a fleeting opportunity, embracing authoritarianism in the name of economic gain and sacrificing specific democratic values such as freedom of speech and the rule of law for the illusion of international influence. The red carpets were rolled up, the state carriages returned to their stables, and the golden plates washed and stored until the next occasion. However, the damage to Britain's democratic culture would prove far more challenging to repair.

Trump's visit was a global spectacle that not only revealed to the world but also to the Britons themselves the conditional, transactional, and ultimately hollow nature of their government's commitment to the cherished values. The carefully crafted image of Britain as a beacon of good in the world, nurtured over decades through its support for international law, human rights, and democratic norms, was significantly tarnished in a mere 72 hours. The special relationship with the United States was preserved, but at a cost that future generations would continue to reckon with long after Trump and Starmer had exited the political arena.

As the lights dimmed over Windsor Castle and life in the ancient town resumed, the only lingering question was whether the British people would tolerate this betrayal of their values or demand a higher standard from their leaders. The answer to this question would not only shape the destiny of Starmer's government but also the very future of British democracy. The seeds of Labour's electoral downfall, sown by months of policy reversals and unfulfilled promises, were watered by three days of grandeur that laid bare the government's moral vacuum. The repercussions of this would soon unfold, casting a shadow of uncertainty over the political landscape.

Chapter 15
Admin Errors and Identity Cards

The leak was meticulously planned, strategically landing in journalists' inboxes on a Monday morning in late August. It was a 2021 email from Gerald Shamash, a Labour Party lawyer, to Morgan McSweeney, who was then running a think tank called Labour Together and is now serving as Keir Starmer's chief of staff. The subject line was deceptively mundane, but the content was incendiary. Shamash was advising McSweeney on how to manage what seemed to be significant breaches of electoral law donations totalling £739,492 that had not been properly declared to the Electoral Commission. His suggested approach was elegantly simple: call it an administrative error.

The email, dated February 2021, was brief, professional, and precise. However, its implications were nothing short of shocking for a Prime Minister who had built his political brand on integrity, transparency, and respect for the rule of law. Shamash wrote, "It may be better if Labour Together cannot deal substantively with questions I pose, then perhaps best to simply base our case on the non-reporting down as admin error." This was documentary evidence that Starmer's inner circle, long before taking power, had been advised to minimise serious regulatory violations by framing them as mere paperwork mistakes. The optics could not have been worse. This was not an ancient issue from a forgotten scandal; it was 2021, when Starmer was already the Labour leader and had been promising to restore trust in British politics, positioning himself as the antithesis to Conservative corruption.

The Electoral Commission had indeed fined Labour Together £14,250 in September 2021 for over 20 reporting breaches related to undeclared donations. At the time, this fine attracted minimal media coverage. Labour was in opposition, focused on criticising Boris Johnson's government over 'partygate' (a scandal involving alleged lockdown-breaching parties at Downing Street) and various other scandals. The notion that Labour's own operation might be cutting corners with electoral law seemed almost trivial compared to the widespread corruption that appeared to characterise Conservative governance, including the 'partygate' scandal and other issues such as the handling of the COVID-19 pandemic. However, context changes everything. What seemed like a minor administrative issue in 2021 looked very different in 2025, with Starmer in Downing Street claiming moral authority while his government struggled in the polls.

The Conservative opposition, still reeling from their historic defeat and desperately searching for lines of attack to regain credibility, seized on the revelations with a palpable intensity. Conservative Party Chairman Kevin Hollinrake declared the evidence "clear" that McSweeney had been "caught red-handed hiding hundreds of thousands of pounds that helped install Keir Starmer as Labour leader." He called for both the Electoral Commission and the police to urgently investigate what he described as a scandal "at the very heart of government" that was "incredibly serious and potentially criminal."

Kemi Badenoch, speaking during Prime Minister's Questions, accused Starmer of presiding over a culture of cover-ups that undermined his promises to clean up politics. "The Prime Minister stood at that dispatch box and told this House that his government would uphold the highest standards of integrity," she declared, her voice rising in theatrical indignation. "Yet we now know that his chief of staff, the man who controls access to the Prime Minister and sets the tone for this government's operation, was advised to treat nearly three-quarters of a million pounds in undeclared donations as an admin error. Is this what integrity looks like in Labour Britain?"

The attack was effective precisely because it targeted Starmer's core political identity. He was not a charismatic campaigner like Tony Blair, a conviction politician like Jeremy Corbyn, or even a particularly skilled parliamentary performer. His selling point had always been competence and integrity, the forensic barrister who would restore order after years of chaos. Strip away that reputation, and what remains? A technocrat without vision, a manager without a mandate, a leader lacking the personal qualities that might inspire loyalty during difficult times. The scandal not only damaged his political image but also raised questions about his leadership and the future of the Labour Party.

Labour's defence was technically correct but politically insufficient. The party insisted that McSweeney's salary during the relevant period was covered by funds from Starmer's 2020 leadership campaign, not by donations from Labour Together. While the Electoral Commission breaches were real, they did not involve personal enrichment or deliberate fraud. These were genuine administrative errors, failures of proper procedures rather than criminal conspiracies. The fine had been paid, the systems had been improved, and lessons had been learned. However, the scandal had already tarnished the party's image and could affect its future electoral prospects. It was time to move on, but the damage had been done.

Deputy Prime Minister David Lammy dismissed calls for a police investigation, stating on Times Radio: "In opposition for 14 years, Labour Together was part of a group of organisations aimed at getting the Labour Party back in touch with the British public and positioned to win again. Labour Together played a crucial role in achieving this, so I'm not surprised the Tories are engaging in muck-raking." Work and Pensions Secretary Pat McFadden defended McSweeney on Sky News, insisting, "The Electoral Commission, which is responsible for overseeing donations, declarations, and everything related to this, looked into these issues three or four years ago."

On September 26, 2025, the Electoral Commission issued a statement that temporarily relieved Downing Street. The watchdog decided not to reopen its investigation, declaring itself "satisfied" with the results of its 2021 probe. This probe, conducted four years ago, had found 'no evidence of any other potential offences' aside from those already adjudicated. However, the political damage had been done. The story had dominated headlines for days, reminding voters of the corner-cutting and rule-bending they believed they had voted against.

Politics is not solely about technical correctness; it is about perception, narrative, and the stories voters tell themselves about their leaders. The narrative emerging from the leaked email depicted a political operation that viewed legal obligations as inconveniences rather than principles to uphold. The Shamash email suggested a mindset where the priority was not whether rules had been broken but whether violations could be justified. It was about calling it an administrative error, minimising the problem, and controlling the narrative. This was standard political crisis management, a tactical approach every party employs when confronted with uncomfortable revelations. However, it also mirrored the kind of behaviour that Starmer had spent years condemning in his opponents.

The timing of the leak exacerbated the damage. It surfaced just as Labour was gearing up for its September conference in Liverpool, an event meant to convey unity, competence, and purpose. Instead, the party arrived at the conference defending its chief of staff against accusations of electoral law violations while the Prime Minister's personal ratings plummeted to historic lows. The narrative of competent governance that Starmer so desperately needed to establish was being systematically undermined by a steady stream of scandals that made his administration appear no better than its predecessor.

Media coverage split along predictable lines, each contributing to the

192

shaping of public perception. The Daily Mail featured the story prominently on its front page and published analysis pieces exploring the culture within Starmer's operation. The Telegraph, eager to criticise Labour, provided extensive coverage highlighting every detail that could embarrass the government. The Guardian, typically more sympathetic to Labour, covered the issue but with less prominence, stressing the technical nature of the breaches and the lack of evidence for deliberate wrongdoing. The BBC, attempting to maintain neutrality amidst accusations of bias from both sides, reported the facts in a manner that satisfied nobody.

What made the admin error controversy particularly damaging was its connection to other recent scandals, including the freebies row over designer glasses and concert tickets, cuts to winter fuel payments, Angela Rayner's stamp duty issues, Sue Gray's resignation, and a series of ministerial departures. Each incident might have been survivable on its own, but together they formed a pattern that voters recognised: a government that claimed one thing while doing another, promising integrity. At the same time, its officials bent rules and accepted gifts, and professing to represent working people while hosting billionaires at state banquets. The weight of these scandals was felt in the public perception of the government.

The political damage was further compounded by Starmer's inability to present a compelling counter-narrative. When Boris Johnson faced similar accusations of hypocrisy, he could rely on charm and bluster, redirect the conversation, and create new controversies to distract from older ones. Jeremy Corbyn, when facing criticism, could point to decades of principled consistency and a political record that resonated with his core supporters, even in the face of hostile media. Starmer, however, lacked Johnson's charisma and Corbyn's convictions. He had competence, or at least the appearance of it, but that competence was precisely what the admin error story called into question.

The leak dominated headlines for three days before being overshadowed by an even more contentious issue: the government's announcement on September 26, 2025, regarding the introduction of mandatory digital identity cards for anyone seeking legal employment in the United Kingdom. The timing was disastrous. Instead of allowing the administrative error story to fade from public consciousness, the BritCard announcement sparked a new controversy that energised critics across the political spectrum, reminding voters of their longstanding suspicions about Labour's authoritarian tendencies.

This announcement was made during the Global Progress Action

Summit in London, a gathering of international leaders and policymakers focused on progressive solutions to global challenges. Labour leader Keir Starmer addressed an audience of progressive leaders from around the world. He stated, 'For too many years, it's been too easy for people to come here, slip into the shadow economy, and remain here illegally because, frankly, we've been squeamish about saying things that are clearly true. This government will make a new free-of-charge digital ID mandatory for the right to work. You will not be able to work in the United Kingdom if you do not have a digital ID. It's as simple as that.'

Critics quickly dubbed the proposed system 'BritCard.' The government argued that it would help address illegal working and immigration abuse while modernising Britain's outdated approach to identity verification. The cards would be mandatory for anyone seeking employment and would initially be digital, stored on smartphones, similar to the NHS app, or on contactless payment cards. Employers would be required to verify workers' identity and right-to-work status through the government's system, with non-compliance resulting in significant fines. The implementation was set to begin immediately, with a full rollout planned by the end of the current Parliament in 2029. Proponents of the system argue that it could significantly reduce illegal working, improve immigration enforcement, and streamline the employment process for both employers and employees.

While the rationale sounded superficially reasonable, illegal working is indeed a genuine problem that undermines legitimate businesses and exploits vulnerable workers, and immigration enforcement requires modern tools. Britain's historical context is unique. The British public has long been deeply suspicious of identity cards, viewing them as foreign impositions that are at odds with British traditions of liberty and privacy. The memory of wartime identity cards, which were not abolished until 1952, remains a part of the national consciousness. More recently, Tony Blair's attempt to introduce ID cards through the Identity Cards Act 2006 has served as a cautionary tale about governmental overreach and the limits of technocratic ambition. This historical context underscores the deep-rooted nature of the public's suspicion and its potential impact on the acceptance of the proposed digital ID system.

Blair's ID card scheme was launched with similar rhetoric about modernisation and security. The cards were intended to help prevent terrorism, reduce identity fraud, improve public service delivery, and generally make Britain more efficient and secure. However, practical problems quickly arose. Cost estimates soared from £3 billion to over £5 billion, the technology proved to be more complex than anticipated, and privacy campaigners raised alarms about the creation of a vast government database containing biometric information on every citizen. Civil liberties groups warned about 'function creep,' the inevitable expansion of a system initially designed for limited purposes. These concerns highlight the potential risks and drawbacks of a digital ID system, underscoring the need for caution and thorough consideration before its implementation.

By the time the Coalition government took power in 2010, public opposition to ID cards had become so strong that scrapping them was one of their first priorities. The Identity Documents Act 2010 repealed Blair's legislation, dismantled the ID card database, and refunded fees to the few thousand individuals who had voluntarily obtained cards. This costly and contentious experiment was relegated to history, serving as a poignant reminder of the consequences that arise when governments disregard public opinion and proceed with schemes that seem rational on paper but are deeply unpopular in practice.

Now, fifteen years later, Keir Starmer proposed reviving the idea. The government insisted that the BritCard would not be identical to Blair's scheme. It would be digital-first, cheaper to implement, and more narrowly focused on employment verification, rather than serving as a universal ID card. This means that the card would be used to verify a person's identity and eligibility to work, potentially streamlining the hiring process and reducing instances of illegal employment. However, critics argued that these distinctions were merely semantic. A mandatory identity card system was still a mandatory identity card system, regardless of whether it existed on a phone or in a wallet. The principle remained the same, and many believed it to be fundamentally flawed.

The public reaction was immediate and overwhelming. A parliamentary petition titled "Do Not Introduce Digital ID Cards," created months earlier by Maxim Sutcliff and having previously garnered modest support, suddenly gained traction. The parliamentary petition system allows citizens to voice their concerns and influence government policy by collecting signatures in support of a particular cause. Within 24 hours of the announcement, it collected 400,000 signatures. Within 48 hours, that number had risen to 800,000. By the end of the first week, 1.6 million people had signed. The numbers continued to climb relentlessly: 1.8 million, 2 million, 2.2 million, making it one of the fastest-growing petitions in the history of the parliamentary petition system. By the time Labour MPs began arriving in Liverpool for the conference, the petition had exceeded 2.4 million signatures, demonstrating a level of public opposition that could not be ignored or dismissed as fringe activism.

The petition's growth reflected a genuine anxiety that transcended traditional political divides. Conservative voters who valued liberty and limited government signed alongside Labour supporters who felt betrayed by a government they had elected to protect civil liberties. Liberal Democrats, Greens, and even some Reform UK supporters found common ground in opposing what they perceived as an authoritarian power grab. The coalition against the BritCard was ideologically diverse but politically powerful, united by a shared suspicion of state surveillance and distrust of governmental competence.

Civil liberties groups mobilised with remarkable speed and coordination, suggesting they had been preparing for this fight. Big Brother Watch, Liberty, Privacy International, and other organisations issued a joint statement condemning the proposal as "wholly un-British" and warning about the risks of normalising surveillance. Rebecca Vincent, interim director of Big Brother Watch, was particularly scathing, calling the scheme "uniquely harmful to privacy, equality, and civil liberties."

Silkie Carlo, director of Big Brother Watch, had warned earlier in the summer about exactly this scenario: "This government promised to protect our freedoms and rebuild trust. Instead, they're building the architecture of a surveillance state. Digital ID cards will track where we work, what we purchase, and how we interact with society. This is not about immigration; it is about control."

Liberty added its voice to the chorus of opposition, with legal officer Jasleen Chaggar telling journalists, "We all have something to fear from mandatory digital ID systems that require us to surrender our privacy rights to access public services to which we are entitled. A database that connects all our government records and logs our interactions using a single unique identifier would be a civil liberties nightmare, leaving us exposed to mass surveillance, tracking and profiling, security breaches, and data theft."

The legal community raised concerns about discrimination and human rights. Employment lawyers warned that the system would create new barriers for vulnerable workers, particularly those without stable housing or reliable access to technology.

Immigration lawyers have underscored that the individuals most likely to be targeted by enforcement are often those least equipped to navigate complex bureaucratic systems. Human rights organisations have pointed out that mandatory ID schemes in other countries have historically been used to discriminate against minorities and track political dissidents, potentially leading to severe violations of civil liberties.

The technology sector has expressed scepticism about the government's ability to implement such a system securely. Cybersecurity experts have cited a long history of government IT projects that have exceeded budgets, been delivered late, and failed to function as intended. Examples include the NHS patient records system, the rollout of Universal Credit, and the contact tracing app during the COVID-19 pandemic. The British government has demonstrated a consistent record of technological incompetence. Why would the BritCard initiative be any different?

The historical parallels are striking. Comparisons to Blair's failed scheme have appeared in every news article, opinion piece, and parliamentary debate. Keir Starmer, who served as Director of Public Prosecutions under Blair's government, has been accused of not learning from the mistakes of that era. The government's assertion that BritCard would be different rang hollow to anyone who remembers the promises made about the 2006 scheme. At that time, we were assured that costs would be controlled, privacy would be protected, and the system would be limited in scope. None of those promises was fulfilled. Why should anyone believe similar assurances now?

The Blair connection runs deeper than mere policy parallels. The think tank that developed the BritCard proposal is Labour Together, the same organisation at the centre of a donations scandal. This group published a detailed 30-page report in June 2025 advocating for the scheme. The report argued, "The Labour Government has the opportunity to build a new piece of civic infrastructure, something that would become a familiar feature of daily life for everyone in the country." Morgan Wild, Labour Together's chief policy adviser, claimed, "Through a national effort to provide everyone with proof of their right to be here, BritCard can stop [Windrush-style injustices] from ever happening again."

However, Labour Together's credibility is now in shambles. How can the public trust a policy proposal from an organisation that failed to properly declare three-quarters of a million pounds in donations? The symbolism of this situation is damning. The same group that couldn't adhere to basic electoral law is now designing a system to monitor every working person in Britain.

Protests erupted outside Downing Street within days of the announcement, underscoring the strength of public opposition to the BritCard scheme. Although these demonstrations were smaller than those against Trump's visit, they were more sustained, with activists maintaining a continuous presence that served as a powerful visual reminder of public dissent. Protesters held placards reading "No to ID Cards," "Protect Privacy," and "This Is Not China." They chanted slogans that combined civil liberties rhetoric with personal concerns: "Our data, our choice!" and "Big Brother Starmer, we won't obey!"

Media coverage of the protests was extensive, reflecting the breadth of the issue and the diversity of perspectives. Sky News and Channel 4 emphasised the breadth of opposition, interviewing everyone from Conservative MPs to left-wing activists to ordinary citizens who had never previously engaged in political activism. The Guardian ran features on the history of British resistance to identity cards, placing the current controversy within a broader tradition of defending privacy and limiting state power. The BBC and The Times framed the story more cautiously, giving government ministers space to protect the policy while also covering the opposition, providing a comprehensive view of the issue.

Culture Secretary Lisa Nandy became the government's primary spokesperson for the policy, appearing in numerous interviews to advocate for BritCard. Her appearances revealed the difficulty of promoting a fundamentally unpopular policy to a sceptical public. Speaking to LBC's Nick Ferrari, she dismissed concerns that ID cards could be used to restrict access to public services, stating, "It's only for employment that you'll be required to produce it. It will definitely not be the case that elderly or retired people, for example, will need one to get an NHS appointment or pension entitlement."

On GB News, Nandy confirmed that "all British adults will have a digital ID by the end of this Parliament, but it's not like an ID card scheme where you would be required to carry it around and show it to access services." She emphasised the practical reasons for the initiative: "The problem with national insurance numbers is that they're not linked to anything else. They're not linked, for example, to photo ID. So you can't verify that the person in front of you is actually the one whose national insurance number you're looking at, and we've seen a real rise in identity theft." The digital ID, on the other hand, could provide a more secure and efficient way to verify one's identity, potentially reducing instances of identity theft and fraud.

However, when pressed for details, the government's position appeared contradictory. Nandy told Sky News that the system would be both mandatory and voluntary: "The plan is to ensure that everybody has it, but you can choose whether you use it." She assured BBC Breakfast: "We're not envisioning for a moment that this will be mandatory," even as Starmer announced it would be required for employment. The government's stance is that while the digital ID will be available to all, its use may be voluntary in some contexts and mandatory in others, such as employment. The contradictions were significant. If you couldn't work without it, how could it be considered voluntary?

Home Secretary Shabana Mahmood, who had replaced Yvette Cooper in the September cabinet reshuffle, voiced her support for the initiative. Mahmood has long favoured ID cards, having backed Blair's scheme when she first entered Parliament. "My long-term personal political view has always been in favour of ID cards," she told journalists at a Five Eyes intelligence alliance meeting. "In fact, I supported the last Labour government's introduction of ID cards. The first bill I spoke on in Parliament was the ID cards bill that the then Conservative Lib Dem coalition scrapped."

The Conservative opposition, still establishing itself under Kemi Badenoch's leadership, found that opposing BritCard provided them with an opportunity to credibly claim to be defending British liberty against Labour's alleged authoritarianism. Badenoch branded the proposal a "desperate gimmick" that would do "nothing to stop the boats." Writing on social media, she stated: "Conservatives will oppose any push by this organisation or the government to impose mandatory ID cards on law-abiding citizens. There are arguments for and against digital ID; many people already use digital identities for banking and online services. We're certainly not opposed to that. But mandating ID is a different matter altogether."

The Liberal Democrats, often dismissed as irrelevant in British politics, found themselves with a popular cause that resonated with their traditional strengths. Ed Davey, whose party had been part of the coalition that scrapped Blair's ID cards, could legitimately claim to be consistent on the issue. Victoria Collins, the party's technology and science spokesperson, declared: "We cannot support a mandatory digital ID where people are forced to turn over their private data just to go about their daily lives. People shouldn't be turned into criminals simply because they can't have a digital ID or choose not to. This will be especially concerning for millions of older individuals, those living in poverty, and disabled people, who are more likely to be digitally excluded." The digital ID scheme could potentially exacerbate digital exclusion and privacy concerns, particularly for vulnerable groups.

Even Reform UK, whose populist nationalism might have led one to expect support for stronger immigration enforcement, found ways to oppose the scheme. Nigel Farage, always opportunistic in his politics, framed BritCard as evidence that the establishment parties were all the same, committed to expanding state power and restricting individual freedom. "I am firmly opposed to Keir Starmer's digital ID cards," he wrote on social media. "It will make no difference to illegal immigration, but it will be used to control and penalise the rest of us. They want to turn Britain into a digital prison."

The devolved nations voiced their opposition to the proposed BritCard. Scottish First Minister John Swinney objected to what he perceived as Westminster's attempt to impose a British identity on Scots. "I am opposed to mandatory digital ID; people should be able to go about their daily lives without such infringements," he stated. "Furthermore, by referring to it as BritCard, the Prime Minister appears to be trying to force every Scot to declare themselves as British. I am a Scot." Plaid Cymru's Westminster leader, Liz Saville Roberts, echoed this sentiment, saying, "Most people in Wales identify as Welsh only; a 'BritCard' would go down like a lead balloon here." Northern Ireland's First Minister, Michelle O'Neill of Sinn Féin, called the proposal "ludicrous and ill-thought-out."

The public debates surrounding BritCard have highlighted significant concerns about the future of British society. These concerns extend beyond the specific policy, encompassing worries about surveillance capitalism, data breaches, algorithmic discrimination, and the gradual erosion of privacy in an era of pervasive digital tracking. The ID card controversy has become a window through which larger questions about the direction of Britain and citizens' control over this transformation are being examined.

Ordinary individuals interviewed by journalists have shared concerns that reflect a mix of principled objections and practical worries. A nurse in Manchester, for instance, expressed concern about how the system would impact homeless patients she treated, whose chaotic lives made it difficult to maintain any form of identification. A small business owner in Cornwall complained about being forced to act as an immigration enforcement officer, facing fines if he incorrectly checked his employees' papers. A university student in Edinburgh raised the issue of 'surveillance creep,' noting how systems initially introduced for one purpose often expand to serve others. A retired teacher in Wales simply stated that she didn't trust the government with that much personal information. These individual stories bring to life the real-world implications of the BritCard.

The controversy took a political turn when opposition researchers uncovered earlier statements from Keir Starmer criticising aspects of surveillance and state power. In 2010, as Director of Public Prosecutions, he wrote an article for the Guardian defending privacy rights and warning against excessive data retention. In 2015, as a backbench MP, he questioned government proposals for expanded surveillance powers. Now, as Prime Minister, he was advocating a policy that seemed to contradict those earlier positions. The apparent hypocrisy proved politically damaging and personally revealing, suggesting that Starmer's principles shifted depending on whether he was in opposition or in power.

As opposition to the BritCard grew, the government's defence became more pronounced. Ministers argued that other European countries had identity cards without becoming police states, pointing to Estonia's successful e-ID system as a model. They emphasised that the system would cost an estimated £400 million to build, with just £10 million per year to operate, significantly less than Blair's failed scheme. However, each clarification appeared to introduce new problems. If the system was modelled on European counterparts, why had their issues, such as discrimination, privacy violations, and technical failures, not been addressed in the British design? If costs were so low, why should anyone trust these estimates, given the government's past record on IT projects?

According to anonymous briefings to journalists, the government is divided on how to proceed with the BritCard. Some ministers are urging a push ahead, arguing that backing down would make Labour look weak and indecisive. Others are advocating for a tactical retreat, recognising that the political costs of continuing outweigh any potential benefits. Starmer, characteristically, seems paralysed by indecision, unable to fully commit to the policy while also unwilling to abandon it. The result is an ineffective approach: a controversial proposal that has unified opposition without generating substantial support. This internal division within the government provides insight into the political dynamics surrounding the BritCard.

The two controversies, the admin error leak and the BritCard announcement, became intertwined in the public consciousness. Together, they painted a picture of a government that was both incompetent and authoritarian, unable to follow basic rules while determined to impose new restrictions on citizens. The symbolism was devastating. Here was Labour, elected to restore integrity to British politics, caught treating electoral law violations as mere paperwork errors. Here was Labour, supposedly defending civil liberties against Conservative attacks, introducing a surveillance system that civil liberties groups condemned. The contradictions were too glaring to ignore and too fundamental to explain away.

On social media, the reaction was fierce. Twitter was flooded with mockery and outrage. Memes comparing Starmer to Big Brother proliferated, while screenshots of the Shamash email circulated endlessly, often annotated with sarcastic commentary. The petition link was shared tens of thousands of times. Conservative MPs posted clips of Starmer's past speeches about civil liberties alongside news coverage of the BritCard announcement, allowing the hypocrisy to speak for itself. Even Labour activists, who typically support the party, expressed dismay, their tweets shifting between disappointment and growing anger.

"This is not what we voted for," wrote a prominent Labour activist with over 50,000 followers. "We voted for change, for integrity, for protecting civil liberties. Instead, we get the same old authoritarian New Labour playbook. I'm furious." This sentiment was echoed across the political spectrum, uniting left-wing campaigners and libertarian conservatives alike in their opposition to what they perceived as governmental overreach. The disappointment was palpable, a stark contrast to the hope and optimism that had accompanied Labour's election.

As September drew to a close and Labour MPs prepared to head to Liverpool for the party conference, the mood was grim. The conference was meant to be an opportunity to showcase unity, competence, and purpose. Instead, the party arrived defending its chief of staff against accusations of regulatory violations and its Home Secretary against charges of authoritarianism. The narrative of competent government that Starmer desperately needed to establish was being systematically undermined by self-inflicted wounds that demonstrated a government out of touch with its own values and public opinion.

Protests outside Downing Street continued, maintained by a rotating cast of activists determined to keep the issue prominent. The petition continued to grow, nearing 2.5 million signatures and triggering an automatic parliamentary debate. Civil liberties groups announced plans for legal challenges if the BritCard legislation were to proceed. Opposition parties coordinated their attacks, sensing vulnerability. Even media outlets traditionally sympathetic to Labour began running more critical coverage. A palpable sense of a government in crisis emerged, barely fifteen months into its term, creating a sense of urgency and concern among the public.

The twin scandals struck at the very heart of Starmer's promise of integrity. The admin error story suggested that rules were treated as mere suggestions when they became inconvenient. Meanwhile, the BritCard controversy demonstrated a willingness to sacrifice liberty for the appearance of control. Together, they illustrated a government that had learned all the wrong lessons from Blair's era: the technocratic hubris, the disregard for civil liberties, and the assumption that voters would accept objectionable policies if they were marketed correctly.

The historical parallels were also hard to ignore: Blair's ID cards, his approach to immigration, and his faith in technology and modernisation over tradition and liberty. The organisational connections of Labour Together, serving as a bridge between the donations scandal and the surveillance policy, were striking. Labour in 2025 increasingly resembled Labour in 2006, repeating mistakes that had led to the party's loss of public trust and electoral defeat. The difference this time was that the decline was happening much more quickly, compressed into months rather than years.

As backbench Labour MPs arrived in Liverpool, they could feel the shift in public mood. Conversations on doorsteps had already become challenging during the summer. The freebies scandal had damaged the party's reputation, and the cuts to winter fuel payments had angered traditional supporters. However, this situation felt different. The combination of the McSweeney revelations and the BritCard announcement had crystallised a narrative: Labour had become what it claimed to oppose. The erosion of public trust was undeniable, a stark reminder of the gravity of the situation.

In constituency offices across the country, Labour MPs reported unprecedented hostility from their constituents. Voters who had supported Labour in July 2024 were now furious, feeling betrayed. "You said you'd be different," one constituent told their MP during a heated meeting. "You promised to restore trust. Instead, you're tracking us like criminals while your own staff can't even follow donation rules." The MP had no satisfactory response. None of them did.

By late September, as delegates began arriving in Liverpool for what would become one of the most contentious Labour conferences in recent memory, the party's position had deteriorated dramatically from the optimism of July 2024. The landslide victory that had seemed to herald a generation of Labour dominance now appeared to be a historical accident, a moment when voters, exhausted by Conservative chaos, were willing to try anything different. That moment had passed, and the willingness to give Labour the benefit of the doubt had evaporated. Polling numbers reflected a government that had lost public confidence remarkably quickly.

The controversies surrounding admin errors and BritCard would not be the only items on the conference agenda, but they would dominate the atmosphere. MPs arriving in Liverpool understood they would face hostile local media, angry constituency activists, and sceptical voters. The government, which had promised integrity, appeared evasive, and the party, which had vowed to respect civil liberties, seemed authoritarian. The leader who had pledged to competence looked overwhelmed. The gap between promise and performance, rhetoric and reality, between what Labour had said it would be and what it had become, was too wide to bridge with improved communication or tactical adjustments.

As the eve of the conference approached, Labour looked less like a party of principle and more like one trapped in the shadows of Blairite mistakes, doomed to repeat errors rather than learn from them. The forensic barrister who had pledged to restore trust in British politics had overseen the introduction of an identity card scheme that united opposition across the political spectrum. The lawyer known for respecting rules had employed a chief of staff who advised treating regulatory violations as mere administrative errors. The leader who had promised change had delivered continuity with the worst aspects of New Labour: authoritarianism, technocratic arrogance, and a willingness to sacrifice principle for the sake of appearing rigid.

As rain began to fall on Liverpool, delegates attending the conference recognised that they faced more than challenging politics or difficult media coverage. They faced a crisis of identity and purpose that struck at the heart of what the Labour Party was supposed to represent. The controversies surrounding administrative errors and BritCard were not isolated incidents, but symptoms of a deeper malaise: a government that had lost its moral compass barely a year after taking office. Whether Labour could find its way back to the principles that had once defined it, or whether the party would continue drifting further from its roots, remained an open question as the conference began.

Chapter 16
The Liverpool Conference

The rain arrived just when Liverpool needed sunshine. As delegates
streamed into the ACC Convention Centre on the morning of Sunday, 28
September 2025, the grey skies and persistent drizzle mirrored the
Labour Party's political fortunes. This was supposed to be a triumph, the
first conference in government since 2009, celebrating the landslide
victory that had ended fourteen years of Conservative rule. Instead, it felt
like a wake.

The polling numbers told a brutal story, marking a historic moment.
Ipsos reported that Reform UK was leading Labour by 12 points, 34 per
cent to 22 per cent, with Labour's vote share at its lowest since June
2009. The Conservatives, sitting at 14 percent, were also experiencing
historic lows, but this offered little consolation for a government barely
fifteen months old. Keir Starmer's personal satisfaction ratings had
plummeted to the lowest for any Prime Minister polled by Ipsos since the
question was first asked in 1977.

These numbers were not mere abstractions; they represented real
anger, disappointment, and betrayal felt by voters who had given Labour
a chance and now regretted it. As MPs collected their passes and
navigated through security, they carried the weight of disappointing
constituency surgeries, hostile doorstep conversations, and a growing
sense that something fundamental had gone wrong.

Opening Salvos

The conference opened with the traditional rituals, but the
atmosphere was tense. Outside the venue, hard-right demonstrators,
known for their anti-immigration and anti-EU stance, welcomed
delegates, serving as a visible reminder of the political threat gaining
momentum. Inside, Starmer portrayed his party as being in 'the fight of
our lives' against Nigel Farage's politically ascendant Reform UK,
suggesting that Farage intended to 'tear apart' the tolerant version of
Britain that Starmer advocated.

However, the fight was not just outside the party; Labour was also
battling internal divisions, torn between differing visions of its identity
and principles. The backbenchers arrived in Liverpool with pressing

questions that demanded answers: Why had BritCard, a controversial policy on immigration and citizenship, been announced when civil liberties groups were united in opposition? Why were electoral law violations, which had led to significant fines and public scrutiny, being dismissed as administrative errors? And why did competence, which was the cornerstone of Starmer's appeal, seem so elusive?

The McSweeney Shadow

The Morgan McSweeney donations scandal cast a long shadow over the conference, resembling a thick fog. Just days before delegates arrived in Liverpool, leaked emails revealed that McSweeney, Starmer's powerful chief of staff, had been advised by Labour's lawyer, Gerald Shamash, to label £740,000 in undeclared donations to Labour Together as an "admin error."

The emails brought to light some uncomfortable truths. Shamash had written to McSweeney, acknowledging that there was "no easy way" to explain the failure to disclose the donations, especially since the Electoral Commission had explicitly informed McSweeney in 2017 that Labour Together was required to declare any donation exceeding £7,500. The lawyer suggested that it might be "perhaps best" to attribute the issue to an administrative failure.

Conservative Party chair Kevin Hollinrake described it as a "secret slush fund to install Starmer as leader." On September 26, the Electoral Commission announced it would not reopen the investigation, but the damage had already been done. The scandal reinforced the perception that Labour's promises of integrity and transparency were empty and that the new government operated under the same murky rules as the previous one.

During the conference, MPs were careful not to publicly criticise McSweeney. His reputation for ruthlessness was well-established, and he had an extensive network of loyalists. However, in private conversations, the questions piled up. How could Starmer claim to represent a break from the past when his closest aide had overseen such grave violations of electoral law? Why was "admin error" deemed acceptable for Labour, while it would never have been tolerated by the Conservatives?

The scandal was particularly distressing because Labour Together had played a crucial role in Starmer's rise to power. The think tank, misleadingly named to suggest broad party unity, was explicitly designed to steer Labour away from "the hard left" and secure Starmer's position in Downing Street. More than £100,000 had flowed to the organisation while McSweeney was managing Starmer's leadership campaign in 2020. The connections among factional disputes, hidden money, and political ascension were impossible to overlook.

"It stinks," one shadow minister lamented to colleagues over drinks. "We're supposed to be better than this. We're supposed to be the good guys. And our chief of staff is caught red-handed hiding three-quarters of a million pounds? How do I go back to my constituency and defend that?"

The Housing Debacle

The housing controversy erupted on Saturday, September 27, when Housing Secretary Steve Reed appeared on GB News to promote Labour's "build, baby, build" agenda, sporting one of the red baseball caps that had become conference merchandise. The slogan was prominently displayed across the conference venue, featured on promotional materials, and transformed into a rallying cry for delegates. However, the branding could not conceal the substantive problems that became painfully evident during the live interview.

When presenter Camilla Tominey asked Reed how many homes had been built since Labour assumed power 14 months earlier, he could not provide an answer. Pressed for specifics, he replied, "I can't give you an exact figure. I know it's shallow; I'm appalled by it as well, but the fact is, the Conservatives didn't get the applications through." When Tominey continued to press him, Reed snapped, "I am not Wikipedia. Being Housing Secretary doesn't mean I know every single statistic related to the entire housing sector."

The actual figure was 117,390 homes. At that rate, as Tominey pointed out, it would take 13 years to meet the government's target of 1.5 million homes by the end of Parliament. Reed's inability to share such a fundamental statistic became immediate fodder for social media mockery and attacks from the opposition. Here was Labour's Housing Secretary, at the party's own conference, unable to answer the most fundamental question about his portfolio.

The clip spread rapidly across Twitter and news broadcasts. Conservative accounts relentlessly amplified it, and even sympathetic commentators struggled to defend his performance. One Labour MP, watching from the conference floor, remarked to a colleague, "We look like amateurs. How does the Housing Secretary not know how many houses we've built? It's literally his job."

The "build, baby, build" caps ultimately became a symbol of

Labour's problems: slick branding without substance, confident slogans without delivery. The gap between rhetoric and reality was starkly illustrated in a single devastating interview. Delegates who had proudly worn the caps quietly removed them, shoving them into bags or abandoning them on tables at fringe events.

The Sadiq Khan Situation

The Sadiq Khan situation injected a layer of complexity into the conference atmosphere. Just days before the conference, on September 24, Donald Trump's address to the United Nations General Assembly, where he labelled the London Mayor as a 'terrible mayor' and falsely accused London of wanting 'to go to Sharia law,' sparked a strong response from Khan. He swiftly countered Trump's remarks, branding him as 'racist, sexist, misogynistic, and Islamophobic,' and implying that the president seemed to be 'living rent-free inside Donald Trump's head.'

This exchange put Labour in a difficult position. Khan was defending the party's values and standing up against xenophobia and Islamophobia from a foreign leader. However, Starmer, eager to maintain positive relations with Washington amid trade negotiations, took a notably restrained approach. When asked about Trump's remarks, Starmer stated he was "indifferent" to the president's comments and had "more important things to worry about."

Labour MPs, in a display of courage and unity, unequivocally condemned Trump's attack. Rosena Allin-Khan, MP for Tooting, boldly called for the US ambassador to be summoned and confronted about Trump's 'rampant Islamophobia.' Health Secretary Wes Streeting, in a robust social media defence, asserted, 'Sadiq Khan is not trying to impose Sharia Law on London. This is a Mayor who marches with Pride, who stands up for diverse backgrounds and opinions, and who focuses on improving our transport, air quality, streets, safety, choices, and opportunities. I'm proud he's our Mayor.'

The contrast between the passionate response from the backbench MPs and Starmer's tepid reaction highlighted a deeper issue. The party's commitment to diversity and tolerance seemed negotiable when geopolitical convenience dictated it. Although Khan did not deliver a major speech at the conference, his presence loomed over the proceedings, reminding everyone of the battles Labour should be fighting and the principles it should be defending.

In fringe events and corridor conversations, questions lingered: When would Labour stand up for its own? When would principles matter more than political expediency? If the party couldn't defend its own Mayor against racist attacks, what did it stand for?

The Burnham Phenomenon

The Andy Burnham phenomenon dominated the conference in ways the leadership had not anticipated. As the Mayor of Greater Manchester and not an MP, Burnham could not formally challenge for the leadership and had intentionally limited his conference appearances. However, this did not diminish the excitement around him. Whenever Burnham spoke, crowds gathered, drawn by the promise of an alternative vision and a different approach to Labour politics.

During a fringe event on electoral reform, Burnham criticised the "climate of fear" within the Labour Party, where members were "suspended for liking a tweet by another political party" or where "a Member of Parliament loses the whip for trying to protect disability benefits." He asked, "How can you have an open debate about all of those things if there's too much fear within our party and the way it is being run?" His words elicited applause. "There's nothing more unstoppable than an idea whose time has come," Burnham declared, and delegates believed him.

Burnham's unambiguous stance on the UK's potential re-entry into the European Union was another highlight. He openly expressed his desire for the UK to rejoin the EU, stating, 'I'm going to be honest. I want to rejoin. I hope so. I see this country rejoin the European Union in my lifetime. I believe in unions of all kinds.' This direct statement contrasted with the cautious approach of Starmer and struck a chord with the delegates.

Burnham also sparked a crucial discussion about Labour's direction, highlighting the need for unity within the Labour family to tackle the challenges they faced. 'I've been accused of many things in the past week – I've done nothing more than launch a debate,' he stated. 'What I would say to those who think I'm speaking out purely for my own ambition is that I'm speaking for the thousands of councillors worried about going to those doorsteps next May, speaking for the members of the Senedd working hard to keep Wales Labour, and for members of the Scottish Parliament who want a stronger narrative about Labour.'

Burnham, while careful not to overstep, sparked palpable anticipation about his potential return to Parliament. When directly asked about his leadership ambitions, he replied, 'I can't launch a leadership campaign. I'm not in Parliament.' Despite this technical impossibility, speculation continued. Polls suggested he could significantly boost Labour's vote share. MPs whispered about getting him back into Westminster through a by-election, leaving the prospect unspoken but palpable.

Energy Secretary Ed Miliband, when asked about Burnham, cautiously expressed his support: "I am very clear about this. Keir is my friend, my long-standing friend, and I'm Keir's guy, right? I'm for Keir. So if you ask me a leadership question, I'm not interested." However, he added, "We are best when we're a broad church, and we utilise talent from all across the Labour Party."

The Two-Child Benefit Cap Battle

The controversy surrounding the two-child benefit cap highlighted significant internal divisions within the Labour Party and demonstrated the leadership's determination to suppress dissent. A motion to abolish the cap, which was supported by 84 percent of Labour members, according to Survation polling commissioned by the Mainstream group, was blocked from discussion through the conference's priorities ballot process.

Though the procedure was technical, the implications were clear: the leadership would use every tool available to prevent embarrassing votes, even when the policy in question was deeply unpopular among the membership and increasingly difficult to defend politically. The cap forced children into poverty, subjected families to hardship, and violated Labour's stated commitment to social justice. Yet, the conference would not even entertain a discussion about it.

Luke Hurst, the national coordinator of Mainstream, stated, "This outcome shows one thing: the party machine is wildly out of step with the Mainstream of the Labour Party. With each passing day, the continuation of the two-child limit means children are going hungry."

However, dynamics at the conference were shifting as delegates gathered. Education Secretary Bridget Phillipson, who was running for deputy leader, told a fringe meeting that scrapping the cap was "on the table" and acknowledged evidence that the policy was pushing children into poverty. This was the most unambiguous indication yet that the government might reverse its stance not out of conviction, but out of political necessity.

The cynicism surrounding this situation was palpable. If the policy was indeed wrong, why not change it now? Why wait until the political pressure becomes unbearable? Rumours circulating in bars and corridors suggested that Starmer's team governed based on focus groups and opinion polls rather than principles. They would defend the indefensible until it became politically untenable, then claim credit for listening and changing course.

For many delegates, especially younger members and activists who had joined during the Corbyn years, the fight against the benefit cap crystallised their frustrations. This was not the Labour Party they had signed up for; this was not the transformative politics they believed in. The party's machinery's determination to silence debate and prevent discussions on policies affecting the most vulnerable felt like a betrayal of everything Labour was supposed to stand for.

The Palestine Divisions

The motions regarding Palestine ignited bitter conflict and exposed fault lines that threatened to divide the party. Two competing emergency motions were brought to the floor on Tuesday morning, September 30, both calling for action to address the humanitarian crisis in Gaza. Motion 2, proposed by UNISON and seconded by ASLEF, called for a complete suspension of arms sales to Israel and explicitly described Israel's actions as genocide. Conversely, Motion 1 proposed a moratorium on arms sales "that could be used in the conflict" and did not make any allegations of genocide.

The debates were intense and emotional. South Cotswolds CLP delegate Josh Littler-Jennings, supporting Motion 1, emphasised that the only way to ensure peace was to "deliver a two-state solution." Councillor Jennifer Hemingway of Smethwick CLP stated, "Language matters. The October 7 atrocities were the worst terrorist attack in Israel's history. Hamas must never play a part in a future Palestine, and Motion 2 fails to recognise this."

However, Motion 2 received overwhelming support from delegates and trade union affiliates. It passed decisively, while Motion 1 was voted down as the weight of the affiliate vote led to its defeat. This result represented a clear rejection of the leadership's preferred position and a strong statement about where the party membership stood on the Israel-Palestine issue.

Sasha Das Gupta, Co-Chair of Momentum, celebrated the outcome: "Labour Conference voting for the government to employ all means to end Israel's genocide is a significant achievement, marking a watershed moment in the Party since Israel began its acts in Gaza."

In contrast, a spokesperson for Labour Friends of Israel responded with anger: "As we approach the second anniversary of the worst massacre of Jews since the Holocaust, it is shameful, shocking, and inexplicable for the conference to have passed a motion, proposed by trade unions, about the tragic conflict in Gaza that makes no reference to the October 7 Hamas atrocities that sparked it. This motion does absolutely nothing to further the Labour government's aims of ending the war, releasing the hostages, and creating a path to a two-state solution."

The Palestine Solidarity Campaign accused the Labour leadership of attempting to "silence their own members" by limiting the number of speakers in favour of Motion 2. Procedural complaints added to the sense that the party apparatus was working against its own membership, manipulating debate structures to minimise embarrassment even when the votes were not in doubt.

The debates revealed a party deeply divided not just on policy, but on fundamental questions of how to discuss these policies. Every motion, every speech, and every procedural vote became a proxy battle concerning larger questions about Labour's identity and direction.

Trade Union Tensions

The relationship between the Labour Party and its trade union base, which has traditionally served as a source of strength and funding, is becoming increasingly strained. Sharon Graham, the outspoken General Secretary of Unite the Union, arrived at the conference ready for confrontation. Unite, with over a million members, has historically been Labour's most reliable financial backer and organisational powerhouse. However, Graham's patience with Starmer's government is wearing thin.

In interviews at the conference, Graham was candid about her frustrations. Speaking with Sky News's Trevor Phillips, she stated, "Workers are scratching their heads. I'm scratching my head, let alone anybody else, in terms of what choices Labour is making." She added, "People are starting to leave Labour in droves. Why would they pick the pockets of pensioners and not introduce a wealth tax? Labour is not doing what it says on the tin."

Graham's criticisms extended beyond specific policies to question whether Unite's affiliation with Labour could still be justified. "It's getting harder to justify that affiliation," she told Lewis Goodall in another interview. This threat was not to be taken lightly; just months earlier, in July 2025, Unite's policy conference had voted to suspend Angela Rayner's membership and to "re-examine" the union's funding of the Labour Party, with only a handful of delegates opposing the motion.

The backdrop to Graham's discontent is significant. Unite has been crucial to Labour's electoral successes, providing financial resources, volunteer activists, and organisational infrastructure. While the union has delivered for Labour, Graham believes Labour has not delivered for workers. The government's refusal to repeal anti-strike laws, its hesitation on workers' rights, and its reluctance to address wealth inequality suggest a party that has forgotten its roots.

Graham did give a fringe speech advocating for a wealth tax, a passionate address that received sustained applause from delegates eager for redistributive policies. However, this applause did not translate into government action. Rachel Reeves, the iron-fisted Chancellor committed to fiscal discipline, showed no interest in wealth taxes. The gap between what the unions demand and what the government is willing to provide is widening, not closing.

While Unite is the most vocal, it is not alone in its frustrations. Other unions, such as the GMB and Prospect, also have their own grievances and face pressures from their memberships. The trade union movement, once Labour's unshakeable foundation, is now reconsidering its relationship with a party that seems increasingly indifferent to the interests of workers.

The financial implications of Unite's potential disaffiliation are staggering. Unite contributes £1.4 million annually in affiliation fees, a significant sum that Labour can scarcely afford to lose. Internal party documents reveal that Labour is in a 'difficult financial position,' operating under a 'recovery plan' aimed at achieving a 'planned but manageable deficit.' It estimates it needs at least £4 million to adequately resource the 2026 elections.'

If Unite were to disaffiliate, a scenario Graham's comments suggest is increasingly plausible, it could trigger a domino effect. Other unions might follow suit, posing a serious threat to the very essence of Labour as a party intrinsically linked to the trade union movement. With Reform UK gaining ground in working-class communities, Labour can hardly afford to alienate its traditional base.

Youth and Activist Discontent

The conference was marked by a noticeable absence: the energy and enthusiasm of younger members and activists. During the Corbyn years, the event had buzzed with the excitement of young people who believed they could change the world. Momentum, the grassroots organisation created to support Corbyn, had mobilised thousands of activists, generating a festival atmosphere that mixed policy debate with genuine joy.

This energy was largely missing in Liverpool. While Momentum was still active, organising fringe events and supporting candidates for internal party positions, its presence felt diminished, with membership having dropped from a peak of 40,000 to somewhere between 20,000 and 30,000. The young activists who remained were frustrated and disillusioned.

Momentum's conference priorities, such as challenging leadership on child poverty, condemning atrocities in Gaza, and opposing anti-migrant rhetoric, found support among delegates but not from the platform. The gap between grassroots activism and party leadership had never been wider. Many young members felt their voices were systematically ignored, and their concerns were dismissed as naive idealism or factional troublemaking. This disconnect was exacerbated by the party's shift in focus from issues that resonated with the youth, such as climate justice and workers' rights, to more traditional political topics.

A 24-year-old delegate from Manchester, who joined Labour during Corbyn's 2015 leadership campaign, captured the mood: "I used to bring friends to conference. We'd stay up all night debating policy, planning campaigns, and feeling like we were part of something bigger. Now? Most of my friends have left the party. The ones who stayed do so out of stubbornness, not hope. We're here because we refuse to abandon Labour to the careerists, but we're not having fun anymore."

The contrast with the conferences in 2017 or 2019 was stark. Back then, young members filled fringe events focusing on climate justice, workers' rights, and democratic socialism. They sang "Oh, Jeremy Corbyn" with genuine affection, believing that another world was possible and that Labour could be a vehicle for transformative change. The absence of this fervour in the recent conference was palpable, leaving a void in the once-vibrant energy and enthusiasm.

Now, those same venues hosted smaller crowds and older faces. The optimism had turned into cynicism. Young members who remained active did so defensively, trying to protect whatever progressive gains they could and resisting a rightward drift. Their struggle was palpable, as they fought to maintain their ideals in the face of disillusionment, but no longer believed they could reshape the party in their image.

The implications for Labour's future are troubling. Political parties need constant renewal, fresh energy, and new activists willing to knock on doors and organise communities. If young people decide that Labour is not worth their time, where will the next generation of organisers come from? How will the party connect with voters under 35, a demographic that is already deeply sceptical of traditional politics? The decline in youth engagement could lead to a loss of innovative ideas, a disconnect with younger voters, and a weakening of the party's grassroots support.

The Deputy Leadership Contest

The deputy leadership contest has added another layer of intrigue, transforming into a proxy battle for the party's future direction. Following Angela Rayner's resignation in early September due to issues related to stamp duty, a move that sparked debates about the party's direction and leadership, the race to replace her attracted multiple candidates. Still, two emerged as frontrunners: Lucy Powell and Bridget Phillipson.

Powell, the Leader of the House of Commons, represented a more inclusive and consultative approach to party management. She emphasised the need to unite different factions, listen to members' concerns, and rebuild trust between the leadership and grassroots. Burnham supported Powell but was careful to clarify that he had "nothing against Bridget Phillipson." He expressed a desire for "a more inclusive, collaborative approach to running the party, a more democratic approach."

Phillipson, the Education Secretary, was widely viewed as the leadership's preferred continuity candidate. Her position on the two-child benefit cap, indicating that it was 'on the table' for potential removal, suggested she was willing to adapt to political pressures while ultimately remaining loyal to Starmer's vision. Powell, on the other hand, has proposed a more inclusive and consultative approach to party management, emphasising the need to unite different factions and rebuild trust between the leadership and grassroots.

The contest revealed much about the party's internal dynamics. Powell garnered support from members who craved a softer style and wanted to feel heard rather than managed. In contrast, Phillipson attracted MPs who valued stability and worried that excessive internal debate might be perceived as a weakness.

LabourList's annual conference karaoke became an unlikely barometer for support. The event, held at The Bierkeller bar from 8 PM to 1 AM on Monday, September 29, featured signature cocktails named for each candidate: the "Powell Punch" and the "Bridgetini." Organisers promised to reveal which cocktail sold more, turning drink sales into a straw poll of delegate sentiment.

215

Despite the lighthearted atmosphere, the stakes were significant. The deputy leader traditionally serves as a bridge between the leadership and the party, mediating conflicts and maintaining internal cohesion and unity. The choice between Powell and Phillipson is not just a decision about the kind of party Labour wants to be, but also a reflection of your priorities: a party that prioritises unity and inclusion or one that values discipline and message control.

Rachel Reeves: The Iron Chancellor

Rachel Reeves delivered her keynote address on Monday, September 29, to a packed hall of delegates at the ACC. Her speech exemplified her signature style, technically accomplished, filled with economic statistics, and projecting an aura of fiscal responsibility and governmental competence. "Security, security, security" was her central theme, a deliberate echo of Tony Blair's famous "Education, education, education" mantra.

"I will take no risks with the trust placed in us by the British people," Reeves declared, reinforcing her reputation as a fiscal hawk. Under her leadership, the Treasury would be "unequivocal" in its commitment to economic responsibility. She highlighted the economic failures of the Tories under Liz Truss, reminding delegates of the chaos that Labour had inherited.

Reeves announced a 'youth guarantee,' a policy with the potential to significantly reduce youth unemployment and boost the economy. This promise ensures that every young person who has been out of work or education for 18 months will be given an opportunity for guaranteed paid work. She also committed to ensuring that every primary school in England would have a library or library space by the end of parliament, noting that 1,700 schools currently lacked one. Additionally, she renewed her commitment to a youth mobility scheme between the UK and the EU.

While the substance of her speech was solid and the policy announcements genuine, the address felt disconnected from the mood of the conference, as if Reeves were speaking to a different party in a different country. She barely acknowledged the scandals consuming the government, speaking as if the public's primary concern were GDP growth rates rather than the government's trustworthiness. This disconnect highlighted the need for more relevant and timely political discourse.

The applause was polite but not enthusiastic. Delegates stood out of obligation rather than genuine support, underscoring the lack of enthusiasm for Reeves's policies. 'She's talking about fiscal policy while the house is burning down,' one MP whispered to a colleague. 'Read the room.'

Reeves also appeared to take a swipe at Andy Burnham, cautioning against the "dangerous" notion that fiscal discipline could be relaxed. This reference was subtle but unmistakable. Burnham had been advocating for increased borrowing to invest in infrastructure and public services, criticising Labour for being overly reliant on bond market investors. Reeves aimed to draw a line, making it clear that her Treasury would not entertain such thoughts.

The speech also contained concerning hints about the upcoming budget. Reeves spoke of 'the long-term damage done to our economy, which is becoming ever clearer,' subtly acknowledging an impending downgrade in productivity forecasts by the Office for Budget Responsibility. The implication was evident: taxes may need to rise. Despite her promise not to increase income tax, national insurance, or VAT, Reeves appeared to be scrambling to find revenue elsewhere, eyeing banks, gambling companies, and other sectors for potential sources. This potential shift in tax policy could have significant implications for these industries and the broader economy.

For delegates seeking a vision of a different type of politics, Reeves's speech was deeply disappointing. It presented competent managerialism disguised as economic strategy and technocratic fine-tuning masquerading as transformative change. The caution she exhibited, with responsible fiscal management and modest investments in youth employment and school libraries, felt inadequate when the moment called for boldness.

Starmer's Speech: The Struggle for the Soul

On Tuesday, September 30, Keir Starmer delivered his leader's speech at the Labour Party conference. The Prime Minister took the stage at 2 p.m. in the main hall, addressing an audience that had spent four days exposing the depths of Labour's crisis. This was his moment to reset the narrative, rally the troops, and offer a vision compelling enough to unite a fractured party and win back a sceptical public.

The speech began on an emotional note with a tribute to Margaret Aspinall and the Hillsborough families, whose decades-long campaign for justice culminated in the passage of the Hillsborough Law. This law, which imposes criminal sanctions on public servants who conceal the

217

truth, is a significant milestone in the fight for justice and accountability. "The state will see, the state will listen, the state will be accountable to working people," Starmer promised. "Because now injustice has no place to hide." This powerful opening connected Labour's values to tangible achievements, linking Hillsborough to Grenfell, Windrush, Horizon, and the infected blood scandal, a pattern of the state abandoning working-class people.

Starmer then framed the situation: "Britain stands at a fork in the road. We can choose decency or division. Renewal or decline." He positioned this as "a fight for the soul of our country," explicitly comparing it to Britain's post-war reconstruction. The enemy, he asserted, was clear: Reform UK, Nigel Farage, and the "politics of grievance," a term used to describe a political strategy that focuses on stoking resentment and anger among the public rather than offering constructive solutions.

His attack on Farage was direct and personal. "When was the last time you heard Nigel Farage say anything positive about Britain's future? He can't. He doesn't like Britain, doesn't believe in Britain, and wants you to doubt it just as much as he does." Starmer questioned whether Farage actually loved the country and whether he wanted Britain to succeed or fail. He explicitly called out Reform's racism, not only targeting Farage himself but also the violence and hatred that stem from their rhetoric.

On patriotism, Starmer employed a comprehensive strategy that emphasised unity. Cabinet ministers were armed with Union Jacks and St. George's Crosses. 'They're our flags; they belong to all of us, and we will never surrender them,' he declared, reclaiming symbols from the right. He invoked Euro '96 at Wembley, 'Football's coming home' as a moment when England felt united across all divides. He spoke of pride in the Saltire, the Red Dragon, and the Union Jack, emphasising the solidarity of four nations forged by working people. This invocation of national symbols was not about division, but about the unity that they represent, making the audience feel a sense of togetherness.

The policy substance came in waves, each one carrying a personal narrative. He announced the scrapping of Tony Blair's target for 50% university attendance, replacing it with a goal of two-thirds of young people either going to university or earning 'gold standard apprenticeships.' This was not just a policy shift, but a reflection of personal experiences: his father, a toolmaker who felt disrespected for working with his hands; his sister, a care worker doing vital, undervalued work; and his brother, who struggled within an education system that

218

neglected him. 'What I want is a Britain where people are treated with the dignity they deserve for making different choices, choices our country needs, choices we should value, and choices that deserve our respect.' This personal narrative made the policy substance more relatable and engaging for the audience.

The unveiling of the groundbreaking' NHS Online' initiative, a pioneering digital NHS Trust, stands as a pivotal moment in healthcare. This innovative platform, set to deliver an additional 8.5 million appointments, empowers patients to engage with specialists remotely, at their convenience, thereby drastically reducing waiting times. As the speaker aptly put it, 'This marks a new era for our NHS, embracing the future, empowering patients, and slashing waiting times for every individual in our nation.'

Regarding housing, the commitment is unwavering. We pledge to provide housing for all veterans in need, as well as for young care leavers and victims of domestic abuse. This initiative, linked to planning reform and broader economic renewal, is a testament to our empathy and support for the most vulnerable in our society.

The economic policy took centre stage in the announcement, with the speaker underscoring that 'growth is the defining mission of this government.' However, it's not just any growth, but a unique kind that springs from the grassroots and enriches every community, not the elite. He expressed gratitude to businesses for their contributions, particularly in the face of tough budget decisions. He acknowledged the £25 billion increase in payroll tax, defending it as vital for restoring public finances and investing in infrastructure. Furthermore, he unveiled a substantial defence investment, including the construction of Norwegian frigates on the Clyde, ensuring a decade of shipbuilding for Glasgow.

On the topic of childcare, he highlighted the provision of thirty hours of free childcare for every child aged nine months to four years. He recounted visiting a reception class in Nuneaton, where some children arrived already reading books while others were "virtually still in nappies," indicating that inequality is entrenched from a very young age. This investment is framed as a means to level the playing field.

Throughout the speech, the speaker repeatedly used the term 'working class' four or five times instead of the euphemism 'working people.' This choice was intentional, aimed at reclaiming Labour's roots. He positioned 'dignity and respect' as Labour's core values, not just as words, but as guiding principles that resonate with every individual and guide every decision he made.

The speaker took a moment to celebrate Labour's achievements, which include significant investments in clean energy, the establishment of the Celtic Freeport in South Wales, carbon capture initiatives in Merseyside, and the production of offshore wind turbines in Humberside. He also highlighted successful trade deals with India, the US, and Europe, as well as a steadfast commitment to supporting Ukraine. Additionally, he mentioned the extension of free school meals, which has lifted 100,000 children out of poverty, 'the first step on our journey to eliminate child poverty.' He also expressed support for British Steel, introduced new protections for renters, ensured sick pay for the least well-off, ended fire and rehire practices, scrapped zero-hour contracts, and implemented a proper living wage.

On immigration, he navigated a careful path. The speech featured a detailed story about canvassing in an Oldham by-election, where he met a woman who felt she had to prove she wasn't racist before expressing concerns about men from Eastern Europe in her neighbourhood not adhering to local customs. He acknowledged her struggle, stating that "regardless of our intentions, we had become a party that patronised working people." He promised to dismantle smuggling gangs, crack down on illegal employment, remove individuals without the right to stay, and secure Britain's borders. However, he also drew a moral distinction: controlling migration is reasonable, but resorting to violence is thuggish, inciting racial violence is criminal, and suggesting that people cannot be British based solely on their skin colour is outright racism. "If you say they should now be deported, mark my words, we will oppose you with everything we have because you are an enemy of national renewal."

He dismissed the term "broken Britain". Instead, he highlighted examples of British excellence and community spirit from tech investments in Hartlepool and Belfast to Melanie, who runs a carers' meetup in Calderdale, and fifteen-year-old Kaitlyn, who started a girls' football team in Barnet, to George, who delivers food parcels in Telford, and the community members who cleaned up after riots. "Mere politics cannot break Britain... People like this are the real face of Britain."

Regarding fiscal responsibility, he took a firm stance. He declared that the fiscal rules were "non-negotiable. "This isn't a game; it's not a tactic. Those rules protect working people and safeguard our children's future." He recognised the allure of ideological fantasies but firmly rejected them: "I will never allow working people to bear the cost. This is why we changed the party."

He expressed disdain for the Conservatives: "I have had enough of lectures from self-appointed champions of working people who want to dismantle our public services, undermine worker rights, crash the economy like Liz Truss, and who have lied to this country, unleashing chaos and then walking away after Brexit." When he quipped, "Remember them?" the audience laughed. Reform, not the Tories, was now seen as the main opposition.

The speech concluded with a call for unity, reaching out to "patriots, whether you vote Labour or not", who wanted to stand against grievances and work towards renewing Britain. "No matter how many people tell me it can't be done; I believe Britain can come together. We can pursue a shared destination and unite around a common good."

However, the gap between the speech delivered and the urgent needs of the moment was too wide to bridge. Delegates had spent four days confronting the reality of Labour's challenges: scandals, authoritarian policies, insensitivity, and internal divisions. They needed a leader who understood the extent of the crisis, could acknowledge mistakes, and chart a path forward, inspiring them to believe once again. The question arises: Did the speaker effectively inspire belief in the audience?

Instead, they received policy announcements and rhetorical positioning. The opening about Hillsborough was genuinely moving, but then came the avoidance: The BritCard was mentioned only indirectly as a necessary modernisation. At the same time, the McSweeney scandal received no direct acknowledgement beyond vague references to "learning lessons" and "improving systems." The housing debacle was glossed over with promises of renewed focus on delivery.

The patriotic language, while aimed at countering Reform UK's advantage, felt more reactive than proactive. It subtracts from the discourse rather than adds something new. The use of working-class terminology was an attempt to signal authenticity, but it only served to highlight the distance between Labour's leadership and the people they purported to represent. The attacks on the Conservatives and Reform were meant to draw clear lines, but they failed to explain why Labour was squandering its mandate so rapidly.

The policy substance, including commitments to apprenticeships, NHS Online, housing, and defence investment, represented genuine attempts to address real issues. However, they landed in a context marred by mistrust. How could voters believe promises about dignity and respect when the government was implementing mandatory digital identity cards? How could they trust commitments to veterans while Labour was covering up assault scandals? How could they accept the reclamation of national symbols when the government seemed embarrassed by British values?

221

The immigration section highlighted a significant contradiction in Starmer's stance. His anecdote from Oldham acknowledged Labour's past patronisation of working-class people on this issue. However, he then seemed to do precisely that by drawing a 'moral line' that implied anyone with concerns beyond his carefully measured stance was dangerously close to racism. This sent a clear message to working-class voters: your concerns are valid, but only if they align with our approved stance and are expressed in ways we deem acceptable.

Moreover, the rhetoric surrounding fiscal responsibility seemed insincere in light of a budget that imposed £25 billion in payroll taxes on businesses, resulting in rising unemployment and declining investment. The promises of growth 'from the grassroots' seemed distant and intangible, while real communities saw their high streets deteriorate, pubs close, and youth clubs shut down. The celebration of AI revolutionising healthcare felt disconnected from the reality of people waiting months for GP appointments or enduring long waits in the accident and emergency department.

Most importantly, the speech failed to present a vision of what Britain should become, but only what it should avoid. It defined Labour by opposition: not to the Tories, not to Reform, and not to the "snake oil merchants" of both left and right. However, opposing negative things does not equate to having a compelling vision of positive outcomes. The emphasis on "dignity and respect" as core values felt hollow without concrete meaning, and a "Britain built for all" remained merely a slogan rather than a clear ambition.

The speech delivered a level of competence akin to a corporate PowerPoint presentation: it covered all necessary points without eliciting any emotional response beyond relief that it was over. It presented policies without a vision, rhetoric without conviction, and positioning without purpose.

The applause at the end was prolonged yet mechanical, reflecting party loyalty rather than genuine enthusiasm. People stood up out of obligation, not because they felt inspired. The standing ovations Starmer received for criticising Brexit chaos, promising to eliminate child poverty, and defending the NHS were real but celebrated past Labour values and accomplishments rather than confidence in this government's ability to achieve them.

As delegates departed for final receptions and farewell drinks, the consensus was clear: the conference had not resolved Labour's issues. If anything, it had sharpened them. The speech had changed nothing because it had taken no risks. In trying to appease every constituency and sidestep every controversy, Starmer had ultimately satisfied no one. The Left viewed it as mere technocratic tinkering when they were looking for transformation. The Right saw evasion where they wanted accountability. The public perceived a politician managing a crisis rather than a leader confronting it.

As the hall emptied and the stage lights dimmed, one reality remained: Labour had arrived in Liverpool facing a crisis of credibility and was leaving with that crisis intact. There was a clear indication that their leadership either didn't understand the problem or lacked the courage to address it.

The speech had changed nothing because it had risked nothing. In attempting to address every constituency and avoid every controversy, Starmer satisfied no one. The Left saw only technocratic tinkering when they wanted transformation, while the Right perceived evasion where they sought accountability. The public, who had hoped for a leader confronting the crisis, instead saw a politician managing it.

However, the day after the speech revealed something worse than evasion: a sudden and complete retreat. Within twenty-four hours of labelling Reform UK's immigration policy as "racist" and questioning whether Nigel Farage loved Britain, Starmer was backpedalling.

In interviews on Wednesday morning, October 1, the Prime Minister clarified that he did not believe Nigel Farage himself was racist, but rather that his policy of scrapping Indefinite Leave to Remain was racist. Speaking with Sky News, Starmer described Farage as a "formidable politician" but insisted that the policy would evoke feelings of discomfort among minorities. When pressed three times by LBC's Nick Ferrari about whether his rhetoric put Farage at risk, Starmer responded, "No, that's not the case," dismissing Farage's warning that such language would "incite the radical left" and pose a threat to the safety of Reform activists.

Deputy Prime Minister David Lammy also quickly backtracked on Tuesday evening, retracting his earlier assertion to the BBC that Farage had "flirted with Hitler Youth," referencing decades-old allegations that Farage had sung Nazi songs as a schoolboy. "I wasn't at school with Nigel Farage. I don't know what songs he sang at school," Lammy told reporters, suddenly uncertain about accusations he had confidently made just hours earlier.

The climbdown was both comprehensive and humiliating. After spending four days at the conference, building up to a rhetorical confrontation, throwing around terms like "Plastic Patriots" and accusing Farage of not liking Britain, the Prime Minister retreated the moment

Farage pushed back. Writing in the Daily Mail, Farage noted that his opinion of Starmer had "shifted": "We might disagree on our worldview, but until this weekend I believed he was a reasonable human being. Now I'm shocked at his behaviour."

The backpedalling highlighted a fundamental weakness in Starmer's strategy. He aimed to define clear distinctions with Reform UK, reclaim patriotism and working-class identity from the right, and position Labour as defenders against the "politics of grievance." However, when faced with the consequences of his own statements, he quickly retreated.

The pattern was clear: bold rhetoric in speeches, followed by careful retreats in interviews. He criticised Farage as un-British in front of party members, then acknowledged his formidable presence when speaking to journalists. He labelled specific policies as racist during rallies, only to later differentiate between racist policies and racist individuals when challenged. He deployed Lammy to make provocative historical comparisons, only for Lammy to claim ignorance when those comparisons drew scrutiny.

This behaviour was a microcosm of the entire conference: lots of positioning but little conviction. The speech that seemed to change nothing was followed by clarifications that altered everything. Labour delegates, who had cheered Starmer's criticisms of Reform with hope, were left disappointed. They believed their leader was finally drawing clear moral lines and defending Labour values. Within a day, they discovered those lines were negotiable, those values conditional, and that moral clarity was easily abandoned.

For Reform UK, this was a significant opportunity. Farage could now assert that he had been slandered by the Prime Minister, who later, under pressure, admitted that the slander wasn't as clear-cut as it seemed. The millions who voted for Reform or considered it, whom Starmer had termed "frustrated" rather than racist, watched the Prime Minister imply that they were enemies of national renewal, only to retreat when challenged.

For Labour MPs already doubting Starmer's leadership, this confirmed their worst fears: he lacked the political courage to sustain a fight. He would make bold claims and then abandon them. He would draw lines and then blur them. He would attack and then apologise. The pattern was familiar, whether it was the pensioners' winter fuel payments, the welfare reform climbdown, or the McSweeney cover-up, it was always the same: initial commitment followed by a panicked retreat when pressure mounted.

As delegates left Liverpool on Wednesday, returning to

constituencies where Reform was gaining support and Labour was losing ground, they carried with them not just the memory of a speech that failed to inspire but also fresh evidence of a leader who retreated from his own rhetoric within twenty-four hours. The conference had crystallised Labour's crisis, and the aftermath confirmed that it was terminal, leaving the party's future in jeopardy.

The Fringe Circuit

Significantly, the conference's true essence was not confined to the main hall, but rather, it unfolded through the vibrant fringe events that had surpassed the official proceedings in significance. These gatherings were not just supplementary, but integral to the conference, serving as the platform for candid discussions, the battleground for competing visions of Labour's future, and the sanctuary where activists and MPs could express themselves more openly than from the official platform.

Big Brother Watch's sessions on digital surveillance and civil liberties were a magnet for large crowds, with speakers systematically dismantling the case for BritCard. The arguments were not only compelling but also alarming, and the constitutional concerns were not merely serious but grave. Yet, the government's deafening silence in response to these expert opinions was a stark reminder of the disconnect between those in power and those they serve.

Labour Together, ironically, the same think tank at the centre of the donations scandal, hosted sessions on policy development. The optics were unfortunate, but the organisation pressed on, aiming to position itself as a source of fresh thinking. Delegates attended, some out of sincere interest, while others were driven by morbid curiosity to see how this tainted organisation would address its credibility issues.

The Housing Group organised packed events focusing on the target of 1.5 million homes. Delegates asked pointed questions about delivery plans and whether ministers had any realistic idea of how to achieve their pledges. The shadow of the Steve Reed interview, where he struggled to answer basic questions about Labour's housing policy, lingered over the discussions, serving as proof that even at the highest levels, the government lacked answers.

Climate activists coordinated panels on the Green New Deal, a comprehensive plan to address climate change and economic inequality, advocating for more ambitious carbon reduction targets. Union representatives hosted sessions on workers' rights and the Employment Rights Bill. Different Labour factions held competing events, each

225

claiming to represent the party's authentic voice.

The Tony Blair Institute for Global Change, a significant presence at the conference, hosted discussions on government innovation and AI policy. The contrast between Blair-era triangulation and current member sentiment was not just stark, but profound, yet the enduring influence of the Blairite tendency in shaping government policy was unmistakable.

The sheer variety of fringe events, hundreds of them spread across The Pullman, The Hilton, The Leonardo hotels, and ACC meeting rooms, suggested a party filled with diverse ideas and energy. However, this fragmentation also highlighted the difficulty of forging a coherent direction. Every faction had its plan, vision, and policy proposals. The challenge lay in translating any of this into governmental action.

Private Conversations

In the bars and restaurants around Liverpool, honest conversations were taking place. MPs huddled in corners, speaking quietly about what actions could be taken. Some argued for moving forward, insisting that weak leadership would be worse than unpopular policies. Others advocated for tactical retreats, recognising that the political costs of their current approach were unsustainable. A few, still a minority but growing in number, began to question whether Starmer himself was the problem, a concern that was gaining momentum.

"He's a manager, not a leader," one shadow minister told a small group of trusted colleagues over drinks at The Bierkeller. "That's fine when things are going well. But in a crisis, when you need someone who can rally people, change the narrative, and instil belief? He doesn't have that ability."

The issue of Morgan McSweeney came up repeatedly. MPs acknowledged his political effectiveness after all, he had played a crucial role in Labour's return to power. However, they questioned the sustainability of his factional style and confrontational approach to internal dissent. "He's making enemies when we need allies," one MP noted. "Every suspension, every disciplinary case, every blocked motion creates resentment that lingers. We're governing as if we're still in opposition."

Others expressed deep concerns about the approaching local elections in 2026, just eight months away. Polls indicated catastrophic losses were expected. Councillors would bear the brunt of voter anger, losing seats they had held for years. "My councillors are terrified," a Northern MP confided. "They're going door-to-door where people are genuinely furious, not just disappointed. They're asking me what to tell voters, and I don't have answers." The fear and uncertainty about the impending elections were palpable.

The BritCard issue dominated many private discussions. MPs were aware of the theoretical efficiency arguments that a single digital ID could streamline government services, reduce fraud, and modernise outdated systems. However, the civil liberties concerns were significant, and the timing was politically disastrous. "Why now?" one backbencher asked rhetorically. "Why pick this fight when we're already struggling? It's political malpractice." The potential consequences of the BritCard issue were looming large.

Some conversations shifted to contingency planning. What if Reform UK gained control of councils in May 2026? What if the 2029 election appeared unwinnable? Should the party begin positioning itself for opposition, focusing on protecting seats rather than defending an unpopular national government?

The most candid discussions acknowledged what few wanted to say publicly: Starmer might not lead Labour into the next election. This wouldn't have been the result of a leadership challenge, as the rules and political dynamics made that nearly impossible, but rather through resignation. If polling continued to deteriorate and the 2026 elections resulted in catastrophe, Starmer might conclude he had become a liability. The ongoing speculation about Burnham, the careful positioning by cabinet ministers, and the quiet conversations about succession all suggested a party bracing for the possibility of change.

Social Dynamics and Atmosphere

The social aspects of the conference reflected the overall mood of the party just as much as the formal proceedings did. LabourList's karaoke night, a longstanding celebration where MPs and activists sing protest songs and pop hits, felt more subdued this year. The legendary event, hosted at The Bierkeller and featuring cocktails supporting each deputy leadership candidate, still attracted a crowd. Notable appearances included Dawn Butler MP, Emily Thornberry MP, Alison McGovern MP, Stephen Kinnock MP, and Stella Creasy MP, some of whom even took turns DJing.

However, the energy was markedly different from previous years. Many attendees noted the absence of Sue Grey, the former chief of staff, who had been ousted earlier in the year. Grey's departure, while removing a source of tension, also meant losing someone who had attempted to moderate the more extreme factional impulses within the party. Her absence was keenly felt, and it was evident in the conference's atmosphere.

Other conference traditions continued as usual. Morning breakfast briefings at various hotels allowed journalists to question ministers over coffee and pastries. Meanwhile, evening receptions hosted by think tanks, unions, and advocacy groups provided networking opportunities and a bit more alcohol than was entirely professional. The new conference app for 2025 helped delegates navigate the packed schedule and discover last-minute fringe events.

Yet something fundamental was missing. The sense of purpose, the shared mission, and the feeling of being part of something greater than oneself were increasingly difficult to find. Delegates went through the motions, attending sessions and voting on motions, but the joy had faded. The conference felt more like an obligation than a celebration.

First-time delegates, those elected in 2024 who were experiencing their first conference as representatives of the governing party, were particularly disillusioned. Their expectations of triumph and unity were shattered by the reality of dysfunction and deep factional conflicts. The contrast between the party they envisioned joining and the fact they found in Liverpool was jarring, leaving them with a profound sense of disillusionment.

"I thought it would be different," said a first-term delegate from the Midlands, nursing a pint at a hotel bar. "I knocked on thousands of doors telling people Labour would be different, better and more honest. And now I'm here, and it's just... politics. The same old games, the same manipulation, the same disappointment. Just with different people doing it."

Media Coverage and External Perception

The media coverage during conference week was not just critical, it was harsh. Every stumble, contradiction, and indication of disunity was not just reported, but amplified and dissected. The defining image of the conference, Steve Reed's housing interview, was not only shown but also replayed endlessly on news broadcasts and social media. Conservative and Reform UK accounts didn't just comment on it; they seized on it as evidence of Labour's incompetence and unpreparedness for governance, further adding to the weight of public perception on the party.

Owen Jones, a former Corbyn supporter who has grown critical of Starmer's government, wrote a scathing column during conference week: "This government has lost its way barely a year in. The scandals, the authoritarianism, the tone-deafness, all of it's painful to watch." The BBC's political editor reported on "a party in crisis, searching for direction," while The Times published analysis pieces questioning whether Starmer possessed the political skills necessary to lead effectively.

The traditional divide between hostile right-wing media and sympathetic left-leaning outlets had not just blurred; it had largely collapsed. Even journalists who hoped for Labour's success struggled to find positive stories, as the government's actions and statements offered too much damaging material. This collapse of the traditional media divides further underscored the party's struggle for favourable coverage.

International coverage was equally troubling. The New York Times ran an article wondering whether Labour's landslide victory was already becoming a cautionary tale about the limits of centrism. European newspapers highlighted the UK's political instability, the rapid decline in support for the government, and the rise of the populist right. For a government that wanted to position Britain as a reliable partner after the chaos of Brexit, this coverage was deeply detrimental.

Social media metrics told a similar story. Conference hashtags trended, but not in the ways Labour would have liked. The #BuildBabyBuild hashtag became ironic, as it was used to mock the government's failure to deliver. The #LabourConference2025 tag is filled with criticism, memes, and expressions of frustration from both the left and right.

Traditional Conservative supporters were quick to attack Labour, but the critiques from disappointed Labour voters were more devastating. These were individuals who had voted for change, given Starmer a chance, and wanted to believe. Their disillusionment echoed through every tweet, post, and comment: "Is this what we voted for?" "Labour is becoming what it replaced." "I already regret my vote."

The Polling Reality

The polling during conference week unveiled a significant trend that had cast a shadow over Liverpool. Reform UK was successfully retaining 9 out of 10 of its voters for 2024 (89 percent), a result of immense significance. The party was also attracting support from other parties, particularly the Conservatives, with 39 percent of 2024 Conservative voters indicating that they would consider switching to Reform UK. In contrast, the Conservatives, Labour, and Liberal Democrats were managing to hold on to only about half of their expected voters for the 2024 election, a fact that cannot be overlooked.

Gideon Skinner, Senior Director of UK Politics at Ipsos, noted, "Labour's issues run deeper than personnel changes. They are losing votes to both the left and the right, with the public still pessimistic about the state of the economy and the direction of the country."

The YouGov polling revealed a significant paradox for Reform UK. Despite leading in voting intention polls, when Britons were asked to choose between Labour under Starmer and Reform UK under Farage for the next election, 43 per cent favoured Labour for a second term, compared to 37 percent who supported Farage taking up residence at Number 10. This paradox suggests that, although the public was dissatisfied with Labour, they were not yet ready to embrace Reform UK as a viable alternative government, which has significant implications for the future of UK politics.

The personal favourability ratings for major party leaders were universally low, a clear reflection of the deep public disillusionment with the entire political class. Starmer's approval rating was at -44, with only 24 percent holding a favourable opinion and 68 per cent viewing him unfavourably. Nigel Farage registered a net rating of -29, while Kemi Badenoch's was -31. Every major party leader was underwater, a stark indication of the public's dissatisfaction.

Starmer's position was particularly notable; he was the least popular Prime Minister Ipsos had ever polled since tracking began in 1977, worse than Gordon Brown in 2010, Theresa May in 2019, and even Liz Truss, who resigned after 49 days following economic turmoil. The comparison to Truss was especially painful for Labour MPs who had made her a running joke for years.

The regional breakdown of support was equally alarming. Labour was losing support in its traditional strongholds, the North, the Midlands, and Wales, where working-class voters were turning to Reform UK's populist promises. While Labour had substantial majorities in seats it had historically won in the 2024 election, those majorities were quickly eroding, a sign of the party's vulnerability.

In Scotland, Labour's slight gains against the SNP appeared vulnerable. In Wales, Labour's dominance was threatened by both Reform UK and a resurgent Conservative opposition. The overarching narrative was the same: a government that had previously enjoyed significant victories was losing ground rapidly.

The Final Day

The final day of the conference, Wednesday, October 1, brought a mixture of relief and dread. There was relief that the ordeal was over, allowing MPs to return to their constituencies without facing further awkward questions in hotel bars. However, there was also a sense of dread about what was to come, particularly concerning the local elections in 2026 and whether the government could recover from such a disastrous start, which included a series of scandals and a significant loss of public trust.

The closing sessions concluded ongoing business. Constitutional amendments were voted on, and the results of internal elections were announced. Momentum-backed candidates secured some positions but fell short in others, reflecting the movement's waning influence. The Conference Arrangements Committee concluded the proceedings with the customary acknowledgements and thanks.

As delegates departed Liverpool, the rain finally stopped. Evening light broke through the clouds, shining on the waterfront as conference staff began breaking down stages and packing up banners. The symbolism was not lost on anyone; the storm, a metaphor for the political turmoil and public discontent, had passed, but it had left damage in its wake, indicating that the political landscape had been significantly altered.

On the train back to London, MPs occupied first-class carriages, staring at their laptops or phones, processing the events that had just unfolded. A few voiced optimisms, insisting that things would improve, that the media cycle would shift, and that governing was always difficult. However, most understood that something fundamental had changed.

One first-term MP, elected during the 2024 landslide, confided to her seatmate, "I knocked on thousands of doors promising people that we would be different. I pledged integrity, competence, and respect for civil liberties. Now, I have to return and explain digital surveillance, donation scandals, and housing ministers who lack basic statistics. How do I do that? How do I look them in the eye and ask them to keep trusting us?" Her colleague had no answer. Nobody did.

The Aftermath

The petition against BritCard reached 2.6 million signatures by the end of the conference and continued to grow. Civil liberties groups were preparing legal challenges, while the Conservative Party organised campaigns against what they labelled "Starmer's surveillance state." Even media outlets that had traditionally been sympathetic to Labour began to run increasingly critical coverage.

As the conference centre lights dimmed and Liverpool returned to its usual rhythm, rain started to fall again. It would continue through the night, washing away temporary installations and optimistic slogans, leaving the streets clean but emptier than they had been before.

Labour had come to Liverpool hoping to demonstrate purpose and unity. They left, revealing division and uncertainty, an administration searching for direction and finding only more questions. The landslide victory of July 2024, which had seemed to signal a generation of Labour dominance, now appeared to be a historical anomaly, a moment when voters, fatigued by Conservative chaos, were willing to try something different.

That moment had passed. The willingness to give Labour the benefit of the doubt had evaporated. Central to this was a Prime Minister who increasingly seemed unable to manage events, inspire loyalty, or offer the kind of leadership needed to turn the tide.

The conference had exposed the fundamental contradiction at the heart of Starmer's agenda: he had won power by promising change but governed with caution. He campaigned on integrity while presiding over scandals. He pledged to listen but silenced dissent. The gap between his promises and performance was too wide to ignore.

For the activists and members who filled Liverpool's hotels and bars, the conference was a dispiriting experience. They had seen their concerns dismissed, their motions blocked, and their preferred candidates defeated. They watched the leadership prioritise message discipline over democratic debate, spin over substance, and political calculation over principle.

For MPs returning to their constituencies to face angry voters, the conference offered no comfort. The speeches were uninspiring, the policies unimpressive, and the leadership ineffective. They returned to their surgeries and town halls armed with talking points that felt hollow and promises that seemed empty.

For the ministers and special advisers running the government, the conference was a missed opportunity. They had come hoping to reset the narrative, generate positive coverage, and unite the party behind their agenda. Instead, they spent four days in damage control, deflecting criticism and defending the indefensible while support continued to slip away.

Looking Forward

Fifteen months into Labour's government, the decline had already begun. As autumn darkness settled over Britain, the only question remaining was how far and how fast the descent would occur. Liverpool had not provided answers; it had only intensified the urgency of the questions and the acute nature of the crisis, making the path forward more uncertain than ever.

The 2026 local elections loomed just seven months away. Labour councillors across the country faced the threat of electoral annihilation, potentially losing seats they had held for decades. The May results would serve as the first real test of whether Labour could recover or whether the decline would continue.

Looking beyond 2026, the prospect of a general election emerged. Constitutionally, it need not occur until 2029, but political realities could necessitate an earlier contest. If Reform UK continued to rise, if local election losses proved catastrophic, or if internal pressure became unbearable, any of these factors might trigger an early election that Labour would almost certainly lose.

All possible scenarios appeared grim. Starmer could struggle on, hoping for economic recovery or the implosion of Reform UK to salvage his premiership. He could resign, instigating a leadership contest that would consume months while the government drifted aimlessly. Alternatively, he could call for an early election, gambling that voters would prefer Labour to Reform UK when faced with a choice.

None of these options offered much hope. The damage inflicted in fifteen months of governance was extensive. Once lost, trust is nearly impossible to rebuild, and enthusiasm, once extinguished, rarely reignites. The coalition that had secured Labour's landslide victory, comprising frustrated Conservatives, hopeful progressives, and pragmatic centrists, had fractured beyond repair.

As conference attendees dispersed from Liverpool's rain-washed streets to their homes across Britain, one undeniable truth remained: Labour had squandered a once-in-a-generation opportunity. Given the power to transform the country and address inequality, rebuild public services, and restore faith in politics, they delivered instead scandal, surveillance, and disappointment.

The party that promised to be different proved to be all too familiar. The government that vowed integrity was consumed by compromises. The leadership that committed to listening stopped hearing what was being said.

As the trains departed from Liverpool Lime Street Station, carrying MPs and delegates back to their constituencies, uncertainty loomed large over the future of Labour.

Chapter 17
When the Media Turned Their Backs

Little more than a year ago, Keir Starmer stood at the pinnacle of British politics. In July 2024, his Labour Party achieved a remarkable victory, winning a landslide majority of 174 seats and securing a total of 411 seats in the House of Commons, the most significant victory of this century. The media landscape seemed ripe for a Labour revival, a revival that would soon be overshadowed by a dramatic turn of events. After 14 years of Conservative chaos, scandals, and economic turmoil, even newspapers that had historically supported the Tories began to consider the prospect of change. Notably, The Sun, a prominent right-wing tabloid that had famously claimed, "If Kinnock wins today, will the last person in Britain please turn out the lights?" in 1992, offered Starmer a tentative endorsement.

However, by September 2025, the Prime Minister found himself in an extraordinary predicament. An Ipsos poll indicated that only 13% of Britons approved of his performance as Prime Minister. In comparison, a staggering 79% expressed dissatisfaction, marking the worst rating for any British Prime Minister since records began in 1977. This sudden and drastic shift was worse than Rishi Sunak's ratings before the election, worse than John Major's low points in 1994, and even worse than Liz Truss, the woman famously outlasted by a lettuce.

Initially, the media had been cautiously optimistic about the former human rights barrister, who had promised to restore integrity to British politics. However, a dramatic shift occurred, and the media turned against him with a vengeance. From broadsheets to tabloids, and from traditional broadcasters to social media platforms, the narrative changed from hopeful scrutiny to open hostility. Even outlets that traditionally supported Labour began to question whether Starmer had the necessary qualities to lead. This chapter examines the reasons behind the dramatic shift in the British media's stance towards Keir Starmer and his Labour government.

To truly grasp the shift in media perception, one must first comprehend the monumental challenges that Starmer was handed. The Conservative government's legacy was a staggering one: NHS waiting lists had reached unprecedented levels, prisons were bursting at the seams, infrastructure was crumbling, and public services were in dire straits after enduring years of austerity. The national debt had soared, economic growth was sluggish, and Britain's global standing had diminished.

Upon assuming office, Starmer was met with a stagnant economy, stubbornly high inflation, and a cost-of-living crisis that was hitting ordinary families hard. Real wages had remained relatively unchanged since the 2008 financial crisis. The effects of 14 years of underinvestment were starkly visible in Britain's infrastructure, from railways to schools and hospitals. The new government was left to grapple with a staggering £22 billion shortfall in public finances that the Conservatives had conveniently omitted during the election campaign.

Starmer and Chancellor Rachel Reeves faced an unenviable dilemma: raise taxes to fund the much-needed public services or maintain fiscal discipline and allow these services to deteriorate further. The media's response was as predictable as it was inevitable. They would criticise the government, no matter which path they chose. And criticise they did.

The media's disenchantment with Starmer's government did not stem from policy failures but rather from perception issues, which political observers refer to as "the optics." In the brutal arena of modern British politics, appearances hold as much weight as actual achievements. Starmer's initial months in office were marred by controversies that fueled narratives of hypocrisy and elitism.

Within weeks of taking office, Starmer became embroiled in what the press eagerly labelled "donorgate" or "wardrobegate." In September 2024, it was revealed that the Prime Minister had accepted over £107,145 in gifts, benefits, and hospitality since December 2019, more than any other MP, and two-and-a-half times the amount of his nearest rival.

The details of the expenditure were particularly damning: £20,000 in accommodation costs, which included the use of an £18 million Covent Garden penthouse owned by Labour donor Lord Waheed Alli; £5,000 worth of clothing for his wife, Victoria, which was initially undeclared, violating parliamentary rules; £2,435 for designer spectacles; tickets to Taylor Swift concerts, Arsenal football matches in corporate boxes, and even Coldplay gigs. Lord Alli, a millionaire media entrepreneur, had been given unrestricted access to Downing Street via a security pass, where he hosted parties for other Labour donors, raising immediate concerns about 'cash for access'-the idea that wealthy individuals could gain influence by providing gifts or donations, and cronyism-the practice of appointing friends or associates to positions of authority, both of which are considered unethical in politics.

The British press, ranging from the Daily Mail to The Guardian, pounced on the story with enthusiasm. The timing of the revelations was particularly unfortunate. They came to light just as the government was cutting winter fuel payments for millions of pensioners and pursuing benefit cuts. This contrast was politically toxic: here was a Prime Minister who had campaigned on restoring integrity to politics while accepting luxury freebies and instructing pensioners to tighten their belts, leading to widespread accusations of hypocrisy-the practice of claiming to have moral standards or beliefs to which one's own behaviour does not conform.

Labour backbencher Rosie Duffield resigned the Labour whip over the scandal, accusing Starmer of "sleaze, nepotism, and apparent avarice" that were "off the scale." In her resignation letter, she expressed shame over what Starmer and his inner circle had done to tarnish and humiliate the once-proud party. Veteran Labour politician Baroness Harman, while defending Starmer's character, noted that "doubling down and trying to justify it is making things worse."

The conservative press had a field day. Reform MP Lee Anderson called Starmer "the UK's number one sponger." At the same time, GB News ran segments contrasting the Prime Minister's acceptance of free designer clothes with his decision to "snatch" winter fuel payments from pensioners. Even after Starmer repaid £6,000 worth of gifts in October 2024, the damage had been done; the repayment only served as evidence that something had been amiss in the first place.

George Eaton of the New Statesman argued that while no parliamentary rules had been broken, the controversy posed a serious political problem for Labour, leaving them open to accusations of hypocrisy that conflicted with the government's message of budget austerity. The timing, coinciding with the cut to winter fuel payments, was "awkward" at best, catastrophic at worst.

Yet, the freebies scandal did not fade away. Investigative outlet Novara Media revealed in June 2025 that Starmer had continued to accept free VIP football tickets worth nearly £10,000 even after the initial scandal. Although he had stopped accepting freebies in September 2024 due to media scrutiny, he quietly resumed this practice in November. Reports showed him attending Arsenal matches from the directors' box throughout early 2025, including a Champions League semi-final just two days before Labour lost the Runcorn by-election, a seat that had been one of the party's 16 safest and was seen as a significant loss for the party.

The optics were devastating. While Labour faced historic electoral defeats, pensioners shivered through winter without their fuel payments, and cuts to disability benefits loomed, Keir Starmer was in corporate boxes watching football. A prominent Labour MP told Novara Media, "Given the furore just ten months ago over Starmer's freebies, and the public's reaction, this really feels like they are looking at the letter of the law rather than the spirit of the law. This kind of behaviour erodes public trust in politicians, including Starmer himself, and feeds the narrative of the far-right that all politicians are in it for themselves." The public's disappointment in Starmer's behaviour was palpable.

Even Starmer's justifications felt unconvincing. When confronted about accepting tickets to Arsenal matches, he claimed that security concerns made it impossible to sit among ordinary fans. Former Labour leader Jeremy Corbyn dismissed this explanation, telling The Guardian, "I don't like corporate boxes in football or anywhere else. Sometimes you have to say to security, 'I'm a human being too.'" This contrast highlighted a deeper issue: Starmer's disconnect from the very people he claims to represent was stark and disheartening.

As if the controversy over freebies were not damaging enough, the BBC reported in September 2024 that Sue Grey, Starmer's chief of staff, earned £170,000 per year, about £3,000 more than the Prime Minister. Gray, who gained notoriety for her investigation into Boris Johnson's "partygate" scandal, joined Starmer's team amid accusations from Conservatives that her probe had been politically biased.

The revelation that Gray earned more than the Prime Minister was not just a matter of numbers. It was a symbol of Labour's skewed priorities and raised serious questions about Starmer's effectiveness as a leader. If he couldn't even negotiate his chief of staff's salary to be lower than his own, how could he be expected to negotiate with world leaders? The symbolism was damaging, and the media quickly seized on it, leaving the public concerned about Labour's leadership.

If the scandal, which involved allegations of Starmer accepting luxury gifts, damaged his reputation for integrity, his decision to cut winter fuel payments threatened to destroy Labour's historic bond with working-class voters and the elderly. This policy, announced by Chancellor Rachel Reeves in July 2024 as part of measures to address a £22 billion budget shortfall, exemplified everything that could go wrong with Labour's media narrative.

Previously, all pensioners received between £100 and £300 to help cover their heating bills during the winter. Under Labour's new rules, only those receiving pension credit or other means-tested benefits would qualify. The government estimated that this change would save approximately £1.3 billion in 2024-25 and £1.5 billion in subsequent years. However, the human cost, in terms of the lives and well-being of our elderly citizens, was significant.

In November 2024, Work and Pensions Secretary Liz Kendall admitted in a letter what analysis had shown: compared to the numbers that would have been in poverty without this policy, an additional 50,000 pensioners would be pushed into relative poverty after housing costs in each of the years 2024-25, 2025-26, and 2027-28. In the years 2026-27, 2028-29, and 2029-30, that figure would rise to 100,000 additional pensioners facing poverty. For all measures of poverty, an additional 50,000 pensioners would be pushed into poverty each year from 2024-25 to 2029-30.

The timing of this policy change was not only unfortunate but also particularly cruel. The energy regulator Ofgem announced a 1.2% increase to the energy price cap in November 2024, following a 10% increase in October. Pensioners who had relied on the winter fuel payment for years found themselves unable to adequately heat their homes. Charities warned that elderly individuals were facing life-threatening conditions from cold weather and malnutrition, as they chose between heating and eating, and NHS A&E departments were overwhelmed with cases of hypothermia.

The media response was swift and harsh. Trade union leaders condemned the policy. Unite General Secretary Sharon Graham called on the government to "do a U-turn," while TUC General Secretary Paul Nowak urged the Chancellor to "rethink" her plans. Age UK warned that "very significant numbers of older people" were "too frightened to turn on their heating when it was cold, making life utterly miserable for them and putting their health at risk."

The conservative press took advantage of the situation without mercy. The Daily Mail ran headlines contrasting Starmer's acceptance of luxury gifts with images of pensioners freezing in their homes. GB News featured emotional interviews with elderly people unable to afford heating. Even Labour-supporting outlets like The Guardian published critical pieces questioning the morality and effectiveness of the policy.

The contrast between Starmer's acceptance of luxury gifts, including a pair of designer sunglasses worth £ 2,000, and the poverty faced by pensioners became a central theme in political discourse. As one segment on GB News put it: "Keir Starmer has talked a lot about difficult decisions, but while he's snatching the Winter Fuel Allowance from pensioners, it seems the only difficult decisions he's been making are which £2,000 pair of designer sunglasses to accept from one of his friends.

In September 2024, the Commons voted on a policy that saw up to 50 Labour MPs struggling to support it, with about 30 expected to refuse to back the decision. This internal dissent, as reported by the Times, was a significant test of Starmer's authority. Despite Labour's considerable majority, the 'significant number of absences' indicated the 'extent of disquiet' within the party, a matter of concern for all those invested in Labour's unity.

This policy ultimately led to Labour's devastating loss in the Runcorn and Helsby by-election in May 2025, a seat that had been the party's 16th safest. Starmer's potential U-turn in May 2025, aimed at increasing the number of pensioners eligible for winter fuel payments, came too late. By then, the damage to Labour's reputation and Starmer's personal standing was irreversible, a grave situation that the party and its supporters had to face.

While domestic policy missteps provided ammunition for the media, it was Starmer's handling of immigration and civil unrest that gave them an even greater opportunity to attack. The emergence of the 'Two-Tier Keir' label, suggesting differential treatment in policing and justice, dominated media coverage throughout 2024 and 2025. This media influences fundamentally reshaped the public perception of both Starmer and his government, highlighting the power of the media in shaping public opinion.

In August 2024, following the alleged murder of three young girls in Southport by a 17-year-old, violent riots erupted across England. Far-right groups exploited the tragedy, spreading misinformation on social media and organising violent protests targeting mosques and asylum hotels. The disorder was alarming, as police officers were injured, buses were set ablaze, and communities were terrorised.

Starmer's response was characteristically legalistic but politically tone-deaf. He held regular press conferences denouncing all those involved as "far right," pledging to raise a "standing army" of police officers, and introducing authoritarian facial recognition technology along with "preventive action" to apprehend prospective rioters before any crime occurred. His government claimed to have made 1,000 arrests, with courts working overtime to issue swift, severe sentences. Some rioters received 15-month sentences for individual Facebook posts, like Julie Sweeney, a grandmother and sole carer, whose inappropriate social media comment resulted in serious jail time.

The crackdown was intense, but Starmer notably missed multiple opportunities to acknowledge that while violence was unacceptable, it might reflect underlying grievances related to immigration that needed to be addressed. This oversight would prove costly.

The situation escalated when Elon Musk, the owner of X (formerly Twitter), weighed in. Responding to footage of the disorder, Musk tweeted that "civil war is inevitable" in the UK and criticised Starmer for not protecting all communities equally. He accused the Prime Minister of operating a "two-tier" policing system, coining the term "Two-Tier Keir."

Downing Street's response that Musk "does not speak for Britain" and dismissed his comments as unjustified only intensified the controversy. Musk doubled down, sharing posts that attacked UK authorities for arresting rioters while seemingly tolerating other forms of disorder. With 193 million followers on X compared to Starmer's 1.8 million, Musk's intervention significantly amplified the "two-tier" narrative.

The accusation of "two-tier policing" gained traction as it resonated with existing concerns. Just two weeks before the riots in Southport, disturbances in Harehills (Leeds) involving members of the Roma community saw police retreat. At the same time, a bus was set ablaze, and officers were attacked. Yet, Starmer made only a perfunctory statement regarding that incident, in stark contrast to his high-profile response to the events in Southport. The perceived double standard was undeniable.

Similarly, months of "pro-Palestine" protests in London, some featuring anti-Semitic chanting and Hamas symbols, received relatively little criticism from Starmer. One organising group, the Muslim Association of Britain, was founded by a former Hamas chief, yet suggestions that these events could be labelled "hate marches" were dismissed. This was contrasted sharply with the swift and harsh crackdown on anti-immigration protesters.

Reform UK leader Nigel Farage seized the opportunity, repeatedly asking in Parliament whether Britain had "two-tier policing and a two-tier justice system." His question provoked groans from Labour benches, but opinion polling indicated that the accusation had resonated with the public. YouGov found that the perception of two-tier policing had become widespread. Many remembered Starmer taking the knee during the 2020 Black Lives Matter protests, an image his critics wouldn't let him forget, especially after dozens of police officers were injured.

The situation deteriorated further when Starmer attempted to preempt critics on immigration. In May 2025, he delivered a speech and released a white paper warning that uncontrolled immigration risked turning Britain into an "island of strangers." Critics quickly noted that his language echoed Enoch Powell's infamous 1968 "Rivers of Blood" speech. The white paper outlined measures to reduce immigration, including doubling the time required to qualify for indefinite leave to remain from five to ten years.

The media response was swift and polarised. Right-wing outlets praised Starmer for finally "getting tough" on immigration, while progressive media and Labour's own support base expressed outrage. Critics accused Starmer of "feeding into far-right, anti-immigrant narratives" and abandoning Labour's traditional values. Muslim voters, historically a reliable Labour constituency, deserted the party in significant numbers. Analysis showed that Labour's vote share declined by 21 percentage points in council wards with over 20% Muslim residents.

The contradictions in Starmer's positions were glaring. When Reform UK proposed abolishing indefinite leave to remain entirely, Starmer labelled it "racist." Yet Labour's own policy of doubling the qualifying period to ten years drew criticism for being similar. Critics questioned how Labour could deem Reform's policies racist while implementing comparable ones. The confusion and apparent hypocrisy provided the media with ample material for coverage.

By late 2025, the label "Two-Tier Keir" had become entrenched. Opposition MPs frequently used it, and social media was filled with memes. Even former Labour supporters began to question whether Starmer truly understood or cared about their concerns. The Spectator noted that "two-tier policing is not an issue that blunt denials will make go away," arguing that any hint of two-tier justice would inevitably evoke the cry of "two-tier Keir."

Beyond optics and immigration, significant policy decisions have left vast segments of Labour's traditional support base feeling deeply disappointed. A troubling pattern has emerged: Starmer makes promises in opposition, only to abandon them once in government. Initially, the media offered Labour the benefit of the doubt, but they have increasingly documented these U-turns with hostility.

Perhaps the clearest example of Labour's betrayal of its traditional values is the decision to maintain the Conservatives' two-child benefit cap. Introduced in 2017, this Dickensian policy prevents parents with more than two children from receiving benefits or tax credits for additional children. The impact on families is severe, with charities estimating that abolishing the cap could immediately lift 300,000 children out of poverty.

While in opposition, Labour vehemently opposed the cap. Starmer spoke passionately about child poverty. Yet, within weeks of taking office, he not only retained the cap but also went further. In July 2024, Labour expelled seven MPs who voted to abolish it, including veteran campaigner Diane Abbott. The SNP's Stephen Flynn, who proposed the amendment, highlighted that ending the cap would immediately lift 300,000 children out of poverty. Starmer's response? "Financial constraints."

By July 2025, the situation had deteriorated further. The government announced a £5 billion cut to Universal Credit, but then reversed the decision within days due to a powerful public backlash. A More in Common poll revealed a net approval rating of -43, with 70% of voters perceiving the government as chaotic. Although the U-turn was politically necessary, it was reputationally disastrous.

The Guardian, a newspaper that has traditionally supported Labour, did not hold back: "For Labour, with its history of building Britain's welfare state, to maintain Tory benefit caps and even attempt further cuts raises fundamental questions about what the party stands for." They emphasised, "Will the kids eat or not?" And Starmer's answer has been a firm "not."

Other betrayals followed. Women Against State Pension Inequality (WASPI) campaigners, who had been promised compensation for sudden changes to pension ages, were informed that the government couldn't afford it. Many of these women, now in their 60s and 70s, saw their retirement plans shattered by Conservative policy changes. The Labour Party had pledged to rectify this injustice, but once in power, would it? Silence.

Veterans, who had placed their trust in Labour's 2024 manifesto promise to 'support our veterans,' were left deeply disappointed. Leader Keir Starmer's vow in opposition to address Gulf War illness and repeal legislation that limited veterans' legal claims against the Ministry of Defence had given them hope. However, nine months into power, neither promise had been fulfilled. Thirty-three thousand Gulf War illness sufferers remained without assistance, and veterans seeking justice watched as these promises faded away, leaving them feeling abandoned and disillusioned.

Most painfully for those who suffered unimaginable loss, Starmer broke his vow to bereaved Hillsborough families. He had committed in 2022 and again in 2024 to enacting a Hillsborough Law that imposes a duty of candour on public bodies to prevent cover-ups by April 15, 2025, the 36th anniversary of the disaster. When the deadline passed without any action, campaigner Charlotte Hennessy, who lost her father James in the tragedy, called the delay "a disrespect" to the 97 victims' families.

As the list of broken promises continued to grow, media coverage shifted dramatically from scepticism to open contempt. Outlets across the political spectrum began documenting Starmer's betrayals. The conservative press had a field day, but even media outlets sympathetic to Labour became disillusioned, reflecting the growing public sentiment of disappointment and betrayal.

A piece on the progressive blog "The Canary" captured the sentiment: "Starmer's Labour is in the pocket of millionaires." Current Affairs magazine published a scathing analysis titled "Keir Starmer is a Disgrace to the British Labour Party," arguing that "to 'take all the Left out' is to remove its soul." Journalist Neil Wilby compiled an extensive analysis, labelling Starmer "Four Tier Keir," categorising broken promises by severity, and noting his approval rating of only 27% as of March 2025.

Even billionaire investor John Caudwell's praise became a damaging indictment. On BBC Newsnight before the 2024 election, Caudwell stated: "What Keir has done is taken all the left out of the Labour Party. He's come out with a set of values and principles in complete alignment with my views as a commercial capitalist." Starmer responded that he was "delighted." For a Labour leader, such praise from a billionaire capitalist should have been politically toxic. The fact that it wasn't reveals not only how far Labour had drifted from its roots but also the powerful influence of the media narrative that had shifted to portray Starmer as a "Red Tory" rather than a progressive leader.

While Starmer faced the brunt of media criticism, Chancellor Rachel Reeves became a focal point for economic discontent. Her tenure demonstrated how relentless media scrutiny can destroy political careers by highlighting perceived failures.

In her first Autumn Budget in October 2024, Rachel Reeves announced a £25 billion increase in employers' National Insurance contributions, a payroll tax that immediately impacted businesses' bottom lines. The rationale behind this decision was to fund essential public services without raising income tax. However, the outcome was an unexpected and severe economic devastation.

Unemployment rose, job vacancies decreased, and hiring intentions plummeted. The Confederation of British Industry (CBI), representing employers, reported that the tax burden on businesses reached 30.5% in the latest financial year, the highest level since the turn of the century. Business confidence, which Labour had worked hard to build during the election campaign, evaporated overnight, causing a sudden shift in the economic landscape.

The media response was brutal and played a significant role in shaping public opinion. Business sections ran countless stories highlighting companies cutting jobs, cancelling investment plans, and considering relocating abroad. The Financial Times, typically supportive of Labour's economic strategies, questioned whether the government understood the fragility of business confidence. The Telegraph featured opinion pieces suggesting Reeves should be dismissed. Even outlets that usually favoured Labour began to wonder if the Chancellor had overstepped her bounds.

Reeves' personal approval ratings plummeted. By July 2025, her net favorability dropped to -45, comparable to Kwasi Kwarteng's disastrous ratings in October 2022, following the mini-budget that crashed the pound. In September 2025, YouGov reported her satisfaction rating at just 13%, with 69% of respondents dissatisfied, resulting in a net rating of -56. These statistics were disastrous for a Chancellor supposedly working to stabilise the economy after Conservative turmoil.

Labour had campaigned on the promise of delivering economic growth. "Growing the economy" was one of Keir Starmer's six key missions. Yet by 2025, economic growth was still sluggish. The Office for Budget Responsibility's forecasts for the deficit had deteriorated instead of improved, leading to increased borrowing and potential future financial instability. The first two quarters of 2024 saw growth rates of only 0.9% and 0.5% far from transformative. By 2025, the economy was flat-lining.

Bond markets grew increasingly anxious. The UK was paying a premium to borrow, reflecting investor concerns about fiscal sustainability. This premium, which was higher than that of other comparable economies, was a clear sign of the market's lack of confidence in the UK's economic management. Rachel Reeves's attempt to present Labour as the party of budgetary responsibility had faltered. Each time she promised restraint, another spending commitment or tax increase seemed to follow.

The media narrative shifted from "Labour will fix the economy" to "Labour doesn't understand the economy." Conservative critics seized the opportunity. Business leaders who had previously supported Labour publicly expressed regret. The government's business day at the 2024

Labour conference, where corporate delegates were charged £3,000 to attend but denied access to cabinet ministers, became a symbol of Labour's strained relationship with the private sector. This event, intended to showcase Labour's commitment to the business community, instead highlighted the growing disconnect between the party and its traditional supporters.

Importantly, voters were not experiencing any improvement. A YouGov poll in December 2024 found that when asked which party would be better at managing the economy, Labour and the Conservatives received almost equal ratings—23% for Labour and 24% for the Conservatives. The results were similar for the question of keeping prices down: 19% for Labour and 20% for the Conservatives. This was remarkable. After 14 years of Conservative economic mismanagement, Labour was unable to convince voters that it would perform better. The media's relentless focus on Labour's economic failures undermined the party's traditional advantage

By mid-2025, the economic narrative had solidified into a widely accepted view: Labour struggled to manage the economy, Rachel Reeves appeared out of her depth, and Keir Starmer lacked the political courage to make necessary decisions. Bill Blain, a strategist at Wind Shift Capital, told CNBC in May 2025, "Starmer lacks capable cabinet colleagues who can create the illusion of a strong leadership team. Some are beginning to settle into their roles, but most appear to be out of their depth. This is particularly true of Rachel Reeves, who is naturally not a risk-taker. The bigger issue is that Labour presents its approach as doing the right thing by controlling spending, but it has backfired, making it appear insensitive to its voters. They are perceived as cruel."

The media consensus was unmistakable: Labour had sacrificed competence for ideology, abandoned growth for austerity, and betrayed workers to appease bond markets. Whether this view was accurate or not, it dominated coverage and shaped public perception. The Guardian reported in June 2025 that "Labour's drop in the opinion polls during its first 10 months in power is the largest of any newly elected UK government in 40 years." For a government that had won a landslide just months earlier, this collapse was unprecedented.

As Labour's popularity fell, Reform UK's profile rose. The media's focus on Nigel Farage and his populist movement provided a stark contrast to their increasingly hostile coverage of Starmer. This shift illustrated how media narratives can create self-fulfilling prophecies.

Nigel Farage, the architect of Brexit and a persistent challenger to the establishment, founded Reform UK as a successor to UKIP. Initially dismissed as a protest party, Reform gained traction as disillusionment with mainstream politics intensified. By September 2025, Ipsos polling showed Reform UK leading with 34% support, while Labour had plummeted to just 22% the lowest recorded for the party since June 2009.

The media was captivated by Farage. His combative style, willingness to express unpopular opinions, and mastery of soundbites made him a constant source of headlines. While Starmer delivered earnest but monotonous speeches about fiscal responsibility, Farage was tweeting provocative statements on immigration, deriding "Two-Tier Keir," and attending Trump rallies in America. Television producers recognised that Farage boosted ratings, and newspaper editors knew he sold copies. Social media algorithms favoured his controversial remarks.

Significantly, Reform UK retained 89% of its 2024 voters while attracting substantial numbers from other parties, especially the Conservatives, with 39% of 2024 Tory voters switching to Reform. In contrast, Labour managed to retain only 50% of its 2024 voters, losing support to Reform UK (13%), the Greens (12%), the Liberal Democrats (10%), and even the Conservatives (8%).

The difference in media treatment between Starmer and Farage was striking. When Farage made contentious remarks about immigration, he was portrayed as "saying what people really think." Conversely, when Starmer attempted similar rhetoric, he was criticised for abandoning Labour values and echoing far-right talking points. Farage's simplistic solutions to complex issues were seldom scrutinised as thoroughly as Labour's policies. His party's lack of detailed costings or practical implementation plans went largely unchallenged.

Loughborough University's Centre for Research in Communication and Culture, which meticulously analyses election media coverage, noted a glaring disparity during the 2024 election campaign. Reform UK, a relatively minor party, received more TV and press coverage than the fourth largest party, the Liberal Democrats, and remained the party that received the highest number of positive evaluations overall.' This trend persisted into 2025, highlighting a significant imbalance in media coverage.

The BBC and other broadcasters, committed to maintaining 'balance,' provided Reform UK airtime in proportion to their polling numbers, which only increased their visibility and legitimacy. However, the real game-changer was the role of social media algorithms, which further amplified Nigel Farage's provocative content. This technological influence overshadowed Keir Starmer's commendable yet uninspiring leadership, which received far less attention and often negative coverage.

By the summer of 2025, polling suggested that Reform UK would win the next general election. YouGov's MRP (multi-level regression with post-stratification) projection indicated that nearly two-thirds of Labour MPs would lose their seats if an election were held at that time. The media began treating this outcome as inevitable, spawning endless speculation about Starmer's leadership and whether Labour would collapse entirely.

The traditional media's shift against Starmer was exponentially amplified by social media, where narratives spread faster than fact-checkers could debunk them. This environment allowed for coordinated criticism of the Prime Minister from multiple directions, underscoring the significant role of traditional media in shaping public opinion.

Elon Musk's X platform became a hub for anti-Starmer sentiment. Following their clash over the Southport riots, Musk frequently shared posts that criticised the Prime Minister. With Musk's massive following and X's algorithmic promotion of controversial content, these posts garnered millions of views. The hashtag "Two-Tier Keir" trended repeatedly, and memes mocking Starmer's perceived elitism and alleged disconnect from ordinary voters proliferated. These memes and the hashtag significantly contributed to the public perception of Starmer as an out-of-touch elitist. This narrative was further amplified by the reach of social media.

Interestingly, there is evidence that X's algorithms may have shielded Starmer's own feed from the worst criticism. In July 2024, the progressive outlet Skwawkbox published an analysis revealing that negative replies to Starmer's posts were often hidden behind "Show probable spam" warnings, even when these replies were not spam. This practice, whether due to algorithmic bias, paid prioritisation, or deliberate platform manipulation, had significant implications. Despite Starmer's posts typically receiving far more negative replies than positive engagement, an indication of deeply unpopular tweets, most of the critical responses were filtered from view. This contributed to the perception that Starmer was being protected even while criticised, fueling narratives about establishment cover-ups and the potential impact of platform manipulation on political discourse.

Meanwhile, Starmer's own social media presence was painfully lacklustre. The Spectator noted in January 2025 that while Starmer claimed to follow 410 users on X, only 69 were visible. He didn't appear to follow key cabinet members, such as Wes Streeting, Rachel Reeves, David Lammy, or Yvette Cooper. His posts were formulaic, corporate, and devoid of personality. In the week leading up to January 6, 2025, he managed to tweet just 15 times. In contrast, Farage maintained a relentless social media presence, often engaging directly with his followers and responding to their comments. Even Boris Johnson's chaotic but engaging Twitter feed, filled with personal anecdotes and witty remarks, highlighted Starmer's digital disconnect and the need for a more engaging social media strategy in contemporary politics.

The Labour Party's response to criticism on social media underscored its vulnerability in the face of the collapse of its narrative. Chief Whip Alan Campbell's letter to Labour MPs, cautioning them against engaging with Elon Musk's provocations, highlighted the party's sensitivity to the digital battlefield. The plea, 'It is important that you do not do anything that risks amplifying misinformation on social media and do not get drawn into debates online,' effectively acknowledged the party's struggle to maintain its narrative in the digital age.

The Online Safety Act 2023, a key initiative of Starmer's government, sparked a bipartisan backlash, raising serious concerns about free speech. Critics from across the political spectrum, from civil liberties groups to right-wing commentators, accused Labour of using the Act to suppress criticism and control online discourse. The government's announcement of plans for mandatory digital ID cards in 2025, ostensibly to combat illegal working, further fueled the backlash. The united front of both the left and the right, with Jeremy Corbyn and Nigel Farage leading the charge, and the 2.4 million Britons who signed a petition opposing the measure, underscored the widespread concern about the potential impact of these policies on UK politics.

The media narrative on Starmer solidified, painting him as a figure attempting to control speech, silence critics, and impose authoritarian measures on a free society. Whether this portrayal was accurate or not, it significantly shaped the public's perception. It reinforced the 'Two-Tier Keir' narrative, highlighting the power of media in shaping public opinion and the challenges faced by political figures in managing their public image.

Beyond specific policy failures or scandals, a more fundamental issue plagued Starmer's relationship with the media: no one quite knew who he was or what he stood for. This vacuum of personality and ideology allowed critics to fill it with their own narratives.

Professor John Curtice, Britain's most respected polling expert, perfectly captured the problem in September 2024: 'The mystery of Keir Starmer, who is he? What does he stand for? We are maybe two-thirds of the way through the novel, but we are still not sure where the body lies.' This 'mystery' refers to the public's uncertainty about Starmer's character, beliefs, and vision for the country. Starmer, Curtice noted, had made a virtue of being pragmatic rather than ideological, but this absence of 'Starmerism' left voters confused.

The biographical details were known: he is a successful barrister, former Director of Public Prosecutions, human rights lawyer, and was knighted for his services to law and criminal justice. However, these credentials, while impressive on paper, did not translate into political charisma or a compelling vision for Britain. When asked about his favourite novel, Starmer apparently didn't have one. Previous prime ministers had decorated Number 10 with photos of their political heroes; Starmer claimed he didn't have any political heroes.

This personality deficit proved catastrophic in modern media coverage, which increasingly focuses on character and narrative over policy details. Boris Johnson, despite his failures, was undeniably charismatic. Tony Blair had star quality. Even Theresa May's awkwardness became a defining characteristic that the media could work with. Starmer was simply... there. Competent, but uninspiring.

Bill Blain's May 2025 assessment of Sir Keir Starmer on CNBC was stark: "Starmer has great positives, signing trade deals, for one. But he is dull, boring, and precise. He is competent, but he lacks personality and political charisma... Farage has charisma in spades. So did Boris Johnson." In an age where media coverage prioritises personality over policy, this became a significant disadvantage for Starmer.

Starmer's background as a barrister, while shaping his political approach, also presented unique challenges. His instinct is to carefully parse language, avoid commitments that couldn't be legally defended, and respond to questions with qualifications and caveats. At the same time, it was legally sound, which made him appear evasive, calculating, and cold. This aspect of his background, often overlooked, had a significant influence on his political style.

When challenged about accepting freebies, Starmer maintained that he followed the rules and declared everything correctly in the end. This was legally correct but politically disastrous. When pressed about cutting winter fuel payments, he emphasised fiscal necessity and future economic growth, which was technically defensible but morally tone-deaf. When questioned about two-tier policing, he called it a "non-issue" and moved on. While legally safe, this approach was politically damaging.

The media, accustomed to politicians who engage emotionally and ideologically, found it difficult to deal with Starmer's lawyerly precision. He wasn't exactly lying, but he wasn't being fully honest either. He adopted a barrister's mentality: presenting the most favourable case for himself and the Labour government while technically staying within the bounds of truth. This complexity made it challenging for both voters and journalists to fully grasp his positions.

Al Jazeera's September 2025 analysis expressed this frustration: "Starmer looks like a man struggling to explain either the law or what he intends to do for the people who voted for him. On a practical level, Labour has lost the confidence of the business community it once sought to win over before the election." The very lawyerly traits that had made Starmer successful in legal practice, precision, caution, and rhetorical defensiveness, were undermining his political career.

Perhaps most damaging was the inability to clearly articulate what 'Starmerism' actually meant. This term, akin to 'Blairism' or 'Thatcherism,' would have encapsulated Starmer's political ideology and policy approach. Tony Blair had the 'Third Way.' Margaret Thatcher had neoliberalism and privatisation. Even Boris Johnson had 'levelling up,' however vague that may have been. What did Starmer stand for?

The Guardian's pre-conference editorial in 2025 noted that Starmer 'generally took an Anglo-American rather than a European position.' This was a reference to the American centrist approach of developing prosperity through deregulation, rapid infrastructure development, and market-led growth without emphasising the redistribution of income and wealth. In other words, Starmer's policies and rhetoric sounded more like those of a Clinton-era Democrat or a Blairite than a traditional Labour leader.

This ideological ambiguity meant that different groups projected their own hopes and fears onto Starmer. Progressives saw him as abandoning Labour's socialist roots. Business leaders perceived him as unreliable and prone to tax hikes. Working-class voters viewed him as an elitist lawyer disconnected from their lives. Pensioners regarded him as someone who would cut their benefits while accepting luxury gifts. Nobody saw a leader they could rally behind.

The media, lacking a clear narrative about what Starmer represented, defaulted to the most damaging perception: he was a calculating opportunist with no fixed principles, willing to say anything to get elected and then do whatever was politically expedient. The fact that he had ruthlessly transformed Labour from Jeremy Corbyn's socialist project into a centrist electoral machine expelling left-wing members, blocking left-wing candidates, and moving rightward on almost every issue only reinforced this negative image. This lack of a straightforward narrative left the public in a state of confusion and uncertainty about Starmer's true political stance.

Keir Starmer's relationship with the media has suffered significant damage due to catastrophic management and communication failures. His approach to press conferences, interviews, and public statements has not only alienated journalists but also eroded the confidence of voters. The impact of his media strategy on public opinion is undeniable.

In August 2024, Starmer addressed the nation from Downing Street, warning that the upcoming October budget would be 'painful.' This statement represented a significant breakdown in communication. Instead of inspiring confidence that the Labour Party would address Britain's challenges, he essentially told voters to brace themselves for hardship, a move that could potentially alienate a significant portion of the electorate. The media, as expected, seized upon this.

"I frankly don't want to take the tough decisions we will have to take," Starmer said, as if voters wanted to hear their Prime Minister express reluctance about governing. He framed the reduction in winter fuel payments as a necessary sacrifice, implying that pensioners should accept this loss because they "rely on a functioning NHS, good public transport, and strong national infrastructure." In essence, he was asking them to suffer now for the greater good in the future. The optics were terrible, and the messaging was even worse

The conservative press capitalised on this. The Daily Mail ran headlines like 'Pain Ahead' and 'Harsh Medicine.' Even outlets that typically support Labour questioned whether it was politically wise to warn of pain before delivering it. The media's role in shaping public perception is crucial and cannot be overstated. Voters do not elect governments to manage decline; they elect them to deliver prosperity. Starmer's messaging suggested that Labour was preparing the public for failure instead of promising success.

When the gifts scandal erupted, Starmer's defence only exacerbated the situation. He claimed he needed to accept corporate box tickets to Arsenal due to security concerns, suggesting it would be unsafe for him to sit in the stands with ordinary fans. This implication that the Prime Minister was too important or too threatened to mingle with the public played directly into narratives about elitism.

When pressed by journalists, Starmer remarked that voters would "think I am pretty self-centred" if he insisted on sitting in the stands while taxpayers footed the security bill. However, this reasoning was convoluted. If the security concerns were genuine, why attend football matches at all? Why not purchase tickets in a secure area using his substantial salary? His defence satisfied no one and generated more negative coverage than simple silence might have.

When he eventually repaid £6,000 worth of gifts, Starmer stated, "We are now going to bring forward principles for donations because, until now, politicians have used their best individual judgment on a case-by-case basis. So I made the decision that until the principles are in place, it was right for me to make those repayments." This bureaucratic explanation, suggesting that the repayment was about future protocols rather than admitting past mistakes, only reinforced perceptions that he was legalistic and evasive rather than contrite and honest.

One of the low points in Keir Starmer's media management came when he justified accepting £20,000 in accommodation donations from Lord Alli, a prominent figure in the Labour Party, by referencing his son's GCSE exams. During an interview on BBC Radio 4, Starmer stated: "My boy, 16, was in the middle of his GCSEs. I made him a promise, a promise that he would be able to get to his school, do his exams, without being disturbed. We have lots of journalists outside our house, and I'm not complaining about that; that's fine."

The notion that Starmer required an £18 million penthouse in Covent Garden to assist his son with his studies was swiftly met with ridicule. Most British teenagers, unlike the Prime Minister's son, take their GCSEs while living in regular homes with typical distractions. The idea that luxury accommodation was a necessity to shield the Prime Minister's son from 'disturbance' seemed out of touch and elitist. The Spectator's article, 'Starmer Uses Son's Exams as Excuse for Freebies,' underscored the media's incredulity and invited a more critical view.

These communication failures were not isolated incidents; they represented a pattern. Starmer consistently struggled to gauge public sentiment and failed to understand how his explanations would resonate with ordinary voters. His media team appeared either unable or unwilling to prevent these unforced errors. Consequently, a steady stream of negative coverage, including criticisms of his handling of Brexit negotiations and his stance on national security, emerged, undermining public confidence.

To understand the media's shift against Starmer, it's crucial to examine the British press landscape and how different outlets altered their coverage during Labour's first 15 months in government. The media's influence on public perception cannot be overstated; understanding their role is crucial to becoming more politically aware.

The Daily Mail, Telegraph, Express, and Sun have long been antagonistic toward Labour. During the 2024 election, most of these outlets reluctantly acknowledged that the Conservatives deserved to lose, with some even giving lukewarm endorsements to Labour. However, this support was always transactional and temporary. These papers are committed to defending conservative interests, and Labour's tax increases, welfare policies, and regulatory approach inevitably provoked opposition.

What is truly surprising is not that these papers turned hostile, but the speed and thoroughness with which they did. Within weeks of the election, the Mail was running front-page attacks on 'Two-Tier Keir.' The Telegraph labelled Starmer's government as 'worse than the Conservatives.' The Express warned readers of a 'socialist Britain.' The Sun, which had controversially backed Labour during the campaign, quickly reverted to its traditional Conservative allegiance.

The right-wing press, with its relentless focus on immigration, benefit scroungers, and threats to British values, wielded a significant influence. Their portrayal of Starmer as weak on crime, soft on immigration, and hostile to British interests, along with their amplification of Elon Musk's criticisms, significantly shaped public perception. As Reform UK rose in the polls, they provided favourable coverage of Farage, further influencing the political landscape. This was not just journalism; it was a powerful form of political warfare.

Equally significant was the shift in stance among centrist and centre-left outlets, notably The Guardian. Traditionally supportive of Labour, The Guardian's growing criticism was a notable change. While they still favoured Labour over the Conservatives, their editorial board began to question whether Starmer's government truly represented Labour values. Articles dissected broken promises, analysed polling collapses, and featured internal Labour critics, marking a significant shift in their coverage.

The BBC and other broadcasters, known for their commitment to impartiality, increasingly framed their coverage around Labour's failures. Starmer's plummeting approval ratings became a persistent story, and business dissatisfaction generated numerous segments. The winter fuel payment cut was presented as evidence of either incompetence or cruelty. While the BBC remained theoretically balanced, the overwhelming weight of negative news overshadowed any favourable coverage, highlighting a stark contrast with their usual impartiality.

The Times and Financial Times, as establishment publications that had cautiously backed Labour, became disillusioned with the government's economic management. Their business pages documented job cuts due to National Insurance increases, and their political coverage highlighted cabinet dysfunction and policy U-turns. These were not just partisan attacks but sober assessments of failure, which made them more damaging than the sensationalism of the Daily Mail.

Even left-wing outlets like Novara Media and The Canary turned hostile, accusing Starmer of betraying Labour's socialist heritage, abandoning the working class, and implementing 'Tory policies with a red rosette.' Their exposés of ongoing misconduct and broken promises to vulnerable groups generated headlines in mainstream media, amplifying criticism from Labour's traditional base and significantly impacting public perception.

British broadcast regulations require political balance, which paradoxically worked against Starmer. As Reform UK's polling improved, the party received more airtime. Farage became a regular presence on Question Time, Sunday morning political shows, and news analysis programs. His criticisms of the government were broadcast without equivalent scrutiny of Reform's own policies.

The BBC, ITV News, Sky News, and Channel 4 played a significant role in shaping public perception of Keir Starmer's leadership. Their extensive coverage of his difficulties, particularly the decline in his approval ratings, contributed to a narrative of failure. When Ipsos revealed that Starmer had the lowest Prime Ministerial approval rating ever recorded, it made headlines. YouGov's findings showed that Labour voters were turning against the party, sparking panel discussions. Additionally, by-elections that resulted in humiliating defeats prompted broadcasters to analyse the implications for Labour's survival.

This 'balance' led to negative stories about Labour receiving as much, if not more, coverage than the party's actual policy achievements. For instance, a trade deal with India received only a brief mention, while a pensioner struggling without winter fuel payments prompted extensive segments featuring emotional interviews. These segments, with their focus on human stories, brought the political narrative to a personal level. Media organisations were not being unfair; they were simply reporting the news. However, the news was overwhelmingly negative, and their coverage amplified that negativity.

Starmer's troubles extended beyond domestic policy. His handling of the Israel-Gaza conflict, especially his initial refusal to call for a ceasefire and his cautious criticism of Israeli actions, resulted in not just domestic backlash but also international media condemnation. This global scrutiny highlighted the far-reaching impact of UK politics.

Starmer had built his career on a foundation of human rights credentials. As Director of Public Prosecutions, he earned respect for his progressive approach to justice. However, his response to the situation in Gaza appeared to abandon those principles. Initially, he declined to call for a ceasefire, asserting Israel's right to defend itself. When questioned about civilian casualties, he offered legalistic answers regarding proportionality and international law instead of delivering heartfelt condemnations.

Progressive media outlets worldwide took notice. American publications like The Intercept and Current Affairs published scathing articles criticising Starmer's perceived complicity in what they described as genocide. Middle East Eye consistently analysed the situation, suggesting that Starmer was "running out of road" due in part to his handling of Gaza, which alienated Labour's Muslim voters and progressive base. Observers noted the stark contrast between Labour's harsh treatment of pro-Palestine protesters in the UK and its mild criticism of Israeli military actions.

The impact on Labour was severe. Muslim voters abandoned the party in significant numbers. In council wards with large Muslim populations, Labour's vote shares plummeted. Independent candidates running on pro-Palestine platforms began winning seats that Labour had held for decades. The media reported extensively on this fragmentation, framing it as evidence that Starmer had miscalculated badly.

By mid-2025, facing a potential electoral disaster, Starmer made a significant rhetorical shift regarding the Gaza Strip. The government formally recognised Palestinian statehood and intensified its criticism of Israeli policies. However, this change came too late to repair the damage. Pro-Palestine campaigners viewed the actions as insufficient, while pro-Israel supporters felt betrayed by the abrupt shift. The media, always quick to shape public opinion, portrayed it as yet another instance of Starmer lacking conviction and merely responding to polling pressures.

Labour's media relations suffered further when the party barred journalists from Declassified UK from attending the 2025 Labour conference. This ban marked the second consecutive year that Declassified, known for its critical investigations into UK arms sales to Israel and the government's involvement in Gaza, had been denied access.

Press freedom groups condemned this decision. Labour MP Richard Burgon stated, "Declassified has provided crucial reporting on Israel's war on Gaza and our government's involvement. It is deeply concerning that their accredited journalists have been denied entry to the Labour

Party conference." This action suggested that Labour was attempting to control media narratives by excluding critical voices, which undermined its claims of transparency and accountability.

This exclusion was not an isolated incident. Declassified, known for its critical investigations into UK arms sales to Israel and the government's involvement in Gaza, also revealed that they had been denied parliamentary press passes, with internal emails indicating that officials cited their 'in-depth investigations... from a particular standpoint' as the reason for the rejection. Similarly, the London arms fair had denied them access. This pattern indicated a coordinated effort to exclude journalists whose coverage challenged government positions, highlighting the importance of independent journalism in a democratic society.

Mainstream media outlets, even those that disagreed with Declassified's political stance, critically reported on this censorship. Press freedom is a fundamental principle for journalists across the political spectrum. When Labour appeared to restrict access based on political beliefs, it led to cross-party media condemnation and reinforced narratives about authoritarian tendencies within the party.

By autumn 2025, Starmer's approval ratings had entered a damaging downward spiral. Each poll that reported historic lows generated media coverage, further harming public perception and leading to worse polling results. This cycle of negative publicity, perpetuated by the media's obsession with polling data, a relatively recent phenomenon, created a self-reinforcing feedback loop that accelerated Labour's decline.

The statistics are brutal:

- Ipsos: 13% satisfaction, 79% dissatisfaction (net -66)—the worst Prime Minister rating since 1977
- YouGov: 23% favourable, 67% unfavourable (net -44)—multiple record lows.
- More in Common: net approval of -43 following the Universal Credit U-turn.
- City AM/Freshwater Strategy: net approval of -41.

Even among Labour's own voters, the picture is catastrophic. By May 2025, 50% of those who voted Labour in 2024 had an unfavourable view of Starmer, a 17-point increase since April. This marks the first time Starmer recorded a net negative approval rating among Labour voters, with half of them now regretting their choice.

Cabinet colleagues fared no better. Rachel Reeves had a -56 net rating, comparable to Kwasi Kwarteng's disastrous approval rating after the mini-budget. Angela Rayner received a -32, her worst score ever, while Yvette Cooper had -22 and Wes Streeting -19. The entire government is underwater.

In contrast, opponents saw improvements. Nigel Farage's favorability rating rose to 32%, the highest recorded by YouGov since he assumed leadership of Reform UK. Andy Burnham, the mayor of Manchester, achieved a rare positive net rating (+7) and sparked speculation about a leadership challenge. Even Jeremy Corbyn, previously reviled by the establishment and media during his tenure, now has a better net favorability score (-35 to -37) than his successor.

These numbers generated headlines that became self-fulfilling prophecies. Outlets reported: "Starmer: UK's Most Unpopular PM on Record" (CNN), "Approval Rating Hits Historic Low" (various), and "Worse Than Liz Truss" (multiple sources). Each headline reinforced the public perception that Starmer was failing catastrophically.

The media coverage rarely provided context. Few outlets mentioned that Starmer had inherited multiple crises, that the opposition was fragmented, or that comparable governments historically faced similar mid-term difficulties. The narrative was straightforward: Starmer was the worst prime minister ever, full stop.

This became a meta-story that journalists found irresistible. The panel discussed why Starmer was so unpopular. Columnists analysed what had gone wrong. Political experts appeared on broadcasts to dissect Labour's decline. The coverage itself, an endless discussion of Starmer's unpopularity, likely contributed to making him even more unpopular.

YouGov's John Curtice noted that Labour had "suffered the worst-ever fall in support for a newly elected government." This was not an opinion; it was a measurable fact. The media reported it endlessly, ensuring that every Briton was aware of their government's historic unpopularity. In an era when media consumption shapes political reality, this coverage may have been more consequential than the underlying factors causing the unpopularity.

As media coverage grew increasingly critical and polling numbers plummeted, speculation about Keir Starmer's survival as leader became a daily topic of discussion among political journalists. This coverage, whether accurate or not, further undermined the Prime Minister's authority and the Labour Party's effectiveness.

By spring 2025, multiple media outlets were reporting on potential leadership challenges within the Labour Party. The Guardian mentioned that Labour MPs were privately questioning Starmer's ability to remain in charge. The Telegraph suggested that Angela Rayner was positioning herself as a potential successor, while The Times indicated that Andy Burnham, the popular mayor of Greater Manchester, might consider a challenge.

These reports, often based on anonymous sources and speculation, created a climate of constant crisis. The media, with its fixation on Labour's internal dynamics, played a significant role in shaping public perception. Every Labour MP who provided even a mildly critical defence of the government was labelled a potential rebel. Likewise, any ambitious shadow cabinet minister was portrayed as plotting against Starmer. This focus on internal politics meant that substantive policy discussions were overshadowed by Westminster gossip.

Despite YouGov polling showing that Labour members remained surprisingly supportive—71% felt the party had performed well in government, the perspectives of the membership mattered little compared to the electoral survival of the MPs. With projections indicating that two-thirds of Labour MPs would lose their seats if an election were held, backbenchers became increasingly restless. Media coverage of this unease only intensified their anxiety.

Particular media attention was directed at Andy Burnham. A Cabinet minister under Gordon Brown and Ed Miliband, Burnham had twice unsuccessfully run for the Labour leadership. As mayor since 2017, he had built a reputation for competence, authenticity, and a connection with working-class voters, qualities that Starmer seemed to lack.

Burnham's net favorability rating of +7 made him unique among British politicians. YouGov polling indicated that 54% of Labour members would prefer him to replace Starmer in a leadership election, a significant margin over any other candidate. The media eagerly embraced this story: the popular northern mayor who could rescue Labour from the out-of-touch London lawyer. This portrayal of Burnham by the press had the potential to significantly influence public opinion and, consequently, the Labour Party's internal dynamics.

Although Burnham repeatedly denied any interest in challenging Starmer, insisting that he wanted to focus on his work in Greater Manchester, such denials only fueled further speculation. The media scrutinised every Burnham speech for signs of leadership ambition. Each policy difference he voiced with the government was depicted as a potential platform for a future leadership bid. This coverage served two purposes: it undermined Starmer and promoted a narrative of internal chaos that further damaged Labour.

Unexpectedly, Jeremy Corbyn, who had been expelled from Labour for failing to fully accept an EHRC report on antisemitism , emerged as a factor in media coverage. In July 2025, Corbyn announced plans to launch 'Your Party' as an alternative to what he termed the 'control freaks' of Labour. This announcement sparked extensive media coverage, with speculation about how many Labour MPs might defect to Corbyn's new venture and the potential impact of such defections on Labour's internal dynamics.

The polling data revealed a striking irony: a quarter of Britons held favourable opinions of Jeremy Corbyn, a man who had been expelled from Labour by Starmer and relentlessly criticised during his leadership. Notably, Corbyn's net favorability score was higher than that of Keir Starmer. This dynamic allowed the media to spin damaging narratives, fuelled by the irresistible irony that the man Starmer had expelled was now more popular than the current Prime Minister.

Even Labour-supporting media outlets couldn't ignore the internal dissent within the party. They published articles questioning whether Starmer's aggressive transformation of the party—expelling Corbyn's allies, blocking left-wing candidates, and shifting to the right—had been worthwhile. These articles created the impression that the party was on the brink of civil war, amplifying the potential for political upheaval.

The media's abandonment of Keir Starmer and his Labour government represents a perfect storm of political, economic, and communication failures, intensified by a fragmented and hostile media landscape. Within 15 months, Starmer transformed from a landslide election winner into the most unpopular Prime Minister ever recorded—an extraordinary decline that reflects both his genuine failures and the immense power of relentless negative media coverage.

The media's shift against Starmer wasn't arbitrary or coordinated; it stemmed from multiple factors:

1. Broken Promises: The disparity between what Labour promised in opposition and what it delivered in government created valid grounds for criticism. Issues like WASPI pensions, veteran support, the Hillsborough Law, and the two-child benefit cap highlighted Starmer's betrayals and provided journalists with ample material.

2. Poor Optics: Scandals such as the freebies controversy and cuts

to winter fuel payments made Starmer appear hypocritical and out of touch. In modern politics, perception often matters more than reality, and Starmer's management of his public image was disastrously ineffective.

3. Economic Difficulties: Rachel Reeves' tax increases, coupled with ongoing economic stagnation, undermined Labour's central claim to competence. Disillusionment within the business community generated negative coverage across the media spectrum.

4. Immigration Controversy: The 'Two-Tier Keir' narrative, which accused Starmer of having different standards for different people, along with Elon Musk's intervention and Starmer's own inflammatory rhetoric, fueled a media frenzy that damaged his reputation across political divides.

5. Personality Deficit: Starmer's lawyerly demeanour, perceived lack of charisma, and unclear ideological stance left a void that critics readily filled with negative narratives. Modern media requires compelling characters, and Starmer did not fit that bill.

6. Polling Death Spiral: As approval ratings began to decline, media coverage of that decline intensified, creating a self-reinforcing cycle of negativity.

7. Rise of Reform UK: Nigel Farage's adeptness with the media and the polling success of Reform UK provided journalists with an alternative narrative to cover. The rise of Reform implicitly underscored Labour's failures and the growing competition in the political arena.

8. Social Media Dynamics: The algorithms of platforms like X (formerly Twitter), which often prioritise controversial or harmful content, Musk's criticisms, and viral content amplified negative narratives beyond the reach of traditional media. Labour's inability to effectively compete in the digital space proved to be catastrophic.

Britain's fragmented media landscape ensured that criticism of

261

Labour came from all directions. Right-wing papers accused the party of being socialist while implementing austerity measures. Left-wing outlets condemned Keir Starmer for betraying progressive values. Business media highlighted economic incompetence, while broadcasters, committed to balanced reporting, gave equal weight to both criticism and achievements. Social media platforms amplified the most inflammatory content, and the international press covered Labour's struggles with Gaza and its authoritarian tendencies.

No government could survive such coordinated hostility. The fact that much of the criticism was legitimate, rooted in real policy failures and broken promises, made it impossible to dismiss as mere partisan attacks.

The story of Starmer illustrates a profound aspect of modern British politics and the media. A government that won a landslide majority became historically unpopular within a year. A leader who promised integrity became associated with hypocrisy. A party built initially to represent working people alienated them through harsh cuts to vulnerable populations.

While the media didn't cause these failures, they certainly magnified them. In an era dominated by 24-hour news cycles, social media virality, and an obsession with polling, negative narratives can destroy political careers with unprecedented speed. The traditional media's business model increasingly relies on controversy and conflict rather than nuanced policy analysis. Social media algorithms tend to favour inflammatory content over thoughtful debate. The outcome is a political environment where governments can plummet in public opinion before having a chance to implement their programs.

Whether Starmer will survive to contest the next election remains uncertain. As of September 2025, media speculation suggests a leadership challenge is likely. Reform UK is leading in the polls, indicating they could form the next government, a scenario that seemed unthinkable just months ago. Labour MPs are concerned about their seats, and cabinet ministers are witnessing a decline in their approval ratings.

The media, having turned against Starmer, now actively speculates about his demise. Whether this represents journalistic necessity reporting on political realities or serves as a self-fulfilling prophecy is up for debate. What's certain is that the fragmented and hostile British media landscape has played a central role in Labour's extraordinary collapse

For future historians studying this period, the key question will not be whether the media abandoned Starmer; that is beyond dispute.

Instead, they will ask: Did the media turn against him because he deserved it, or did their actions make this outcome inevitable? Was it a case of journalism, or was it political warfare? In a time when media coverage shapes political reality as much as it reflects it, does the distinction even matter?

Unfortunately, the answer, much like the Starmer premiership itself, remains frustratingly unclear.

Chapter 17
Reform UK's Inexorable Rise

By October 2025, fifteen months after Labour's landslide victory, the political landscape had undergone drastic changes. Reform UK, the populist movement led by Nigel Farage, had gained a commanding lead in opinion polls, consistently reaching 30-35% in national surveys. Labour, which had won 411 seats in July 2024, had now fallen to third place, with support dwindling to the low 20s. The pressing question facing Britain was no longer whether Reform UK threatened Labour's dominance, but the potential risks to British democracy if Reform UK were to ascend to power.

Would Reform UK moderate their stance once in power, as some optimists hoped? Or would they pursue a radical agenda that had garnered their support, fundamentally reshaping Britain in ways that would be hard to reverse? Historical examples, unfortunately, provide little reassurance. Populist movements that came to power rarely moderated; they often radicalised, interpreting their electoral success as a mandate for even bolder actions. Examples from Viktor Orbán's Hungary, Recep Erdoğan's Turkey, and Narendra Modi's India have shown how democratic elections can result in governments that systematically dismantle the checks and balances that protect democracy.

Britain's constitutional structure offered fewer safeguards than many assumed. The principle of parliamentary sovereignty meant that a government with a sufficient majority could legislate almost anything it wanted. There was no written constitution limiting governmental power, and the courts could not strike down primary legislation as unconstitutional. The House of Lords could delay but not prevent a determined government from implementing its agenda. Reform's promises to 'reform' institutions such as the civil service, judiciary, regulators, and even Parliament itself indicated a strong awareness of these constitutional possibilities, raising concerns about the future of these institutions.

The Cultural Reckoning

Beyond concerns related to institutions, there are deeper questions about British identity and social cohesion. The success of Reform UK, a political party that emerged in response to these questions, reflected not only policy preferences but also a fundamental disagreement about what Britain is and what it should be. The flags on lampposts, the Tommy Robinson marches gaining traction in 2024 and 2025, and the protests against asylum hotels all demonstrate a nation grappling with changes that it has not debated correctly or democratically chosen.

The diversity that has transformed British cities over recent decades, generally peaceful and often enriching, has also posed challenges for communities experiencing rapid demographic shifts. However, this change has not been accompanied by an honest national conversation about integration, identity, and belonging. Politicians have either celebrated multiculturalism without reservation or opposed it with evident xenophobia. The space between these extremes, where most Britons actually reside, has been shamefully unrepresented in mainstream political discourse, highlighting the need for more inclusive political representation.

Reform UK stepped into this void with a message that resonated deeply, even if it was unsettling. Their stance that Britain should prioritise British people, British culture, and British interests seemed obvious to their supporters, while it appalled many progressives who viewed such prioritisation as inherently discriminatory. The debate over whether national preference is a legitimate democratic choice or a dangerous form of ethnic nationalism remains unresolved, a tension that Reform skillfully exploited.

These tensions were exacerbated by a generational divide that deepened through 2025. Young Britons, who have grown up in diverse cities where multiculturalism is the norm and who view Brexit as self-harm, struggled to understand older voters' attachment to a Britain primarily rooted in memory. On the other hand, older Britons, who felt their communities had changed without their consent and whose concerns were often dismissed as bigotry, resented being lectured on tolerance and openness.

Reform UK's effectiveness lay in its ability to address the experiences of older voters without alienating them through overtly racist policies. Nigel Farage understood that most people did not harbour personal hatred toward immigrants; instead, they felt their communities had changed too quickly, leaving them feeling they had lost control and that their concerns were unrepresented. By validating those feelings while offering concrete solutions such as 'Operation Restoring Justice,' which promised to deport 600,000 illegal immigrants and process asylum claims offshore, Reform built a coalition that transcended traditional political boundaries. 'Operation Restoring Justice' was a policy aimed at addressing the concerns of many Britons about the perceived lack of control over immigration and asylum processes.

The Economic Reality Check

Beyond the rhetoric and emotion surrounding Reform's policies, there were complex economic realities that would eventually pose significant challenges. Britain's economy was deeply integrated into global systems that could not simply be disregarded through nationalist posturing. The country imported 40% of its food, relied on international supply chains for manufacturing, and needed foreign investment to fund public services.

Reform's promise to reduce immigration, increase protectionism, lower taxes, and simultaneously improve public services was not grounded in economic reality. A decrease in the workforce would lead to labour shortages in critical sectors such as healthcare, agriculture, hospitality, and construction, which were already facing significant workforce gaps by autumn 2025. Increasing trade barriers would raise costs for both consumers and businesses. Tax cuts would diminish revenue, while an ageing population would increase pressure on spending. The mathematics of their proposals simply did not add up, no matter how appealingly Nigel Farage presented them.

Throughout 2025, economic experts from across the political spectrum raised concerns about Reform's plans. The Institute for Fiscal Studies estimated that "Operation Restoring Justice", a key part of Reform's policy, would cost around £28 billion to implement, far exceeding any claimed savings from reduced welfare spending. In its October 2025 assessment, the Office for Budget Responsibility expressed concerns that Reform's economic proposals could lead to a recession. Additionally, the Bank of England highlighted concerns about inflation if policies limited labour supply while increasing demand.

However, Reform's supporters remained sceptical of expert opinions. They recalled predictions of catastrophic outcomes following Brexit that had not materialised, at least not in an apparent or immediate way. They had also experienced the economic policies of supposedly competent governments, such as Conservative austerity and Labour's continuation of strict fiscal policies that had left them feeling poorer. They preferred Farage's straightforward and confident messaging over the complex warnings from experts, which included concerns about labour shortages, increased costs, diminished revenue, and inflation.

This created a troubling dynamic where Reform could make impossible promises, be corrected by experts, and then use those corrections as proof of an elite conspiracy against ordinary people. The phrase "They said Brexit would be a disaster, and Britain survived" evolved into "They're saying our immigration policy won't work because they don't want it to work." This feedback loop was self-reinforcing and resistant to factual correction, fostering a post-truth political environment where trust became more valuable than evidence. In such an environment, policy decisions are not based on reality but on what people are willing to believe, leading to potentially disastrous outcomes.

Labour's Self-Inflicted Wounds

The rise of Reform was not just a result of Labour's significant failures but a reflection of the public's growing discontent. Each major scandal, policy reversal, and authoritarian action in 2025 not only reinforced Nigel Farage's critiques but also resonated with the public, driving them towards Reform.

The cuts to winter fuel payments in September 2024, affecting 10 million pensioners, didn't just spark immediate outrage-it ignited a fire of public discontent that persisted. Starmer's justification for these cuts only added fuel to the fire, especially when contrasted with above-inflation pay rises for junior doctors and train drivers. The message was clear: Labour was perceived as rewarding union supporters while punishing vulnerable pensioners, fueling public outrage.

The Alli scandal in 2024 exposed a stark contrast within Labour's leadership. Lord Alli's lavish donations to Starmer, spent on designer goods and luxury accommodation, stood in stark contrast to the loss of fuel allowances for pensioners. Angela Rayner's holiday in Ibiza, funded by Alli, Bridget Phillipson's extravagant birthday party, and Rachel Reeves' clothing donations further highlighted this contrast, leaving the public feeling indignant.

The disability benefits debacle in early 2025 further damaged Labour's reputation for fiscal prudence disguised as cruelty. Plans to remove Personal Independence Payments from 400,000 disabled individuals, justified by claims of encouraging people to "get back to work," ignored the reality that many recipients had conditions preventing employment. Although the policy was eventually scaled back under pressure, the damage had already been done; Labour appeared willing to target the vulnerable while rewarding the well-connected.

Most damaging was Labour's authoritarian shift throughout 2025.

The implementation of the Online Safety Act led to a series of high-profile prosecutions for social media posts, which criminalise opinions rather than genuine incitement. The announcement of the 'BritCard,' a mandatory digital ID system combining NHS records, benefits data, and online activity, in June 2025, met with immediate backlash. Civil liberties groups condemned it as a form of surveillance infrastructure, while the public viewed it as Orwellian overreach, significantly impacting their privacy and freedom.

These policies transformed Nigel Farage from a fringe agitator into a prophetic voice. His warnings about Labour's authoritarianism, which had been dismissed as paranoid conspiracy theories during the 2024 campaign, now appeared prescient. His promise to "restore British freedom" resonated with voters who felt their liberties were being systematically eroded by a government that had initially claimed it would restore competent governance.

The Devolved Nations

Reform UK's rise manifested differently across Britain's devolved nations, highlighting how Labour's failures resonated through various constitutional and cultural contexts.

In Scotland, where Labour had won 37 seats in 2024, a modest recovery from the SNP's long-standing dominance, the party's rapid decline in popularity created opportunities for both nationalist and populist movements. Anas Sarwar, the leader of Scottish Labour, found himself defending Westminster policies that were toxic within the Scottish political culture. The Winter Fuel Cuts, a controversial policy that reduced fuel subsidies for households, had a significant impact on Scotland, particularly due to its harsher winters. Additionally, the BritCard proposal, a digital ID scheme that seemed to force Scots to identify as British under Keir Starmer's branding, was politically damaging.

John Swinney's SNP, despite facing its own scandals following Nicola Sturgeon's resignation, benefited from Labour's setbacks. His rejection of the BritCard, "I am opposed to mandatory digital ID. Furthermore, by calling it BritCard, the Prime Minister seems to be attempting to force every Scot to declare ourselves British. I am a Scot", resonated strongly with voters. By October 2025, polls indicated that the SNP was recovering to 35-38%, while Labour had fallen to third place behind the Conservatives. Reform UK remained weak in Scotland, polling at 6-7%, but even that modest support posed a threat to Labour in

Central Belt constituencies.

Wales presented a different dynamic. Labour had governed continuously since devolution in 1999, but by October 2025, it faced its most serious challenge in a generation. Vaughan Gething's brief tenure as First Minister from March to July 2024 ended in resignation over donation scandals that foreshadowed Westminster's troubles. These scandals, involving alleged misuse of public funds, tarnished the Welsh Labour brand. His successor, Eluned Morgan, inherited a Welsh Labour brand tarnished by its associations with failures in both Cardiff Bay and Westminster.

Plaid Cymru capitalised effectively on Labour's vulnerabilities. Their leader, Rhun ap Iorwerth, positioned Plaid as defenders of Welsh interests against "London Labour." Polling in the autumn of 2025 showed Plaid gaining traction in traditional Labour strongholds, such as Rhondda, Blaenau Gwent, and Merthyr. However, the more serious threat came from Reform UK. Their polling in Wales, ranging from 11% to 13%, predominantly came from former Labour voters in post-industrial communities and coastal towns. Constituencies in the M4 corridor and along the North Wales coast, which had been Labour strongholds since the party's inception, now appeared vulnerable.

In Northern Ireland, the unique political landscape meant that Reform UK gained little support. However, Labour's failures still had a profound impact on the province. The ongoing dysfunction at Stormont worsened under Labour's watch, with Westminster providing minimal attention. Labour's authoritarian policies heightened tensions, especially given Northern Ireland's history of state surveillance. Republican communities that had experienced decades of monitoring by British security services were particularly alarmed by the Online Safety Act and the BritCard proposal. Sinn Féin's Michelle O'Neill described these proposals as "ludicrous and ill-thought-out," marking rare public criticism from a party that typically maintained careful relations with Labour.

The Opposition Landscape

Jeremy Corbyn, serving as an independent MP for Islington North after being expelled from the Labour Party's parliamentary party, became a symbol of missed opportunities. His principled opposition to the government's authoritarian direction, consistent criticism of benefit cuts, and steadfast support for Palestinian rights positioned him as a focal point for disillusioned left-wing voters through 2025.

Corbyn's "Peace and Justice Project" gained renewed significance as mainstream Labour moved away from progressive ideals. His rallies attracted thousands, particularly young people disenchanted with Starmer's broken promises. Videos of his parliamentary speeches criticising government policies frequently went viral, and his social media presence rivalled that of Cabinet ministers.

However, Corbyn's role seemed more akin to that of a prophet than a politician. At 76, he made no effort to launch a new party or organise a challenge to Labour from the left. The missed opportunities were glaring, as an effective left-wing party could have harnessed the anger that Reform UK was channelling towards the right. Yet, the British left remained fragmented among Labour loyalists, Corbyn supporters, and various small parties that struggled to gain traction.

The Green Party of England and Wales emerged as a genuine progressive alternative. Their co-leaders, Carla Denyer and Adrian Ramsay, articulated a coherent critique of Labour's failures while presenting a positive vision of environmental justice and social democracy. By October 2025, the Greens polled between 8% and 10%, marking historic highs, driven by Labour voters who could not support Starmer's government but were reluctant to consider Reform's nationalism.

In their four constituencies, Brighton Pavilion, Bristol Central, North Herefordshire, and Waveney Valley Green MPs established themselves as principled opponents. They voted against the Online Safety Act, vigorously opposed BritCard, and consistently challenged benefit cuts. By-election victories in Oxford East and Cambridge North in September 2025, both won from Labour with swings exceeding 20%, demonstrated the Greens' potential to become the progressive choice in university constituencies, sparking a sense of hope among the audience.

Ed Davey's Liberal Democrats, who won 72 seats in the 2024 election, faced strategic decisions about their positioning amid Labour's decline. Their success was primarily driven by affluent Southern constituencies, the 'Blue Wall' that collapsed as Tory voters sought more moderate options. Their opposition to BritCard combined civil libertarian principles with an appeal to privacy-conscious affluent voters.

The Liberal Democrats' polling, which indicated 11% to 12% support by October 2025, suggested they had maximised support from their traditional base but struggled to reach new demographics. While their MPs were popular and well-regarded in the constituencies they held, they found it difficult to gain attention in a media landscape dominated by Labour's crisis and Reform's rise. Davey's criticism of

Labour was measured but lacked the aggression that could have attracted greater attention.

The May 2026 Question

Towards May 2026: The Path to a Hung Parliament and Coalition Arithmetic

As October 2025 drew to a close, attention shifted to the local elections scheduled for May 2026. This would be the first major electoral test of Labour's governance and the surge of Reform UK, a pivotal moment that could reshape the political landscape. The elections would determine control of numerous English councils, with thousands of council seats contested, as well as mayoral elections in several regions. Additionally, crucial elections for the Scottish Parliament and the Welsh Senedd were scheduled to take place on the same day, further underlining the significance of the event.

The stakes were high for all parties involved. According to YouGov's September 2025 MRP projection, Reform UK would win 311 seats in a general election held at that time, falling just 15 seats short of an absolute majority. In contrast, Labour would face a disastrous collapse to just 144 seats, a loss of 267 from their landslide victory in 2024. These projected seat counts could have profound consequences for the future political landscape.

Scenario One: A Potential Game-Changer Reform-Conservative Coalition

What could the potential Reform-Conservative Coalition mean for the UK political landscape? If Reform UK, projected to win 311 seats, combines with the Conservatives, who are expected to secure 46 seats, the total would amount to 357 seats. This is the same number of seats that the Conservatives won alone under Theresa May in the 2017 election, when they depended on a confidence and supply arrangement with the Democratic Unionist Party. It's a scenario that could raise concerns and prompt thoughtful consideration of the potential outcomes and historical comparisons.

Scenario Two: The Anti-Reform Rainbow Coalition

The alternative approach to preventing the Reform Party from gaining power would require an unprecedented "grand coalition" of all other parties, a unity government formed solely to stop Farage from entering Downing Street.

However, the arithmetic reveals significant challenges. Combining Labour's projected 178 seats with the Liberal Democrats' 76 seats and the SNP's 38 seats would often fall short of a majority in most simulations. This uncertainty adds a layer of complexity to the already daunting task of forming an anti-Reform coalition.

This highlights the mathematical difficulty of forming an anti-Reform coalition, but the political obstacles are even more daunting. Such a coalition would necessitate:

1. Labour and Conservative Cooperation: The two parties that have dominated British politics for over a century would need to govern together, setting aside fundamental disagreements on economics, social policy, and Brexit.

2. Scottish Independence Tensions: The SNP's involvement would likely require concessions regarding Scottish independence, which both Labour and the Conservatives oppose. The SNP has shown signs of recovery, with YouGov projecting them to win 37 seats, up 28 from 2024, making them a crucial partner with significant leverage.

3. Liberal Democrat Positioning: With projections of winning 78 seats, the Liberal Democrats would hold a position of power as potential kingmakers. Their past coalition government with the Conservatives from 2010 to 2015 significantly harmed their electoral standing, making them cautious about any arrangement that could be perceived as betraying their voters.

4. Ideological Incoherence: A government that spans from Conservatives to Greens would lack a coherent program beyond the singular goal of 'stopping Reform.' How would such a coalition agree on issues like taxation, environmental policy, defence spending, or welfare reform? The resulting coalition agreement would likely be ambiguous, satisfying no one and vulnerable to collapse at any moment. This lack of a clear direction could lead to internal conflict and instability.

5. Democratic Legitimacy: Reform would relentlessly portray this coalition as an establishment conspiracy aimed at denying the will of the people. With Reform leading in 91% of simulations and winning more seats than any other party, this narrative could gain traction.

The May 2026 Crucible

The volatility observed in the May 2026 elections was unprecedented. Reform UK was projected to win 311 seats, including 82 constituencies where the margins of victory were less than five percentage points. This suggested that future swings in voter preference could dramatically alter outcomes. According to YouGov's projections, 143 constituencies had winners receiving less than 30% of the vote, with Reform UK's average margin of victory being just seven percentage points. This fragmented and chaotic electoral landscape meant that the local elections in May 2026 could either propel or hinder Reform's momentum, potentially reshaping the UK's political landscape.

The psychological impact of the May 2026 results would be just as significant as the actual changes in seat distribution. Should Reform gain control of numerous councils, perform well in mayoral contests, and demonstrate strength in the Scottish and Welsh elections, several dynamics would intensify:

Conservative Defections: Each victory for Reform would embolden Conservative MPs who were considering defection. The remaining 45 Conservative MPs would face tremendous pressure to choose their side, whether to join Reform and possibly secure ministerial positions or stay with a faltering party and risk electoral failure. The prospect of a Reform-Conservative coalition, while potentially beneficial for Reform, could actually accelerate the decline of the Conservative Party, as ambitious MPs calculated that Reform's branding might have more future potential than that of the Conservatives.

Labour's Leadership Crisis: Labour was projected to hold just 144 seats, losing over two-thirds of the seats gained in their 2024 landslide victory, which would inevitably lead to leadership challenges against Keir Starmer despite recent reshuffles. Internal disputes would be harsh, with questions arising about whether their collapse was due to Starmer's centrist approach or a lack of radicalism. The party would face pressure to decide whether to move left to recapture lost voters or risk driving more voters toward the Reform party. The potential for Labour to fracture between those advocating cooperation with other parties to block Reform and those insisting on maintaining its independence, even in opposition, is a significant concern.

The Media Narrative Shift: The media coverage would transition from questioning "Can Reform win?" to analysing possible coalition scenarios. Every statement from Conservative or Labour figures would be closely scrutinised for indications of coalition willingness. Nigel Farage would dominate media discussions, positioned as the Prime Minister-in-waiting, while his opponents struggled to present a coherent alternative. The normalisation of Reform as a viable governing party would accelerate, making previously unthinkable arrangements suddenly appear pragmatic.

Tactical Voting Pressures: Projections from Electoral Calculus indicated that tactical voting, whether for partisan reasons or specifically to block Reform, could cost Reform several dozen seats and prevent it from achieving an overall parliamentary majority. However, it's also possible that Reform could gain more seats than projected, potentially securing a majority. The outcomes of the May 2026 elections would reveal whether anti-Reform tactical voting was emerging on a significant scale or if the fragmented electorate made coordinated voting impossible.

The Endgame: Paralysis or Realignment

The May 2026 elections will serve as a critical turning point in the journey toward a hung parliament. This election will not be the final outcome but rather the moment when Britain's political realignment becomes undeniable and irreversible, a shift that will shape the future of the nation. The results will compel immediate decisions regarding coalition arrangements that politicians have been avoiding.

If the Reform-Conservative coalition path prevails, British politics may witness a formal merger or alliance on the right, potentially creating a dominant political force for years to come. However, this could also lead to the dissolution of the Conservative Party, a scenario that would significantly alter the political landscape. On the other hand, if a rainbow coalition emerges, Britain would face unprecedented political instability, with a government lacking public confidence and vulnerable to collapse at any moment.

Another possibility is that no stable coalition forms, leaving Britain in a state of constitutional limbo. The country's political future and decision-making processes could be uncertain, potentially leading to gridlock and a lack of progress on key issues. Such a situation requires another general election within months. With Reform UK projected to be the largest party in 91% of simulations, such a re-election could further strengthen Nigel Farage's position as voters react against the establishment parties for creating chaos.

While the May 2026 elections may not clarify who will govern Britain, they will undoubtedly limit the options to stark and unappealing choices. The era of comfortable two-party politics is over. We have entered a new era characterised by coalitions, minority governments, and ongoing negotiations, none of which anyone knows how to manage effectively.

The Institutional Question

One significant uncertainty surrounding Reform's potential governance involved the institutions essential for implementing their agenda, which held professional values that could conflict with Reform's policies.

Senior police officers, as of 2025, expressed private concerns about being asked to carry out operations that might violate human rights laws. The planned deportation of 600,000 individuals would require massive police resources, extensive detention facilities, and coordination with the military. Some officers questioned whether such operations could be conducted humanely or legally, especially if Britain were to withdraw from the European Convention on Human Rights, as proposed by Reform.

Military leaders faced similar dilemmas. While the armed forces have traditionally refrained from political engagement, Reform's policies raised questions about constitutional obligations. If a Reform government ordered military deployment for immigration enforcement, would the officers comply? If such policies were to violate international law, would military lawyers approve of the operations? The potential for civil-military tension, a serious and significant concern, was evident.

Reform's rhetoric about "reforming" these institutions, removing "politically correct" leadership, ending "woke" training, and prioritising "operational effectiveness" over "diversity" suggested an awareness that overcoming institutional resistance might be necessary. The parallels to authoritarian governments that purged professional leadership in favour of political loyalists were concerning to democratic observers.

However, this situation also represented a potential check on Reform's power. British institutions maintain significant independence and a professional culture. Civil servants could slow policy implementation through bureaucratic resistance, judges could rule actions as illegal, and police could refuse orders that violate professional standards. These checks, while uncertain in their effectiveness against a determined populist government, do exist as possibilities, offering a sense of reassurance to the audience.

The Path Forward

The rise of the Reform movement could lead to three distinct scenarios, each carrying significant implications for the future of British democracy.

Scenario One: The Populist Breakthrough. Reform wins a plurality or majority in the next general election, successfully implements its agenda, and consolidates enough support. Immigration rates fall dramatically due to aggressive enforcement, and border control is re-established. Working-class communities feel heard. The economy adapts to these new conditions, experiencing some disruption but avoiding catastrophic collapse. However, the risk of Britain evolving into an illiberal democracy, similar to Hungary, is a cause for concern. While elections continue, institutions weaken, the media faces pressure, and opposition is constrained through regulatory and legal mechanisms, posing significant challenges to the future of British democracy.

Scenario Two: The Prevented Crisis. The rise of Reform prompts mainstream parties to address legitimate grievances before populists seize power. Labour, acknowledging its past shortcomings, undergoes a leadership change and implements genuine reforms, thereby preventing a potential crisis. The Conservatives, under new leadership, offer a competent centre-right alternative, and the Liberal Democrats and Greens expand their support base. While the influence of reform peaks, it does not lead to a breakthrough, and British democracy manages to adapt and survive without succumbing to crisis.

Scenario Three: The Fragmented Future. No party achieves a working majority in the next election. Reform wins the largest share of the vote but does not secure enough seats to form a government.

Coalition negotiations often lead to unstable arrangements, resulting in a period of political instability characterised by frequent elections, policy paralysis, and institutional drift. Democracy persists, but in a weakened and dysfunctional form that inadequately serves citizens and fuels further radicalisation. This scenario underscores the urgent need to address the current political situation to prevent such a future from becoming a reality.

By October 2025, Scenario One appeared increasingly probable, while Scenario Two seemed unlikely without a dramatic transformation within Labour. The party's reshuffle in October, which removed Rachel Reeves and promoted Lisa Nandy and Liz Kendall, was viewed by most observers as merely rearranging deck chairs rather than addressing fundamental issues. The policies that had led to Labour's decline, such as winter fuel cuts, disability benefit reforms, and authoritarian overreach, remained unchanged. Additionally, the culture that gave rise to the Alli scandal persisted.

Conclusion: The Democratic Wager

Reform UK's rise by October 2025 posed a significant challenge to the very foundations of British democracy. Yet, the institutions that had survived wars, revolutions, and crises for centuries stood resilient. Could civic culture defend democratic values when they are threatened? Would voters reject extremism when presented with real choices? These were the questions that tested the strength of our democracy.

The tragedy was that Labour's collapse was entirely self-inflicted. No external crisis, no war, pandemic, or uncontrollable economic disaster had destroyed them. They simply failed to maintain the trust of the voters who had granted them power. The broken promises, scandals, authoritarianism, and betrayals were all choices made by leaders who prioritised power over principle.

Reform UK's rise was a direct result of Labour's failures. Nigel Farage had delivered a consistent message for years without gaining significant traction. However, Labour's incompetence provided him with the opening he needed. Keir Starmer's betrayals validated Farage's critique, and the government's authoritarian shift rendered Farage's warnings prescient.

As October 2025 comes to a close, flags on lampposts continued to flutter in the autumn winds. Reform UK organisers remained dedicated to building infrastructure for political power. Their polling leads continued to grow, and Nigel Farage, the perennial outsider who had transformed British politics through Brexit, prepared for what could be his greatest triumph, not through brilliance, but by capitalising on his opponents' spectacular failures.

The pressing question for Britain was no longer whether Reform posed a threat, but whether British democracy could survive their likely success and what kind of country would emerge from the transformation they promised. The May 2026 elections would begin to reveal the answer, while the general election that must occur by January 2025 would render the final judgment. The potential for change was palpable, and the future of British democratic tradition remained uncertain.

Author's Note

This chapter meticulously examines political developments up to October 2025, drawing from a wealth of publicly available polling data, media reports, and documented events. The polling data, a cornerstone of our analysis, is sourced from established firms such as Ipsos, YouGov, and Survation, ensuring the highest level of credibility. All direct quotations are taken from verified media reports or official statements, further bolstering the reliability of our findings.

The projections regarding the May 2026 elections and future governance are informed speculations based on current trends, not specific predictions. The three scenarios presented serve as analytical frameworks for understanding potential futures, not as definitive forecasts. It is crucial to note that political situations remain fluid and can change rapidly in response to events, leadership decisions, and voter reactions.

The characterisation of Reform UK's rise as a threat to democracy is one analytical perspective influenced by academic studies of populist movements. Reasonable observers may interpret the same facts differently, depending on their values and political beliefs. While this concern reflects a scholarly consensus regarding the risks posed by anti-system parties, it also acknowledges that political actors have agency and that democratic institutions, as history has shown, may prove to be more resilient than anticipated. This resilience should reassure us and give us hope for the future.

Conclusion: The Unravelling of a Promise
The End of the Starmer Experiment

The story of Keir Starmer's premiership will be studied for generations as a textbook case of how quickly political capital can be squandered, how thoroughly public trust can be destroyed, and how completely a government can lose its way. In just fifteen months, Labour transformed from the party of hope and change into a cautionary tale about the dangers of technocratic hubris divorced from principle.

The numbers underscore this dramatic narrative. From a resounding victory in July 2024, when Labour clinched 411 seats, the party nosedived in the polls to third place behind Reform UK and the Conservatives by autumn 2025. Starmer's personal approval ratings have plummeted to the lowest for any Prime Minister since polling began in 1977, surpassing even those of Gordon Brown during the financial crisis, Theresa May during the Brexit chaos, and Liz Truss during her brief 49-day tenure. This unprecedented collapse unfolded with alarming speed and magnitude in the annals of British democracy.

However, statistics alone cannot capture the sense of betrayal felt by millions who voted for change. Cuts to winter fuel payments forced pensioners to choose between heating and eating. Reforms to disability benefits threatened to push 250,000 people into poverty, including 50,000 children. More than 12,000 people were prosecuted for online speech offences, while ministers accepted designer clothes and concert tickets from wealthy donors. The proposed BritCard system, a controversial national identity card scheme, united opposition across the political spectrum due to concerns about privacy, civil liberties, and government overreach. Each scandal, each U-turn, and each broken promise chipped away at the foundation of trust until nothing remained but rubble.

What Went Right for Starmer

To be fair, Labour's failures were not total. The government did achieve some genuine accomplishments that deserve recognition, even if they became overshadowed by larger controversies.

The Hillsborough Law, a significant milestone, introduced criminal sanctions for public servants who conceal the truth during public inquiries. This long-overdue reform, which honoured the families who had fought for justice for decades, was passed with cross-party support and will be remembered as one of Labour's enduring contributions to British law.

The Employment Rights Bill, although watered down from original promises, did deliver some meaningful improvements to workers' rights. The end of exploitative fire-and-rehire practices, stronger protections against unfair dismissal, and enhanced rights for agency workers represented genuine progress. However, trade unions felt the reforms did not go nearly far enough, particularly in terms of collective bargaining rights and protections for gig economy workers.

The resolution of public sector strikes through pay settlements, while politically difficult and expensive, ended the industrial action that had paralysed services under the Conservatives. Teachers, nurses, and civil servants received long-overdue recognition through wage increases that began to address years of real-terms pay cuts.

Infrastructure investments, particularly in clean energy and transport, laid the groundwork for future economic growth. Commitments to wind farms, solar installations, and railway electrification represented genuine attempts to modernise Britain's economy while addressing climate change.

What Went Wrong

These achievements were overshadowed by failures so systematic and comprehensive that they exposed fundamental flaws in the Labour Party's approach to governance.

The most damaging failure was the systematic destruction of trust. Keir Starmer had campaigned on principles of integrity, competence, and transparency, promising to restore faith in politics after years of Conservative sleaze. Instead, his government was embroiled in scandals that made his predecessors appear restrained by comparison.

The "admin error" defence concerning Morgan McSweeney's £740,000 in undeclared donations epitomised the problem. Documentary evidence showed that Starmer's chief of staff had been explicitly advised to downplay serious violations of electoral law as mere paperwork mistakes. The message to voters was clear: rules applied to everyone except those in power.

The freebies scandal, where Starmer personally accepted £107,145 in gifts, benefits, and hospitality, eroded any remaining credibility regarding ethical standards. Designer glasses, Taylor Swift concert tickets, Arsenal football matches, all funded by wealthy donors, while the government cut benefits for disabled individuals and removed winter fuel payments from pensioners. The optics were disastrous, revealing a government that practised the opposite of what it preached.

The sixteen ministerial resignations and sackings between July 2024 and September 2025 created a chaotic revolving door that undermined the government's competence. Scandals involving Louise Haigh's fraud conviction, Andrew Gwynne's offensive WhatsApp messages, Tulip Siddiq's corruption allegations, Dan Norris's criminal charges, Rushanara Ali's landlord hypocrisy, and Angela Rayner's tax problems reinforced the narrative that Labour was no better than the governments it had replaced.

The assault on civil liberties represented Labour's most fundamental betrayal of its stated values. The government, which had promised to defend freedom, instead criminalised dissent with unprecedented zeal.

Section 127 of the Communications Act became a tool for suppressing online speech, leading to over 12,000 arrests in 2023 for offensive messages, a 58% increase from pre-pandemic levels. Sentences for social media posts included Lucy Connolly's 31 months for a single tweet, Jordan Parlour's 20 months for Facebook comments, and Tyler Kay's 38 months for retweets. The severity of these sentences often exceeded those handed down for actual violence during riots.

The Online Safety Act, which received royal assent in March 2025, established an unprecedented digital surveillance system in a democratic society. It introduced age verification requirements for nearly all online services and mandated the use of government-approved identification or facial recognition scans to access social media. Speech that caused "non-trivial psychological harm" was criminalised, effectively turning American tech companies into censors for British citizens.

The BritCard proposal represented the peak of Labour's authoritarian drift. Mandatory digital identity cards were to be enforced for employment, tracking every worker's movements and activities through employer verification and significant fines. The 2.6 million-signature petition against this policy demonstrated public revulsion at the surveillance state Labour was creating.

The government's priorities were damning. While deploying sophisticated surveillance to monitor citizens' online communications, Labour failed to implement basic oversight of the asylum hotel system that sparked much of the unrest. An Ethiopian asylum seeker, Hadush Kebatu, was housed without a proper risk assessment before sexually assaulting a fourteen-year-old girl. This incident not only highlighted the government's neglect but also the real-life consequences of its actions. The message was clear: the government would surveil law-abiding citizens while neglecting to protect vulnerable children.

The systematic abandonment of the ten pledges that had won Starmer the leadership exposed the hollowness at the core of Labour. Each pledge represented a commitment to party members and voters, and each betrayal illustrated the cynicism of Labour's approach to power, leaving the audience feeling disillusioned with the leadership.

Pledges for economic justice, aimed at taxing the wealthy, were instead used to protect the rich. Starmer's first pledge to 'increase income tax for the top 5% of earners' was abandoned entirely. Corporation tax cuts remained in place despite promises to reverse them, and tax avoidance measures were weakened after lobbying from the City. The government, which claimed to represent working people, instead governed for the benefit of its donors, sparking anger in the audience.

Immigration pledges to defend migrants turned into an expansion of detention and the restriction of rights. Indefinite detention continued, detention centres remained open, and safe passage provisions were abandoned. The "no recourse to public funds" condition persisted, and Labour adopted Conservative rhetoric regarding "irregular arrivals" while implementing policies similar to those of the Conservatives.

Typical ownership promises vanished with privatisation, as the railways remained in private hands and underwent increased private investment. Royal Mail was sold to foreign investors, and water companies continued to pay dividends while neglecting infrastructure. Instead of contracting, the NHS outsourcing expanded. The party that had promised public ownership ultimately delivered private profits.

Climate pledges plummeted from £28 billion annually to just £2.5 billion, erasing any semblance of ambition for a Green New Deal. Workers' rights legislation was weakened to the point where even the Confederation of British Industry (CBI) welcomed it. The Employment Rights Bill, which trade unions had advocated for, turned into a modest reform that did little to change the status quo.

Labour's reaction to Israel's military campaign in Gaza reflected moral cowardice disguised as diplomatic pragmatism. While Palestine Solidarity Campaign activists and Muslim communities called for action, Starmer's government offered only rhetoric.

The emergency motion at the October 2024 conference, which called for a complete suspension of arms sales to Israel and characterised Israeli actions as genocide, passed decisively despite leadership opposition. Nonetheless, the government ignored it; arms sales continued, and diplomatic support for Israel remained unchanged. The disconnect between party membership values and government policy was striking.

The recognition of Palestinian statehood in September 2025, while symbolically significant, came too late and achieved too little. It resembled coordinated theatre, an effort by Britain, Canada, and Australia without principled leadership, and was undermined by ongoing material support for Israel's military operations.

Muslim Labour MPs reported unprecedented pressure from constituents who felt betrayed. The Labour Muslim Network documented a rise in allegations of antisemitism being used to silence legitimate criticism of Israeli policy. Members of the Jewish Labour Movement expressed frustration that genuine cases of antisemitism were being conflated with political disagreement. In the end, everyone lost except those who preferred moral confusion over difficult choices

Rachel Reeves's emphasis on fiscal conservatism stifled any potential for transformative change. Her commitment to "iron discipline" in public spending meant perpetuating Conservative austerity, albeit under a different label.

The £22 billion "black hole" became Labour's excuse for every tough decision. However, the Institute for Fiscal Studies noted that many of the fiscal pressures were "entirely predictable" before the election. Labour chose to campaign on unrealistic promises rather than provide an honest assessment of its policies. This gap between campaign rhetoric and governing reality eroded credibility.

The Tech Prosperity Deal, celebrated after Trump's state visit, turned out to be corporate welfare disguised as bilateral cooperation. American companies would invest billions in British facilities that they would have built regardless, creating jobs mainly for highly skilled workers, while British companies faced American tariffs. The imbalance was clear to anyone examining the details.

The £150 billion investment commitment was aspirational rather than contractual in nature. These were simply expressions of intent reliant on market conditions and regulatory environments. In reality, Trump's 10% tariffs were already impacting British exporters on a daily basis. Labour expended political capital on ceremonial gestures rather than substantive economic benefits.

The cuts to disability benefits exposed Labour's willingness to penalise the vulnerable while safeguarding the privileged. Over 360,000 Londoners faced reductions totalling £820 million, with some individuals losing between £3,800 and £5,700 annually. The government's own estimates suggested that 250,000 people, including 50,000 children, would be pushed into poverty.

Sadiq Khan's rebellion against budget cuts, "What we can't do is take away the vital safety net that so many vulnerable and disabled Londoners rely upon", highlighted the depth of dissent within Labour itself. Over 120 MPs signed a "reasoned amendment" aimed at completely eliminating the legislation. The government was forced into humiliating last-minute concessions that ultimately satisfied no one.

Andy Burnham's criticism resonated deeply, echoing the widespread unease felt by 'really good people' across all parts of the party. The names represented all wings of the party, uniting MPs across factional lines in a powerful display of collective dissent. This welfare revolt suggested that the government had not just implemented controversial but necessary reforms, but had breached fundamental Labour values.

The cuts to winter fuel payments ignited a firestorm of public anger, crystallising the disconnect between Labour's priorities and the needs of the people. The reduction in recipients from 10.8 million pensioners to just 1.5 million left the elderly facing a harsh choice between heating their homes and buying food, while ministers accepted free designer clothing. The symbolism of this disparity was devastatingly unjust.

Unite the Union's Sharon Graham captured the mood: "Picking the pockets of pensioners is not a tough choice; it is a mistake." Her threat to disaffiliate Unite from Labour, which would result in a £1.4 million annual fee withdrawal, demonstrated how thoroughly the government had alienated its traditional base.

Donald Trump's state visit in September 2025 laid bare Labour's moral bankruptcy to international audiences. The decision to bestow honours upon a president whose administration had systematically attacked democratic norms, separated children from their parents at the border, and attempted to overturn an election was a global embarrassment and represented the lowest point of Starmer's premiership.

The appointment of Peter Mandelson as US Ambassador, coupled with revelations of his correspondence defending Jeffrey Epstein and referring to him as "my best pal," added layers of scandal that surpassed usual political embarrassment. Starmer's initial defence of Mandelson, before eventually sacking him, showcased either catastrophic vetting failures or a willingness to overlook connections to convicted pedophiles for the sake of diplomatic convenience.

The guest list for the state banquet featuring Blackstone CEO Steve Schwarzman, Apple CEO Tim Cook, NVIDIA CEO Jensen Huang, and media mogul Rupert Murdoch revealed whose interests Labour truly served. These were the beneficiaries of the Tech Prosperity Deal. This controversial agreement provided these tech giants with preferential access to British markets, while ordinary citizens faced benefit cuts and declining public services.

The contrast with the 5,000 protesters outside Windsor Castle could not have been starker. "Trump is not welcome here," they chanted, voicing values that 70% of Britons shared, according to polling. Yet their government chose pageantry over principle, diplomatic theatre over democratic sentiment.

American progressive commentators took notice. Alexandria Ocasio-Cortez tweeted, "Promising progressive policies to win elections then implementing conservative policies in government is not politics; it's fraud," a post that was retweeted 250,000 times. Bernie Sanders remarked to CNN: "What we're seeing in Britain is a cautionary tale about what happens when politicians abandon their principles for the sake of power."

Labour's challenges have transcended mere policy failures, leading to a profound disconnection from the communities they purported to represent. The Union Jacks and St. George's crosses that adorned lampposts and roundabouts throughout 2025 were not just symbols of a nation feeling its identity was under threat, but also urgent calls for Labour to reconnect with its people.

The protests against asylum hotels, culminating in Tommy Robinson's 'Unite the Kingdom' march with 150,000 participants in September, laid bare a widespread anger that Labour either could not or would not address. The party's response, criminalising online speech, deploying riot police, and prosecuting protesters, was a tactical error that focused on symptoms rather than addressing the root causes of the discontent.

Nigel Farage's Reform UK effectively capitalised on Labour's failures. Their "Operation Restoring Justice," which promised 600,000 deportations within five years, immediate detention for asylum seekers, and withdrawal from the European Convention on Human Rights, offered simple solutions to complex problems. By contrast, Labour's more technocratic responses appeared weak.

The polling trends were alarming. By September 2025, Reform UK led Labour 34% to 22%. Among those who voted Labour in 2024, only 54% remained satisfied with their choice. In working-class constituencies that Labour had held for generations, voters were abandoning the party in favour of Farage's populist promises.

Disillusionment within the Muslim community was particularly pronounced. Labour's failure to take meaningful action regarding Gaza, combined with their disproportionate targeting under speech laws, fostered a sense of betrayal. The Labour Muslim Network documented rising alienation, with mosques in Birmingham and Leicester forming parallel voter blocs and declaring they would "no longer campaign for any party that criminalises our pain."

Young activists who had joined Labour during the Corbyn years felt that they had been systematically betrayed. Momentum's membership dropped from 40,000 to between 20,000 and 30,000. The 2025 conference in Liverpool lacked the energy and enthusiasm that had characterised gatherings during the Corbyn era.

A 24-year-old delegate from Manchester summed up the mood: "I used to bring friends to the conference. We'd stay up all night debating policy, planning campaigns, and feeling like part of something bigger. Now? Most of my friends have left the party. The ones who stayed do so out of stubbornness, not hope."

The betrayal regarding tuition fees has particularly damaged Labour's standing with young voters. Keir Starmer's pledge to 'support the abolition of tuition fees' during his leadership campaign was a promise that resonated with many. However, by November 2024, Education Secretary Bridget Phillipson's announcement of fee increases shattered the trust of young voters, making it urgent for Labour to regain their confidence.

Jo Grady of the University and College Union did not hold back: "Keir Starmer repeatedly pledged to abolish the toxic system of tuition fees and was elected leader of the Labour Party based on that promise. It is deeply disappointing that he is now reneging on that commitment, a move that would harm the very people Labour claims to represent."

By October 2025, only 24% of 18-24-year-olds believed Labour "respected cultural freedom." Trust in Labour to uphold civil liberties among Muslims and ethnic minorities dropped below 30%. The party was losing the diverse, young coalition that should have been its future.

The deteriorating relationship between Labour and trade unions posed a threat to the party's organisational foundation. Sharon Graham's Unite had been Labour's most reliable financial backer, contributing £1.4 million annually in affiliation fees, along with campaign resources and volunteers.

By the 2025 conference, Graham openly questioned whether continued affiliation could be justified, stating, "It's getting harder to defend that affiliation," during an interview with Lewis Goodall. Unite's July 2025 policy conference voted to suspend Angela Rayner's membership and to "re-examine" their funding of Labour, with only a handful of delegates voting against the motion.

Various unions expressed their frustrations alongside Unite. The GMB and Prospect also raised concerns about pay restraint and workers' rights. The Communication Workers Union suspended its donations pending a policy review. Even traditionally moderate unions, such as UNISON, voiced concerns about the government's direction.

The strike wave that erupted in spring 2025, comprising teachers, NHS workers, civil servants, and university staff, tested Starmer's resolve in ways that parliamentary rebellions could not. This new wave of industrial action threatened chaos in the streets, schools, and hospitals across the UK. Labour had come to power promising to end the strikes that had plagued Conservative rule. Instead, within a year, they faced even more extensive industrial action from their own traditional supporters

The government's response highlighted its priorities. There was no additional funding for NHS and teacher pay rises, despite recommendations from the Pay Review Body. Sir Jim Mackey, the CEO of NHS England, insisted on a "much more resistant" approach, denouncing previous strikes as being "net positive" for doctors, as some managed to earn back lost wages through overtime. He urged hospitals to maintain operations during strikes with skeleton staff in A&E, putting patients at risk.

This marked a significant shift in Labour's approach, one that was perceived as a betrayal by many. The party, which had spent years criticising Tory attempts to break strikes, was now adopting similar methods against healthcare workers. Nurses and doctors, who were already struggling to make ends meet after years of real-terms pay cuts, found themselves at the receiving end of the very tactics they had once fought against.

British journalism largely failed to hold Labour accountable with the scrutiny that the situation warranted. The same newspapers that had endorsed Starmer's leadership campaign or remained neutral during the 2024 election struggled to provide consistent critical coverage. This lack of accountability was particularly evident in the way they covered the government's handling of the strike wave and its impact on healthcare workers.

The BBC, balancing accusations of bias from both sides, reported facts with a studied neutrality that satisfied no one. The Times and the Telegraph covered scandals but often shied away from challenging fundamental elements of government policy. The Financial Times offered some scrutiny of economic policies but was reluctant to question diplomatic decisions, such as Trump's visit.

Only the Guardian and a few smaller outlets provided sustained critical coverage, though their reach was limited compared to broadcast media. This sanitised reporting reflected broader trends where access to power was traded for essential independence. Journalists who might have asked uncomfortable questions instead focused on reporting ceremonial protocols and the menus of state banquets.

The Lobby system, which granted privileged access to government information in exchange for cooperation, ensured that most political reporters maintained cordial relationships with the very power they were supposed to scrutinise. No one wanted to be excluded from briefings or shut out of essential background conversations, relationships that made their jobs feasible.

International media faced fewer constraints. The New York Times published pieces questioning whether Labour's landslide victory was already turning into a cautionary tale about the limits of centrism. The Washington Post declared, "If Orwell were alive today, he'd be prosecuted under Britain's speech laws." The Atlantic accused the UK of abandoning Enlightenment principles under the guise of safety.

Labour's failure to pursue constitutional reform exacerbated its other shortcomings. There was no movement toward repealing voter ID laws, which disproportionately affect minority voters. The lack of progress on proportional representation, despite the efforts of the Make Votes Matter campaign, was a missed opportunity for a fairer political system. Additionally, there was no mention of reforming the House of Lords, despite its clear democratic deficit.

The lack of reform in communication legislation contributed to a renewed deadlock in the Northern Ireland Assembly, also known as Stormont. In Wales, Plaid Cymru criticised the UK Government for refusing to grant expanded devolved control over media and policing. In Scotland, SNP First Minister John Swinney opposed mandatory digital ID, stating, "By calling it BritCard, the prime minister seems to be attempting to force every Scot to declare ourselves British. I am a Scot."

Organisations like Compass, the Electoral Reform Society, and Republic, which were once ardent supporters of Labour's commitment to democratic renewal, now accuse the party of betrayal. The party that once championed reform had become a defender of the status quo, which served its interests.

By October 2025, the pressing question was no longer whether Starmer's premiership would survive but rather how and when it would end. Polling trends showed no signs of reversal, with Reform UK maintaining significant leads. The upcoming 2026 local elections posed a threat of catastrophic losses that could prompt questions about leadership.

Three scenarios seemed possible, none of which provided hope for Labour's recovery.

Scenario One: The Long Goodbye

Starmer could continue in office, hoping for either an economic recovery or an implosion of Reform UK to save his premiership. Rachel Reeves's forthcoming budget might include growth measures that ultimately boost the economy. A second term for Trump could create diplomatic opportunities, and mistakes from Farage might remind voters why populism ultimately fails.

However, this scenario required Labour to demonstrate the competence it had consistently failed to show. Every day brought new scandals, U-turns, and evidence that the government was out of its depth. The discipline needed to weather the storm, avoiding mistakes, maintaining message control, and projecting confidence, had proven beyond Labour's capability.

The psychological toll on ministers was already evident. Angela Rayner resigned in September, and Sue Gray departed in October. More resignations seemed not just possible, but inevitable as scandals continued to accumulate. Cabinet meetings had turned into exercises in crisis management rather than strategic planning. The government was focused on firefighting rather than governing.

Scenario Two: The Honourable Retreat

Starmer could resign, paving the way for a fresh start and allowing the party to elect a successor with a new mandate. There are precedents for this: Theresa May stepped down after her Brexit failures, Gordon Brown resigned following an electoral defeat, and Margaret Thatcher left office after losing the support of her cabinet.

This scenario would require admitting failure and accepting that the promise of change had turned into betrayal. For someone like Starmer, a lawyer who has built his career on projecting competence and control, this admission would be devastating. However, it might represent the least damaging option for Labour, inspiring confidence in the potential for a new leader.

The key question is who could succeed him. Andy Burnham is the obvious candidate, but he is not an MP and therefore cannot formally challenge under party rules. Getting him back into Westminster through a by-election would take months. Other potential candidates, such as Rachel Reeves, Wes Streeting, and David Lammy, also carry their own baggage from the government's failures.

A leadership contest during a government crisis would consume valuable time while policy drifted and public anger grew. Nevertheless, it could demonstrate Labour's adaptability and willingness to change direction, rather than defending the indefensible, reassuring the audience of the party's commitment to change.

Scenario Three: The Early Election

Starmer could opt for an early general election, betting that voters would prefer Labour to Reform UK when presented with a choice. The assumption would be that, although voters are angry, they aren't ready to hand power to Farage's populist insurgency.

However, this scenario seems unlikely. Polls indicate that Labour would face a catastrophic loss. Reform UK's 34% support would likely translate into hundreds of seats under Britain's first-past-the-post electoral system. The Conservatives might recover enough to be competitive, potentially reducing Labour to third-party status or worse.

The constitutional precedent for calling an early election is weak. Governments typically don't call elections they expect to lose. Although the Fixed-term Parliaments Act has been repealed, restoring the Prime Minister's prerogative to dissolve Parliament, using it for political suicide would be unprecedented.

Keir Starmer's tenure as Prime Minister is coming to an end, not due to a single catastrophic failure, but rather the accumulation of betrayals too significant to overlook. The forensic barrister who promised competence has delivered chaos. The lawyer who vowed integrity has overseen scandals. The leader who committed to listening has silenced dissent.

The tragedy is that it didn't have to come to this. Labour had a genuine mandate for change in July 2024. Voters had allowed them to demonstrate that progressive politics could work, that government could serve ordinary people instead of wealthy donors, and that integrity in public life was possible.

Instead, Labour chose the path of least resistance. Instead of confronting wealth inequality, they protected the rich. Rather than defending civil liberties, they built a surveillance state. Rather than keeping their promises, they dismissed them as "administrative errors." And rather than leading with principle, they followed polling data and focus groups.

The consequences extend beyond Labour's electoral prospects; the party's failures have eroded public faith in democratic politics itself. When voters trust you with the power to deliver change and you betray that trust, you don't just lose the next election; you convince people that change is impossible, that all politicians are the same, and that democracy is a sham.

This situation presents an urgent opportunity for Reform UK. Farage offers simple answers: closing the borders, deporting immigrants, tearing up international law, and restoring British sovereignty. Although these solutions are simplistic and often authoritarian, they resonate with voters because they are clear and decisive, unlike Labour's muddled and equivocal responses.

The contrast between Starmer's technocratic caution and Farage's populist certainty increasingly favours the latter. Voters do not want to hear about fiscal constraints and political realities; they want leaders who understand their anger and promise to act on it. Labour's failure to connect with public emotions has created an opening that Farage is brilliantly exploiting.

The historical parallels are concerning. The 1930s witnessed democratic governments across Europe struggling to address economic distress and social dislocation, creating opportunities for authoritarian movements that offered simplistic solutions. The failures of democratic politicians directly contributed to the rise of anti-democratic alternatives.

While Britain in 2025 is not Weimar Germany, the pattern is similar: economic anxiety, cultural displacement, and political disappointment are creating conditions conducive to extremism. Labour's failures have made Reform UK viable in ways that should terrify anyone who values British democracy.

The May 2026 local elections will serve as the most crucial test of Labour's standing. Current polling suggests losses of monumental proportions, hundreds of councillors losing seats they have held for decades, councils falling under Reform UK control, and traditional Labour heartlands rejecting their own party.

If these losses materialise as predicted, the pressure on Starmer will become unbearable. Backbench MPs facing electoral annihilation will demand change; trade unions may reconsider their affiliations, and donors will question whether Labour is worth supporting. The party machinery that has protected Starmer will begin to fracture.

However, even if Starmer somehow survives the 2026 elections, the 2029 general election looms as a potential for change. On current trends, Labour would lose hundreds of seats, Reform UK would gain its first significant parliamentary representation, and the Conservatives might recover enough to compete. Britain's political landscape could be transformed for the better.

The most optimistic scenario for Labour involves Reform UK peaking too early, with voters reconsidering their anger when faced with actual choices and economic recovery improving the government's standing. However, this requires luck and circumstances beyond Labour's control. It hinges on voters forgetting fifteen months of betrayal and disappointment.

The more likely scenario involves Labour losing power, probably in 2029 if not sooner, having squandered a once-in-a-generation opportunity. The party that promised transformation would have delivered continuity. The movement that claimed to represent working people would have served corporate interests. The government, which vowed to uphold integrity, would have destroyed public trust.

Labour's failures provide harsh lessons about the limitations of technocratic politics detached from principle. Competence without vision results in only efficient mediocrity. Management without values produces hollow gestures. Processes without purpose achieve nothing of true significance.

Starmer, like Labour, believed that simply being better administrators than the Conservatives would suffice. He thought that avoiding obvious mistakes would satisfy voters and that technocratic competence could replace political courage. However, as we've seen, this approach has proven to be a failure on all counts.

Democracy demands more than efficient management. It requires leaders who can inspire, who understand that politics is fundamentally about values and choices, and who recognise that governing involves making trade-offs between competing goods rather than merely optimising agreed-upon objectives.

Labour's adoption of authoritarian policies, the prosecution of speech, surveillance systems, and mandatory digital IDs, reveals a deeper issue. When governments lose moral authority by breaking faith with their supporters, they tend to compensate through control. When they can't inspire voluntary compliance, they impose mandatory measures. When they can't win arguments, they criminalise dissent.

This is how democracies begin to fail, not through military coups or violent revolutions, but through the gradual accumulation of authoritarian measures justified by efficiency and safety. Each action may seem reasonable on its own. The Online Safety Act protects children. Identity cards prevent fraud. Speech prosecutions maintain social cohesion. However, together they create a framework of oppression that future governments can misuse.

Labour has constructed this framework while claiming to defend democracy. They have prosecuted speech under the guise of preventing hate crimes. They have set up surveillance systems while promising modernisation. They have criminalised dissent while insisting on maintaining order. The precedents they've established will not just haunt British politics for generations, but also shape the future of democracy in the UK.

There is something almost Shakespearean about Starmer's downfall. Here was a man of genuine achievement, a successful barrister, human rights lawyer, and Director of Public Prosecutions who dedicated his career to defending justice and the rule of law. He had prosecuted the powerful, defended the vulnerable, and built a reputation for integrity and competence.

Yet, in his pursuit of political power, he made compromises that seemed tactical but ultimately proved fatal. He accepted questionable donations, employed advisors who bent the rules, made promises he couldn't keep, and prioritised victory over values until that victory became hollow. This sequence of compromises is a stark reminder of the disillusionment that can result from the pursuit of power at any cost.

The tragedy is that Starmer likely believed he was making necessary compromises. He thought that winning power required an accommodation with reality and that governing demanded pragmatism over principle. He convinced himself that betraying promises was justified by the larger goal of maintaining Labour in government.

However, power without principle is meaningless. Victory without values is a form of defeat. A government that exists solely to maintain itself serves no purpose. Starmer achieved the office but lost the opportunity to use it for good. This is a profound loss that many feel in the wake of his tenure. The man who promised to restore trust in politics systematically undermined it. The lawyer who championed the rule of law oversaw its weaponisation. The advocate for human rights contributed to the establishment of a surveillance state. The leader who vowed to bring change delivered only betrayal. This sense of betrayal is a powerful emotion that many feel in the wake of Starmer's actions.

History will not be kind to Keir Starmer. He will be remembered not for his achievements, such as the Hillsborough Law, employment rights reforms, or infrastructure investments, but for his failures: the winter fuel cuts, disability benefit reforms, speech prosecutions, digital surveillance, the sixteen scandals, and broken promises. These actions stand in stark contrast to the values Labour was supposed to stand for, and ultimately, Starmer systematically betrayed them.

He will be remembered as the man who had the opportunity to transform Britain but instead chose to manage its decline. His leadership, marked by unfulfilled promises, could have defended democratic values while building an authoritarian infrastructure. He pledged integrity but delivered corruption, promised competence but produced chaos, leaving a trail of disappointment in his wake.

Most damningly, he will be remembered as the Prime Minister whose failures made Nigel Farage's success possible. By betraying Labour's principles, breaking faith with Labour's supporters, and demonstrating that mainstream politics was incapable of delivering change, Starmer created the conditions for populist extremism to flourish.

The forensic barrister who promised to fix British politics instead broke it beyond repair. The son of a toolmaker, who was supposed to understand how things worked, dismantled the machinery of trust that is essential for democracy to function. The leader who claimed to represent change became the embodiment of everything wrong with British politics.

Keir Starmer's time as Prime Minister is ending not with the bang of dramatic failure but with the whimper of accumulating disappointments. The landslide victory of July 2024, which initially seemed to herald a new era of Labour dominance, has become a historical footnote, illustrating the fragility of political power and the speed with which public trust can be eroded.

As the rain falls on Liverpool, London, and the constituencies where Labour councillors prepare for electoral annihilation in May 2026, the question is not whether Starmer's premiership will end, but what will replace it. Can British democracy survive the damage Labour has inflicted? Can the authoritarian infrastructure they've built be dismantled? Can trust in politics ever be restored?

The answers remain uncertain. But one thing is clear: The Starmer experiment is over. The promise of progressive technocracy has been largely unfulfilled. The notion that competent management could substitute for principled leadership has been tested and found wanting. The hope that Labour could be different, better, and more honest than those it replaced has been systematically destroyed, leaving the future shrouded in uncertainty.

What comes next will depend on the choices voters make in response to Labour's failures. Will they opt for Reform UK's populist authoritarianism or explore alternative options? Perhaps a return to Labour's core principles or a new party with a fresh approach. Will they demand fundamental reform of British democracy, or will they accept its continued decline? Will they abandon politics entirely, or will they find new ways to demand accountability, such as proportional representation, citizen-led assemblies, tighter rules on lobbying and political donations, or even mandatory recall elections for MPs who break public trust? The future is uncertain, but some paths can lead to a more robust and trustworthy political system.

Whatever comes next will be shaped by Labour's failure. The party that promised change delivered betrayal. The government that pledged integrity destroyed trust. The leader who committed to competence produced chaos. In doing so, they may have irreparably damaged British democracy. However, it's important to remember that democracy is resilient and can be rebuilt, even in the face of such significant challenges.

Keir Starmer's time as Prime Minister is drawing to a close. The only question that remains is not just whether British democracy will survive his failures, but how it will be shaped by them in the future.

BIBLIOGRAPHY

Primary Sources

- Government Documents and Official Records
- Crown Prosecution Service. "Jimmy Savile Investigation Report." By Alison Levitt QC. January 11, 2013. The National Archives.
- Department for Work and Pensions. "Winter Fuel Payment Eligibility Changes 2024-25." Official Regulations, September 16, 2024.
- Electoral Commission. "Labour Together Donations Investigation." September 26, 2025.
- GOV.UK. "Director of Public Prosecutions Appointment: Keir Starmer." November 1, 2008.
- Hansard. Parliamentary Debates, House of Commons. Various dates 2024-2025.
- HM Treasury. "Public Spending Audit 2024." July 29, 2024.
- Home Office. "Asylum and Immigration Statistics, Year Ending June 2025."
- Office for Budget Responsibility. "Economic and Fiscal Outlook Reports." 2024-2025.
- Parliament.uk. Petition 730194: "Do not introduce Digital ID cards." Accessed December 2025.
- Court Records and Legal Documents
- *Steel and Morris v. United Kingdom*. European Court of Human Rights. February 15, 2005.
- *Susan Kigula v. Attorney General of Uganda*. Constitutional Court of Uganda. June 13, 2005.
- Electoral Commission Fine Records. Labour Together, September 2021.
- Party Documents
- Labour Party. "Annual Conference 2025 - General Information." September 28-October 1, 2025.
- Labour Party. General Election Manifesto 2019.
- Labour Party. General Election Manifesto 2024.
- Labour Together. "BritCard: A Progressive Case for Digital Identity." June 2025.
- Starmer, Keir. Leadership Campaign Pledges. January 2020.

News Media

British Press
- BBC News. Coverage of Trump UK State Visit, Labour Party Conference, and ongoing political developments. 2024-2025.
- *Daily Mail*. Various political reporting. 2024-2025.
- *Financial Times*. Economic and political analysis. 2024-2025.
- *The Guardian*. Comprehensive political coverage including Owen Jones commentary. 2024-2025.
- *The Independent*. Political reporting. 2024-2025.
- ITV News. Political coverage and interviews. 2024-2025.
- Sky News. Political interviews and coverage. 2024-2025.
- *The Spectator*. Political analysis and commentary. 2024-2025.
- *The Telegraph*. Political reporting. 2024-2025.
- *The Times*. Political coverage and analysis. 2024-2025.

Online and Alternative Media
- Channel 4 News and FactCheck. Political verification and reporting.
- GB News. Political interviews and coverage.
- LabourList. Labour Party conference and internal party coverage.
- Left Foot Forward. Progressive political commentary.
- *New Statesman*. Political analysis and interviews.
- Novara Media. Independent political commentary.
- *Private Eye*. Investigative journalism.

International Press
- Al Jazeera. International perspective on UK politics.
- *The Atlantic*. International political commentary.
- CNN. International coverage of UK developments.
- NBC News. US perspective on UK politics.
- *The New York Times*. International political analysis.
- Reuters. International news coverage.
- *Washington Post*. International political commentary.

Polling Organizations and Data
- Electoral Calculus. Electoral projections and analysis.
- Ipsos. Public opinion polling including satisfaction ratings and voting intention. 2024-2025.
- Survation. Opinion polling and survey research.
- YouGov. Public opinion polling and political favorability ratings. 2024-2025.

Civil Society and Advocacy Organizations
- Age UK. Statements on winter fuel payment cuts.
- Amnesty International. Human rights commentary.
- Big Brother Watch. Civil liberties campaign materials and reports.
- Compass. Democratic reform advocacy.
- Electoral Reform Society. Constitutional reform campaigns.
- Free Speech Union. Legal defense fund documentation.
- Labour Muslim Network. Community statements.
- Liberty. Civil liberties legal analysis and statements.
- Make Votes Matter. Electoral reform campaigns.
- Momentum. Grassroots organization materials and conference priorities.
- Muslim Council of Britain. Community responses.
- Palestine Solidarity Campaign. Campaign statements and protest materials.
- Privacy International. Digital rights advocacy.
- Refugee Council. Policy responses.
- Stand Up to Racism. Protest organization materials.
- Stop Trump Coalition. Demonstration materials and statements.
- Unite the Union. Press releases and campaign materials by Sharon Graham.

Trade Union Sources
- Communication Workers Union. Policy statements.
- GMB Union. Policy positions.
- National Union of Rail, Maritime and Transport Workers. Policy statements.
- Royal College of Nursing. Member consultation results.
- Trades Union Congress. Policy statements by Paul Nowak.
- UNISON. Policy positions and endorsements.
- Think Tanks and Research Organizations
- Institute for Fiscal Studies. Economic analysis and policy research.
- Institute for Government. Governance analysis.
- Policy in Practice. Welfare impact modeling.
- Tony Blair Institute for Global Change. Policy papers.
- Academic and Reference Sources
- British Election Study. Demographic electoral analysis.
- *Encyclopedia Britannica*. Biographical information.

- King's College London, School of Mental Health and Psychological Sciences. NHS reform commentary.
- Queen Mary University of London. Political science analysis by Prof. Tim Bale.
- University College London, Constitution Unit. Constitutional analysis by Prof. Meg Russell.
- University of Leeds. Faculty records.
- St Edmund Hall, Oxford. Official records.
- Wikipedia. Supplementary reference (cross-verified with primary sources).
- Legal and Professional Bodies
- Bar Council. Professional standards commentary.
- Doughty Street Chambers. Professional history records.
- Middle Temple. Bar admission records.
- Office for Budget Responsibility. Economic forecasting.

Social Media and Digital Sources
- X (formerly Twitter). Public statements by politicians, journalists, and political figures.
- Facebook. Community organization and protest coordination.
- TikTok. Viral political content and public reaction.
- Parliamentary petition website. Petition signatures and data.

Interviews and Speeches
- Various television and radio interviews with government ministers, opposition leaders, and political commentators on BBC, Sky News, ITV, GB News, and LBC. 2024-2025.
- Conference speeches at Labour Party Conference 2025, Liverpool.
- Prime Minister's Questions transcripts. 2024-2025.
- Archival Sources
- COUNSEL Magazine. Historical records on Keir Starmer's career.
- Death Penalty Project. Records of Uganda death penalty case.
- *New Law Journal*. Professional legal history.

Note on Sources: This bibliography includes all major sources consulted and cited throughout the manuscript. Where specific articles, reports, or broadcasts are referenced in the text, they are dated and attributed inline. All web sources were accessed and verified as available through October 2025. Some internal government documents, leaked emails, and anonymous briefings cited in the narrative are attributed based on contemporary media reporting rather than direct access to original materials. Polling data represents point-in-time measurements subject to methodological limitations and margin of error. Social media sources represent public statements and should be understood as individual perspectives rather than verified facts unless corroborated by additional reporting.